The Best American
Sports Writing
2019

The Best AMERICAN SPORTS WRITING™ 2019

Edited and with an Introduction
by Charles P. Pierce

Glenn Stout, *Series Editor*

MARINER BOOKS

HOUGHTON MIFFLIN HARCOURT

BOSTON • NEW YORK   2019

hmhbooks.com

ISSN 1056-8034 (print)   ISSN 2573-4822 (e-book)
ISBN 978-1-328-50785-3 (print)   ISBN 978-1-328-50870-6 (e-book)

Printed in the United States of America
DOC 10 9 8 7 6 5 4 3 2 1

Contents

Contents

Foreword

WE'VE BEEN DOING it all wrong.

It's no secret, to either readers or writers, that the entire writing industrial complex is in trouble as regards not just sports writing but just about every kind of writing that makes use of letters, sentences, and the occasional paragraph. Jobs are scarce, layoffs have spread like measles among the unvaccinated, and print and online publishers close or merge into the dim-witted mists of capital reorganization every day. The few that remain not only publish less written work every year but often treat it like an enormous bother. Somehow writing itself has become the greatest impediment to the reigning business model, which measures success in IPOs, an office fridge full of double IPAs, and a summer tiny house.

Clearly, the model that worked for so long, one in which writers, usually supported by advertising, were paid in currency for their work, then had children, bought houses, and went to the bar and ran up a tab (although rarely in that order), is no longer sustainable. Not only are there fewer jobs—by some estimates in the last decade half of all journalism jobs have disappeared—but already stagnant pay is going down, and fast. Finalists for the National Magazine Award have asked if I know where they might be able to pitch a story and get paid in cash. I know of legacy outlets that now pay only $100 for stories that run thousands of words, often make the writer wait many, many months for that, and cut a check only after the writer has expended more pretty-please words begging for payment than they used in the original story. Even more brilliant are those outlets that have convinced "people" to produce "content"—which approximates writing through the ingenious use of a familiar alphabet, punctuation, and the occasional space and hard return—for free.

Virtually every writer I know is in the same boat—or, to use a professional writing trick and turn to the online thesaurus in search of an eye-catching synonym to exhibit style (thereby proving that a scribbling MA degree from Pretentious and Prestigious A&M did not go to waste), the same dinghy. Those favored few who aren't in there with the rest of us use their parents' yachts and are therefore not my concern. To those in this dory (a wooden boat favored by my forebears, utilized for the jigging of squid in the North Atlantic, and used here to pump up the word count), let's just say there seems to be a moratorium on far more than codfish. Many former full-time staffers have shed their slickers and jumped ship to become substitute teachers or, even worse, freelancers. And many of the freelancers among us have become housepainters or gardeners. If you don't believe me, I guarantee you that some pretty decent writers are probably raking the leaves in your front yard right now.

There is, of course, a price to be paid. While many useless stories blessedly go untold, unfortunately so do many worthy ones, and countless voices are silenced before they ever get a chance to speak. How, then, to go forward?

A freelancer myself, I tried, as I pondered this question while raking, to identify the through line (another upmarket editorial phrase) and figure out what has remained constant ever since the first word was put in print in exchange for compensation. Then it struck me.

Money.

I rapidly abandoned the notion that the problem would disappear if readers didn't have to pay for writing. I mean, we live in a capitalistic society, and only an idiot or a media company executive would embrace the crass socialism of distributing words for free. Clearly, the problem is not with the reader. He or she is only at the end of this idea supply chain. Fortunately, as an experienced freelancer, I am accustomed to thinking, as so many editors have requested, "outside the box" or, after hours, while drinking at home.

The answer was right in front of me. It was a bitter realization, but the problem was . . . me. By actually expecting to be paid for writing, I had helped bring a once-thriving industry to its knees. God forgive me.

But no more. I declare that the era of the paid writer is over. Instead of staffers and freelancers, I propose a new model, one that over the past decade or so has already been rapidly evolving into reality. Let us now usher in a brave new age.

I call it "Paylance."

See, the whole problem began the moment writers started being paid, creating what is now an entirely unrealistic set of expectations and an unsustainable economic model, one that turned writing from a privilege of the educated class into something far more crass, even a little icky: a "job," like taking out the trash. And therein lies the answer. The problem is, and always has been, paying writers for their words.

Ah, but in the Paylance era, we're turning that on its head. From now on, *the writer pays*. If we want the industry to thrive, we're gonna have to pay for it ourselves. This is only fair.

The benefits are obvious. Instead of a media company paying writers, under the Paylance model the reverse will be true: writers will pay for the privilege of seeing their work in print. Wanna write what we once called "columns" and now call "posts"? Rates are variable, but my startup will likely start at a dollar a word and go up from there, depending on your lack of experience and the size of your inheritance. Got a personal essay about repressed trauma after you were caught coloring outside the lines in kindergarten? Ten grand a page. Pondering a long-form feature, investigative story, or enterprise piece? The floor starts at $50,000, even more if you want to use pictures, and if you insist on calling it "creative nonfiction," the penalty will be ten grand, or more, per page. Want to be on the cover? Tack on another $250,000. Social media push? Negotiable. Author mugshot? $5,000, more if the picture is actually of you. Bylines start at $10,000, but it'll cost you extra for a middle initial or middle name, or if one of your parents was a published author.

But what about advertising, you ask? What do we do with that?

This is where Paylance *really* pays off. Although there is a great temptation to monetize this prematurely, hear me out. Paylance will never lack for advertising, because since the writers *have to pay*, the advertisers *don't*. At least not at first. That means every

print issue will be as fat as an old big city telephone book and
every paragraph of every online story will be separated by an an-
noying old school banner ad or an autoplay video. Page counts
will go through the roof, and so will page views, because every
story will be spread across dozens, if not hundreds, of pages. We'll
provide enough metrics to eat 'em for breakfast and spread it on
your toast. Then . . . heh, heh, heh . . . we'll charge 'em through
the nose, backed up by all the data we need to prove scale.

And get this: under the Paylance model (talk about every writer's dream), editors will have to pay at least a dollar more than you
have to pay to write just for the privilege of editing you. This will
likely result in no editors at all, as it's a well-known fact that most
of those parsimonious bastards don't ever want to pay for anything
or answer an email.

Oh, I know, there are those who will say that such a model isn't
inclusive and will prevent all but the very rich and privileged from
participating. Well, *duh*—just look around. By any measure, this
is already one of the least inclusive industries around, its demo-
graphics frozen like a mammoth in the permafrost. Paylance likely
won't change this, but at least it will be honest and transparent.
Besides, no one in their right mind gets into this racket anymore
anyway unless they have a trust fund, a former roommate on the
board of directors, and enough Xanax to render this realization
moot. As it is, I still wonder if I made the right decision when I
abandoned the glory of concrete and steel for ink and paper. On
an hourly basis, my earning power probably peaked that summer I
worked seventy hours a week at the prevailing wage. Besides, while
I was growing up I simply assumed that anyone who wrote for a
living was already rich, that writing was already out of reach for
someone whose only other discernible talent was the ability to do
backbreaking physical labor in the sun for hours at a time. Guess
I was ahead of my time!

So far, of course, all this is just a dream, a nascent idea waiting for the right visionary to make it reality. But I've got some
experience with many of the acronyms and dots and *Article Subject
Tribune/Reviews* and have learned how this game works. In fact, I
have taken several meetings with vulture—er, *venture*—capitalists
whose gluttonous and unrealistic profit expectations have already
destroyed most other industries (not to mention public education) and who are now eager to exploit—make that *explore*—the

brave new world of media I envision, line up behind the inevitable unicorn, rush it toward extinction, and auction off the carcass to another sucker even more delusionally greedy.

Precisely why we would *need* venture capital under this model is another question entirely. I mean, since the writers are paying for everything, it wouldn't really require much involvement from the investment class. But since XYZ Investment Unequal Equity Partners has already flushed hundreds and hundreds of millions of dollars buying up digital media companies that—yup, you guessed it—now only produce podcasts about the pivot to video (But we're talking to Netflix! And YouTube!)—sending a few hundred million more my way is the soundest investment opportunity available. Besides, these people just can't resist spending on stuff they don't understand. And I'm gonna take it, just like all the acronyms and dots and *Article Subject Tribune/Reviews* have. As Paylance founder and CEO, I plan to grow my beard out, skate up in my worst T-shirt and thrift store shoes, and, after playing a set with my favorite band you've never heard of, preach to our target audience at the annual Tech FyreFest Northwest. I plan on telling them— again—about how we've already turned a profit before we've produced anything (they fall for that *every single time*). As soon as it's over, I'll swill down a couple of ayahuasca cocktails while inappropriately accompanied by a gaggle of Paylance interns who have no choice, pay myself in Bitcoin and other people in unrealized stock options, and prepare for the future the old-fashioned way. Because in the unlikely event that this model should unexpectedly collapse, I plan to transfer my wealth into bullion, bury most of it either in my backyard or in a friendly foreign bank, surround myself with lawyers, and string together so many buzzwords that it'll take six months before anyone realizes I've said nothing and have already skipped away into the limitless future only I was blind enough to see.

Oh, I know. *What about the readers?* That's the one thing, the only thing, the single essential truth that we're not gonna change.

Since most readers are already writers who were once paid to write, we plan on continuing to take you for granted. You can take that to the bank—I already have.

But until this inevitable scenario unfolds, alas, we must proceed under the current model, one that, somehow, is still working. Each year I read every issue of hundreds of general interest and sports magazines in search of writing that might merit inclusion in *The Best American Sports Writing.* I also contact the editors of many newspapers and magazines and websites to request submissions, and I make periodic open requests through Twitter and Facebook. All year long I search for writing all over the internet and make regular stops at the online sources *Longreads, Longform,* and *Sunday-LongReads,* as well as any other place where notable sports writing is likely to be highlighted or discussed. In trying to keep as many doors open as possible, I also take this opportunity to encourage everyone who cares—friends and family, readers and writers, editors and the edited—to send me stories they would like to see appear in this series. Although many writers are loath to do so, you are encouraged to submit not just your own work but also work you encounter that you admire. Work must be seen to be considered, and this invitation is open to everyone. Each story submitted to the upcoming edition must meet the following criteria:

- It must be column-length or longer
- It must have been published in 2019
- It must not be a reprint or book excerpt
- It must have been published in the United States or Canada
- It must be received by February 1, 2020

All submissions from either print or online publications must be made in hard copy and should include the name of the author, the date of publication, and the publication name and address. Photocopies, tear sheets, or clean copies are fine. Readable reductions to 8½″ × 11″ are preferred. Newspaper submissions should be of the hard copy or a copy of the same as originally published —not just a printout of the web version. Individuals and publications should please use common sense when submitting multiple stories. Because of the volume of material I receive, no submissions can be returned or acknowledged, and it is inappropriate for me to comment on or critique any submission. Magazines that want to be absolutely certain that their contributions are considered are advised to provide a complimentary subscription to the address listed below. Those that already do so should extend the subscription for another year.

All submissions must be made by U.S. Mail. I use a PO box because I have a really long driveway that makes winter delivery difficult, compounded by the fact that, after the town changed my street number, the GPS now sends UPS and FedEx drivers into the middle of Lake Champlain. Do not simply submit a link or PDF by Twitter email—some form of hard copy only please. The February 1 deadline is real, and work received after that date may not be considered.

Please submit either an original or clear paper copy of each story, including publication name, author, and date the story appeared, to:

Glenn Stout
PO Box 549
Alburgh, VT 05440

Those with questions or comments may contact me at basweditor@yahoo.com. Previous editions of this book can be ordered through most bookstores or online book dealers. An index of stories that have appeared in this series can be found at glennstout.net, as can full instructions on how to submit a story. This year I played an extremely minor editorial role in two selections, yet as with every other selection, those two were forwarded to the guest editor blindly, not identified by source or author. All submissions are subjected to the same basic criteria that every other *Best American* title uses. They are chosen according to "literary merit," the definition of which is entirely up to the guest editor, who is responsible for the contents and is never confined to selecting stories from among the 70 stories or so I put forward; my selections are only suggestive. For updated information, readers and writers are encouraged to join *The Best American Sports Writing* group on Facebook or to follow me on Twitter @GlennStout.

It was a great pleasure to work this year with Charlie Pierce, whose work I have long admired and who has appeared in these pages many times. My editor called on him to edit this edition after our original guest editor was forced by a small medical issue to withdraw—she'll be on board next year. I also thank all those at Houghton Mifflin Harcourt who have helped with the production of this series, especially editor Susan Canavan and her assistant, Mary Cait Milliff. This marks the final edition under Susan's steady direction, and I thank her for her skillful patience, faith, and trust in me to oversee the production of this series. Siobhan and Saorla have once again shared our home with the rough cut of this edition stacked in boxes tucked all over the place. My greatest thanks go to the writers, both those in these pages and those elsewhere doing this kind of work, who together provide evidence of the value that remains in words.

GLENN STOUT
Alburgh, Vermont

Introduction

TESS HARDING [attending a baseball game]: Are all these
people unemployed?
SAM CRAIG: No, they're all attending their grandmother's
funeral.
  — *Woman of the Year,* 1942

SOMETIMES I THINK that I am the lost child of Tess and Sam.
Not the refugee child who serves as a pivotal plot point in George
Stevens's romantic comedy classic, but a son they had and then
abandoned in the newsroom of *The Day,* the dying newspaper that
Humphrey Bogart tries to save in *Deadline USA.* (Turner Classic
Movies has had a terrible impact on both my self-image and my
work ethic.) Tess Harding, modeled reportedly on journalism giant Dorothy Thompson, has a job trying to make sense out of politics, both national and international. Sam Craig has a job trying
to make sense out of sports in the big city. Over the course of my
spotty career, I have tried to make sense out of both. Ever since
2011, almost completely on the internet, I have tried to do so simultaneously, and believe me, we will get to this whole internet
thing later. Some days, I'm Tess. Some days, I'm Sam. Some days,
I'm a little of each of them. At least both of them wore pants.

Sports is often considered the journalistic equivalent of hooky.
Often, the people whose job it is to make sense out of our games
are seen as attending an endless parade of funerals for an endless parade of phantom grannies. I confess. Sometimes it feels that
way to me too. In the late 1980s, when I was writing columns for
the *Boston Herald,* I remember flying to Detroit to cover an NBA

playoff series between the Celtics and the Pistons. I was waiting at the rental car counter amid the various species of American Business People. They all looked like walking ulcers. If they fell over, I thought, they'd shatter like delicate glass. Me? I was waiting to get a car, drive at a leisurely pace to a hotel, stretch out on a bed, take a nap, order some room service, and cover a basketball game. It was the go-go '80s and I was standing by the side of the road, waving at the maniacs going by on their way to whatever stress-related disease awaited them.

On the other hand, nearly 30 years had passed from the previous time I covered a major political campaign and the snowy New Year's night in 2012 when I drove from the airport to downtown Des Moines. Back in the day, I had been working for the *Boston Phoenix,* one of the country's great alternative newspapers. (As I was driving through the light, dancing snow that night in Iowa, I was unaware that the poor *Phoenix* had only a year to live.) Now I was the recently installed curator of *Esquire*'s new "Politics" blog, which appeared on the sturdy old magazine brand's website, and we will get to this whole internet thing later, I promise you. Back at the *Phoenix,* I'd had a desk and a telephone with six lines and a great old Royal typewriter on which you typed as though your words could crack the earth.

(This was the second of these lovely beasts on which I'd worked. The first one had died a horrible death. During my senior year at Marquette University, I was one of the editors of the student paper. That year the College of Journalism was still in the process of moving into larger quarters on campus. We worked in the basement, and they were remodeling the floor above us. One afternoon I got up to fetch some more copy paper—ask your parents, kids—and I hadn't taken two steps away from the old Royal when a huge chunk of the ceiling fell down and smashed my noble critter into a bent and dented pile. A head popped through the hole above and a guy in a safety helmet said, "Whoa. Sorry, man." This was my introduction to unplanned obsolescence, something with which the profession became sadly familiar as the years went by.)

I walked into the lobby of the downtown Des Moines Marriott, and the first thing I noticed was that the lobby bar was full of people, most of them younger than me, and all of them were huddled over laptops and cell phones like postulants at prayer. Nobody was

Hanging Around, and Hanging Around was one of the big reasons I got into the business. Hanging Around was how you learned things. When I started at the *Phoenix,* thanks to Marty Nolan and the late Dave Nyhan of the *Boston Globe,* I got to Hang Around with David Broder and Jules Witcover and Alex Cockburn and everyone else who was on the trail in 1980. Three years later, as I moved to cover sports full-time, I tried to Hang Around with people like Dave Kindred and the late Ed Pope and Furman Bisher, the columnist from Atlanta who was the subject of one of those newspaper stories that you never hear unless you Hang Around properly.

In 1974 a guy named William H. Williams, speeding his brains out, kidnapped Reg Murphy, the editor of the *Atlanta Constitution.* He demanded a $700,000 ransom, and a guy was dispatched from the newsroom with the cash in a suitcase. Legend has it that, as he was leaving, the guy with the money stopped, looked at the suitcase, and said,

"I feel like Furman Bisher going to spring training."

Hanging Around is a lost art. I worry that, in less than a generation, the people in this business are going to be no different than those incipient coronary occlusions at the car rental counter, measuring out our lives in Keurig pods. Hanging Around is more than a perk. It's also the whole damn job.

Hanging Around, Scene 1: The Churchill River runs out of Hudson Bay through the city of Churchill in Manitoba. On this September day, the water in the river is slate gray and the whales sliding beneath it are pure white, belugas running out of the bay and down the river. There are four people in the boat. Two hockey players, their father, and one reporter hanging on to the gunwales for dear life, Hanging Around because that's the job.

The hockey players are brothers, Terence and Jordin Tootoo, Inuit sons from Rankin Inlet in the new Canadian province of Nunavit. Jordin is the first Inuit player ever drafted into the National Hockey League, and he is preparing to move to Nashville to play for the expansion Predators in that most unlikely hockey outpost. Terence plays for a minor league team in Virginia. Today, though, dressed in black wetsuits, the brothers are here to ride the little white whales, burly and jovial young Ahabs with no malicious intent at all.

After a while, their father spots something else swimming in the river. He hauls the boat around, and we gradually come up on what on close observation is the head of a very healthy-looking polar bear. (Churchill lies on the primary migratory route for polar bears, and there is a thriving tourist economy there based on them.) We circled the bear once, twice, three times. It kept swimming, blithely ignoring us until, at one point, it rolled over on its back and sniffed loudly into the air. It wanted us to know it was there. As far as concentrating the mind wonderfully, Dr. Johnson is full of giblets—being hung has nothing on being dinner at close range.

So, go ahead, hang out with Joel Embiid, the talented, merrily eccentric Cameroonian center for the Philadelphia 76ers, as he tells Clay Skipper about how he once faced down a lion, and then hang out with Skipper while he tells you about it and about how it's a really good story, the only flaw of which is that it isn't remotely true.

> Read enough stories about the Philadelphia 76ers' star big man—or speak to enough people who know him well—and eventually this legend will come up. It's a well-worn thread in the fabric of the myth surrounding Joel Embiid (pronounced jo-ell em-beed). That he has continued to tell it suggests both a playful charm and deft cunning at the heart of the seven-foot man. But keeping such a tale alive also seems unnecessary given the wild and improbable life that Joel Embiid is actually living right now. "I always say, 'My life is a movie,'" Embiid tells me. "Everything happened so fast."

Or hang out with Ichiro Suzuki, the great Seattle Mariners ballplayer from Kobe in Japan, a city destroyed by merciless U.S. firebombing in World War II, and then hang out with Wright Thompson as he discovers by degrees the way Ichiro's native culture shaped the competitive fire in him, and the cost of what it has burned away within him.

> Father and son both appear to be modern men, but their vastly different upbringings offer little common ground. They can't see each other. Just as Nobuyuki cannot understand the pressure of being Ichiro, who once had to be smuggled out of a building wrapped in a rolled-up rug to avoid photographers, Ichiro cannot imagine the bleak early years of his dad's life. Nobuyuki was born during the war in 1942 and grew up in a bombed-out world dominated by hunger, privation, and the shame of

defeat. He wears threadbare slacks and cries when he talks to a reporter about his son. This off-season Ichiro hosted an event in his hometown. He visited only with his mother, Yoshie.

And just like that, you've been around the world.

Hanging Around, Scene 2: The orphanage was on a flat plain outside of Mexico City. The man who ran the orphanage was a priest who also worked as a *luchador,* one of the famous masked Mexican wrestlers. He had been born Sergio Gutierrez, and he wrestled under the *nom de grapple* Fray Tormenta. He wrestled to support the orphanage, which housed around 300 children. The boxer had come to the orphanage to visit with Fray Tormenta to entertain the orphans. His name was Jorge Paez. He grew up as an acrobat in a circus, and he was famous for riding escalators while doing handstands. He was a talented boxer who, ultimately, never quite became a titleholder.

On this day, as he glad-handed the kids, I wandered out behind the main building and found some of the orphanage's kids playing baseball as the sun was going down and the whole place was aflame all the way to the darkening mountains. The ball was a battered thing with strings hanging off it like a floor mop. One of the kids caught one on the nose and his bat shattered. Long ago, on this empty, scalded space, there had been a slaughterhouse. The kids were using the spinal cords of long-slaughtered cattle as their bats and having a grand old time doing it. Little bits of bone flew through the air as the landscape went blood-red around us in the last spasm of desert daylight before night fell out of the mountains on all of us.

So hang around with the victims of a man named Larry Nassar, whose crimes against children went on for decades and nearly destroyed the prestigious sport of U.S. gymnastics when he finally was run down to justice. And hang around with Kerry Howley as she tells you about the human destruction that was so much more terrible and tragic.

She had known how young the other accusers would be, but somehow it hadn't struck her until she walked into that room full of them. They were little girls. Her rage was such that she spoke slowly and almost in a whisper: "What. Have. You. Done." Between sobs she looked him

straight in the eye, cocked her head, and raised her eyebrows, a look
of profound disappointment and deep familiarity. Larry had sat emotionless, listening to other women he'd abused, for hours prior to this.
Sometimes he shook his head, as if to deny their claims. During Trinea's testimony, something changed. He started to shake, and then he
started to cry.

"I think his heart broke because my heart broke," she tells me later.
"I was worried the other girls would hate me because of his reaction to
me." There's pride in her voice, the triumph of having been the one,
out of the hundreds, who actually broke through. This may be her win,
or it may be his. There are a lot of ways to make a person feel special,
and Larry Nassar knows all of them.

Or hang out with Aaron Hernandez, the New England Patriots
tight end who murdered a man, was acquitted of killing two other
people, and then killed himself in his cell at a Massachusetts max-
imum-security prison. And hang out with the *Boston Globe*'s Spotlight team as they explore Hernandez's life when he was a child
caught in a strange and violent home.

Dennis Hernandez had long had concerns that Aaron, as a boy, had
a feminine way about him—the way he stood or used his hands, his
brother said. He also remembered one of Aaron's early ambitions that
sent their father over the edge.

"I remember he wanted to be a cheerleader. My cousins were cheerleaders and amazing," Jonathan said. "And I remember coming home
and like my dad put an end to that really quick. And it was not okay. My
dad made it clear that . . . he had his definition of a man."

The home environment, in general, was deeply homophobic.

"'Faggot' was used all the time in our house," Jonathan said. "All
the time. Standing. Talking. Acting. Looking. It was the furthest thing
my father wanted you to even look like in our household. This was not
acceptable to him."

And just like that, you realize that you've toured the dark energy
that lives in all human beings, that caused us to create angels and
demons in order to have someone, anyone, to share the blame.

Hanging Around, Scene 3: There were whitewashed walls around
the house in a Miami neighborhood. Birds cawed and sang, and
sang and cawed, in the merciless noonday sun. Inside the house
was cool and soothing, and the elderly woman with the guitar was
seated in a cane chair across the living room from me, talking

about the son, and the grandson, she had raised. She was a strong-looking woman, and wiry, the way some people are born to be. Her son's music had changed the way the world looked at an entire island and its culture. His recorded music wafted through the shady room. His son, her grandson, whom she'd raised, was a ferocious tackler on the University of Miami's football team. His name was Rohan Marley. Her son's name had been Bob Marley. Her name was Cedella Booker. When her son died, of melanoma, at 36, she sang his "Redemption Song" at his funeral:

> *Won't you help to sing*
> *These songs of freedom?*

We conducted the interview because that's why I'd come to Miami, to write about her grandson and his late father. But afterwards we talked about life and music and the road she had traveled. I happened to mention that my wife was expecting a baby.

"Jah blessing on your baby girl," Cedella said.

"We don't know that it's a girl," I said.

Cedella smiled and strummed a couple of light chords and nodded. Two months later, my daughter was born.

So hang around, at a merry remove, with Tom Brady, the singular quarterback of the New England Patriots. And then hang around with Caity Weaver as she goes reluctantly to the Super Bowl in Minneapolis and makes her own fun by exacting a promise for a genuine Philadelphia Eagles mini-fridge for her cubicle if she can complete a 26-item scavenger hunt that requires her to do everything from ride a private jet to find a dead bird. Oh, and she engages a book of magic to help her out.

> I bought a commemorative Super Bowl pen (also $6) at a souvenir pop-up shop that spanned two floors of the stadium, and featured ghostly white statues of football players, benched forever in heaven.
>
> The pop-up contained a FedEx booth where customers could pay to have their purchases shipped directly from the game. A FedEx employee allowed me to have a piece of tape for free. (THANK YOU!!!)
>
> I tore a piece off a jumbo paper towel roll left on a table in a women's restroom and went into a stall to perform my dark deeds.
>
> "Draw a large pentagram on the paper and write their first and last name in the center," the instructions read. "Sprinkle a little salt on the name."

"Then, drip some water on to the condiments."

"Place the special item on to the name. Lean down to the paper and chant the bad spell."

Good luck go, Go away. But bring all of the bad to stay. And for this spell, I must pay a price. With something dear, As well as nice. This is my will, So Mote It Be!

"Fold the paper in half hamburger style, and then hot dog style. Repeat until paper is small enough to fit in your pocket."

Or hang out with Joe Branch, who is involved in the cutthroat world of Cubing, the competitive exercise of solving the Rubik's Cube. And then hang out with his father, John, who has found himself in the role of sports parent in a very unusual, but wholly satisfying, context.

He had found acceptance by doing nothing more than being himself. Funny that it would come in a place where he could leave all the reinvention to the familiar 3 by 3 object in his hands, the one that has 43 quintillion possible configurations but that he and all the others could solve in seconds.

The crowd hushed. The race began. In little more than five minutes, Max Park solved all six of the puzzles, leaving the world behind.

"A valiant effort from the dream team," the MC said.

I walked away with no doubt about the best view—that of a parent, watching a child find his place.

And just like that, you discover that the entire journey is nothing more than a tour of the joy of playing games and that, given the nature of the world and its people, it's the furthest thing in the world from playing hooky.

My grandmother was a shepherd. She and her six sisters worked the flocks in the hills around Listowel in north Kerry. She left Ireland in 1901 and arrived in Massachusetts via Liverpool when she was 24 years old. She worked as a domestic and then married a policeman named Patrick Pierce. They had five children and four grandchildren, one of whom was me. She had no formal education; what she knew she learned from the hedge schoolmasters in her village, and from the *shanachies,* the itinerant Irish storytellers who worked for food and a bit of whiskey and who functioned as both entertainment and collective memory.

Years later, sitting in her dining room in a suburban home not far from my own, my grandmother told those stories to me. Ancient stories about Cuchulain and Deirdre of the Sorrows, and stories about her own life in the old country and the new—about how her youngest sister would duck out of work with the sheep to sit under a tree with a book—and the word "book" would have five syllables in the accent of the north Kerry hills—and then about the boxer dog they'd had who would wait by the door for The Sergeant to get home from walking his beat. And she told me about one day when her father took her into Listowel to see Charles Stewart Parnell speak, and this was after Parnell had fallen from grace, and a huge fight broke out, hurley sticks belting people in the chops. Years later I was reading Robert Kee's excellent biography of Parnell, and he described that same riot and in detail, and it was just as my grandmother had told me over tea when I was a boy.

I wish she were alive. I wish she could read the stories in this book and see how the simple act of telling them, the art of the *shanachie,* has survived the onslaught of technology and the cacophony of information and a collective attention span that is dwindling by the day. I wish she were alive so I could tell her about the polar bear in the river, and about the kids swinging cattle bones in the burning desert twilight, and about Bob Marley's mother predicting the birth of the great-granddaughter she never saw. Because all stories have endings, and not all endings are happy ones. I would tell her that, less than a year after we all chased the whales in the cold, gray river, Terence Tootoo took his own life with a shotgun in a field in Manitoba after being arrested for driving under the influence. His suicide note to his brother Jordin read:

> "Jor, go all the way. Take care of the family. You're the man. Terence."

His brother's suicide threw Jordin into a spiral. He became the first Inuk athlete to play in the National Hockey League. He drowned the pain and memories in alcohol and promiscuous, anonymous sex. But then he got sober and has stayed that way for a decade and a half. He has married and raised a family, and in 2014 he published a memoir with the great Canadian sportswriter, Stephen Brunt. This is Jordin's account of Terence's last, terrible night.

> My brother must have thought his life was over. He must have been thinking, So, f—, this is it. All the work I've done has just gone down the drain. And everyone would know. It would be humiliating. I think

he just couldn't deal with that being in the public eye. Everyone thought that Terence was this great guy, and that's how he wanted to be perceived. Everyone makes mistakes, but for him, with all that pressure coming at him from different angles, I just don't think he had the will inside him to fight it anymore. Instead, it was like, F—, this is it. I'm done. I don't want to deal with all of these people thinking I'm not this perfect, perfect guy.

Terence died. Jordin lived and got well and somehow has managed to live with his life, all the good and bad of it, and he's telling people about it in order to help them live with their own, all the good and bad of them. And that's the end of the story that began in the Churchill River, the white whales like smooth veins of ivory below the surface of the water. My part of it anyway.

I wish my grandmother was alive so I could tell her about Jordin and Terence and the whales and what came after. I wish she were alive to read this book, and I am very glad that all of you are. Lose yourselves. Hang out with the people in the stories, and hang out with the people who came to tell them. Drown in the collective memory. No matter how advanced our technology, we will find a way to tell each other stories because there is something essential and human in the telling. We need to tell each other stories. It is a long and proud tradition that we follow from whoever it was that scratched the Epic of Gilgamesh into clay tablets to every pixel that zips onto the computers that we can hold in our hands. Hang around with these people for a while. Have faith in the craft. Find hope in its stubborn, durable magic.

CHARLES P. PIERCE

The Best American
Sports Writing
2019

WRIGHT THOMPSON

When Winter Never Ends

FROM ESPN THE MAGAZINE

Day 1: February 4, 2018

ICHIRO SUZUKI STEPS out of the cold into the small restaurant that serves him dinner most nights. It's winter in Kobe, Japan, where he once played professional baseball and where he comes during the offseason to train. His wife, Yumiko, is back home in Seattle. He is here alone, free from the untidy bits of domestic life that might break his focus. Every day, he works out in a professional stadium he rents, and then he usually comes to this restaurant, which feels like a country inn transported to the city. It's tucked away on the fifth floor of a downtown building and accessible by a tiny elevator. Someone on the staff meets Ichiro at the back door so he can slip in unseen. Someone else rushes to take his coat, and Ichiro sits at a small bar with his back to the rest of the diners. Two friends join him. Inside the warm and glowing room, the chef slips on his traditional coat as he greets Ichiro in mock surprise.

"Thanks for coming again," says the chef, wearing Miami Marlins shorts.

"You guys made me wait outside," Ichiro jokes.

Ichiro is a meticulous man, held in orbit by patterns and attention to detail. This place specializes in beef tongue, slicing it thin by hand and serving it raw alongside hot cast-iron skillets. They do one thing perfectly, which appeals to Ichiro. Tonight he's got dark jeans rolled up to the calf, each leg even with the other, and a gray T-shirt under a white button-down with a skinny tie. His hair looks

darker than in some recent photos, maybe the lighting, maybe a
dye job. Either way, not even a 44-year-old future Hall of Famer is
immune from the insecurities and diminishments that come with
time. This winter is the most insecure and diminished he's been.

He doesn't have a professional baseball contract in America
or Japan. His agent, John Boggs, has called, texted, and emailed
teams so often that one MLB general manager now calls Boggs
"the elephant hunter," because he's stalking his prey. Boggs recently sent an email to all 30 teams. Only one wrote back to decline. Ichiro hasn't spoken to Boggs once this offseason, locked in
on what he and his aging body can control.

The restaurant fills up. Customers take off their shoes. At every
table, signs warn that no pictures can be taken. Ichiro waves at an
older couple. A producer type brings two young women over to
meet him, and Ichiro makes small talk before they bow and re-
cede. He makes some jokes about aging and turns a wine bottle in
his hand to read the label. The waiters, wearing sandals and blue
bandannas, sling plates of raw tongue and mugs of cold beer with
ice flecks in them. The chef installs a fresh gas can and sets down
a cast-iron grill in front of Ichiro.

"This is really delicious," Ichiro says.

He and his companions discuss the future, debating philoso-
phies of business, a new world opening up. Later they turn nostalgic and talk about the past. He started training every day in the
third grade and has never stopped. Once during his career he
took a vacation, a trip to Milan that he hated. This past October,
Marlins infielder Dee Gordon came to get something at the clubhouse after the season. He heard the crack of a bat in the cages
and found Ichiro there, getting in his daily swings. "I really just
hope he keeps playing," Gordon says with a chuckle, "because I
don't want him to die. I believe he might die if he doesn't keep
playing. What is Ichiro gonna do if he doesn't play baseball?"

Former teammates all have favorite Ichiro stories, about how
he carries his bats in a custom humidor case to keep out moisture,
how in the minors he'd swing the bat for 10 minutes every night
before going to sleep, or wake up some mornings to swing alone
in the dark from 1 to 4 a.m. All the stories make the same point:
he has methodically stripped away everything from his life except
baseball. Former first baseman Mike Sweeney, who got close to Ich-

iro in Seattle, tells one about getting a call from an old teammate who'd had an off-day in New York. *You're not gonna believe this,* the guy began. He'd brought along his wife and they walked through Central Park, thrilled to be together in such a serene place. Far off in the distance, at a sandlot field with an old backstop that looked left over from the 1940s, they saw a guy playing long toss. The big leaguer did the quick math and figured the distant stranger was throwing 300 feet on the fly. Curious, he walked closer. The guy hit balls into the backstop, the powerful shotgun blast of real contact familiar to any serious player. He became impressed, so he got even closer, close enough to see.

The man working out alone in Central Park was Ichiro.

His agent and those close to him think he'll sign with a Japanese team if no offer comes from the major leagues. Television crews floated around the Ginza district in Tokyo the night before asking people what they think about Ichiro's future. Ichiro, as usual, is saying nothing. He's a cipher, keeping himself hidden, yet his yearning has never been more visible. His old team, the Orix Buffaloes, wants him back desperately—but Japanese spring training started three days ago and Ichiro remains in Kobe. For a private man, these three days speak loudly about his need for another season in America. Over the years, he's talked about playing until he's 50 but also of his desire to "vanish" once his career ends. Those two desires exist in opposition, and if America never calls, he holds the power to make either of them real. He can sign with Orix, or he can fade away. The choice is his.

These are the things working in his life at dinner, a cold Sunday night between the Rokko mountains and Osaka Bay. Ichiro finally stands to leave. Two customers step into the aisle and bow, not the perfunctory half-bow of business associates and hotel bellmen, but a full to-the-waist bow of deep respect. Is this what the end of a great career looks like up close? Ichiro hates not playing baseball, but he might hate playing poorly even more. When he's slumping, his wife has said, she will wake up and find him crying in his sleep. The first time he went on the disabled list as a major leaguer was because of a bleeding stomach ulcer. That year, he'd led Japan to a victory in the 2009 World Baseball Classic, winning the final game with a base hit in extra innings. The stress ate a hole in his stomach. Weeks later, a Mariners team doctor told him he couldn't play on Opening Day. Ichiro refused to listen, Sweeney says. Before the team ultimately forced him to sit, the doctor tried to explain that a bleeding ulcer was a serious condition that could actually kill him.

Ichiro listened, unmoved.

"I'll take my chances," he said.

Day 2: February 5, 2018

The next morning at 11:46, Ichiro moves quickly through the Hotel Okura lobby. A hood covers his head. This 35-story waterfront tower is where he always stays, an understated gold and black lacquer palace that looks designed by the prop department from *You Only Live Twice*. His green Mercedes G-Class SUV is parked directly in front of the hotel and he climbs inside. The ballpark he rents, literally an entire stadium, is over the mountains, and he takes a right onto Highway 2, then an exit onto Fusehatake. He uses his blinker to change lanes.

The temperature is 38 degrees and falling.

A waterfall in front of the hotel is frozen mid-cascade.

On the drive toward the stadium, it begins to flurry.

Once there, he changes into shorts and steps out onto the field. A hard wind blows. Passing clouds drop the mercury even more. Ichiro isn't here in spite of the brutal cold but because of it. Japanese culture in general—and Ichiro in particular—remains influenced by remnants of Bushido, the code of honor and ethics governing the samurai warrior class. Suffering reveals the way to greatness. When the nation opened up to the Western world in 1868, the language didn't even have a word to call games played for fun. Baseball got filtered through the prism of martial arts, and it remains a crucible rather than an escape. Japanese home run king Sadaharu Oh wrote in his memoir: "Baseball in America is a game that is born in spring and dies in autumn. In Japan it is bound to winter as the heart is to the body."

A group of people always works out with Ichiro. Today there are 11 of them, not one a serious athlete. One is the chef from last night. One is a white guy who runs like a wounded animal. All of them wear long pants, because only a maniac would dress for this weather in shorts. Every day, the workout is the same. They stretch and jog. Ichiro runs the bases, and the rest follow him around the path. He takes 50 soft-toss swings, hitting the ball into a net, then he stretches again and steps into the batting cage.

Five people stand around the outfield with yellow crates and gloves.

Outside the stadium, two fans wait by the road with a gift of chocolate candy. They bring him this every year. A woman named Minako traveled here from Tokyo to find a crack in the bleacher walls wide enough to see through. She too makes this pilgrimage once a winter. As she stands on her toes and trains her binoculars on Ichiro, she wonders aloud whether this might be the end. Ichiro doesn't believe so. Last year he came within one hit of setting the single-season record for a pinch-hitter. The year before, he hit .291 playing in 143 games. His friend and former Orix BP pitcher, Koji Okumura, says Ichiro's swing has changed over the years. He now opens his hips and shows his chest to the pitcher earlier. "His eyesight is deteriorating," Okumura says. "He's trying to adjust to survive. He knows his death as a baseball player is getting closer."

In the stadium, Ichiro cracks line drives around the field. The wind whips around the bleachers, really blowing now. The final group of pitches, 24 in four minutes, comes a ball every 10 seconds. The last ball he arcs high into the air, and miraculously it lands in one of the yellow crates. His friends go nuts, screaming and yelling, and Ichiro raises his arms in celebration and runs around the batter's box in a little half circle.

He walks off the field and disappears into the dugout tunnel.

The temperature continues to fall.

Day 3: February 6, 2018

Ichiro walks through the hotel lobby at exactly the same time as the day before, 11:46 a.m., repeating his routine to the minute. He's a funny, self-deprecating guy who often makes light of his own compulsive behaviors, which extend far beyond his baseball-related rituals. He said in a Japanese interview that he once listened to the same song for a month or more. There's enlightenment in obsession, he says, because focus opens perception to many things. It boils life down.

"I'm not normal," he admitted.

He gets stuck in patterns. In the minors, sometimes his 10-min-ute bedtime swinging ritual stretched to two hours or more. His mind wouldn't let him stop. For years, he ate only his wife's curry before games, day after day. According to a Japanese reporter who's covered him for years, Ichiro now eats udon noodles or toasted bread. He likes the first slice toasted for two minutes, 30 seconds, and the second slice toasted for one minute, 30 seconds. (He calculates the leftover heat in the toaster.) For a while on the road, he ate only cheese pizzas from California Pizza Kitchen. He prefers Jojoen barbecue sauce for his beef. Once Yumiko ran out and mixed the remaining amount with Sankoen brand sauce —which is basically identical—and Ichiro immediately noticed. These stories are endless and extend far beyond food. This past September, a Japanese newspaper described how he still organizes his life in five-minute blocks. Deviations can untether him. Retire-ment remains the biggest deviation of all. Last year a Miami news-paperman asked what he planned on doing after baseball.

"I think I'll just die," Ichiro said.

Today Ichiro walks onto the field in Kobe, right on time, and everyone is waiting. It's uncanny. They bow when he reaches the dugout. It's a Tuesday, even colder than the day before, but the routine doesn't change: the four jogging laps across the outfield, the baserunning, the 50 soft-toss pitches, exactly 50. Except for the cold, these aren't hard workouts, more like a ritualized ceremony among friends. He could choose the best players in Japan to help him, but he doesn't. He doesn't need to get better at swinging a bat. What he needs, and what he seems to find in this rented sta-dium, is the comfort of the familiar, a place where he knows who he is supposed to be.

He is equally precise during the season, to the amusement of teammates. Dee Gordon says Ichiro even lint-rolls the floor of his locker. He cleans and polishes his glove and keeps wipes in the dugout to give his shoes a once-over before taking the field. The Yankees clubhouse manager tells a story about Ichiro's arrival to the team in 2012. Ichiro came to him with a serious matter to discuss: someone had been in his locker. The clubhouse guy was worried something had gone missing, like jewelry or a watch, and he rushed to check.

Ichiro pointed at his bat.

Then he pointed at a spot maybe eight inches away.

His bat had moved.

The clubhouse manager sighed in relief and told Ichiro that he'd accidentally bumped the bat while putting a clean uniform or spikes or something back into Ichiro's locker, which is one of the main roles of clubhouse attendants.

"That can't happen," Ichiro said, smiling but serious.

From that day forward, the Yankees staff didn't replace anything in his locker like they did for every other player on the team. They waited until he arrived and handed him whatever he needed for the day.

These stories are funny individually, but they feel different when taken as a whole. Like nearly all obsessive people, Ichiro finds some sort of safety in his patterns. He goes up to the plate with a goal in mind, and if he accomplishes that goal, then he is at peace for a few innings. Since his minor league days in Japan, he has devised an achievable, specific goal every day, to get a boost of validation upon completion. That's probably why he hates vacations. In the most public of occupations, he is clearly engaged in a private act of self-preservation. He's winnowed his life to only the cocoon baseball provides. His days allow for little beyond his routine, like leaving his hotel room at 11:45, or walking through the lobby a minute later, or going to the stadium day after day in the offseason—perhaps his final offseason. Here in the freezing cold, with a 27-degree wind chill, the hooks ping off the flagpoles. The bat in his hand is 33.46 inches long. He steps into the cage and sees 78 pitches. He swings 75 times.

Up close, he looks a lot like a prisoner.

Day 4: February 7, 2018

Ichiro hits a home run on his final swing today, always quitting on a positive result. Boggs is still weeks away from opening discussions with the Mariners, and an hour northeast of this stadium, Ichiro's father has been following the news of his son's free agency. Nobuyuki Suzuki orchestrated Ichiro's brutal boyhood training regimen, and now they don't speak.

Father and son both appear to be modern men, but their vastly different upbringings offer little common ground. They can't see each other. Just as Nobuyuki cannot understand the pressure of being Ichiro, who once had to be smuggled out of a building wrapped in a rolled-up rug to avoid photographers, Ichiro cannot imagine the bleak early years of his dad's life. Nobuyuki was born during the war in 1942 and grew up in a bombed-out world dominated by hunger, privation, and the shame of defeat. He wears threadbare slacks and cries when he talks to a reporter about his son. This offseason Ichiro hosted an event in his hometown. He visited only with his mother, Yoshie.

Nobuyuki is left with his memories and his museum.

Before Ichiro signed with the Mariners in 2001, the family built a home in Toyoyama to live in and an adjacent two-story museum filled with artifacts, from Ichiro's Star Wars toys to his first glove. It's open to the public for $11 a person. In the early pictures, Ichiro is always smiling. He smiles less as the years pass. There's a gym stocked with unused equipment, intended for Ichiro's workouts and now used to store boxes. Sometimes at night, Nobuyuki comes alone and walks through the exhibits. He dreamed of his son living here forever, and now he's gone. Nobuyuki found out about the Mariners signing the morning of the news conference. He insists he has no regrets and would do everything again if given a chance.

When Ichiro was three, Nobuyuki bought him his first glove, made of shiny leather. It cost two weeks' salary. Nobuyuki taught his son to clean and polish it carefully. It wasn't a toy, he said. It was a tool. He taught his right-handed son to hit lefty, to gain a few extra steps out of the batter's box. They went to a nearby park, every day the same: 50 pitches, 200 soft-toss swings, and 50 fungo drills. At night, they went to a batting cage near the Nagoya airport, and Ichiro would take 250 to 300 swings on a pitching machine. They did this 365 days a year. Sometimes it got so cold that young Ichiro couldn't button his shirt, his fingers too stiff to work. In elementary school, he wrote in an essay that he played with other children only two or three days a year. Once Ichiro didn't want to practice baseball. He wanted to run around with his friends, so he defiantly sat down in the middle of the field. A furious Nobuyuki started throwing baseballs at his son, but fast reflexes allowed Ichiro to avoid them. Ones aimed directly for his face he easily caught.

Ichiro started this life in third grade and hasn't stopped. With people he trusts, he'll talk about how Ichiro Suzuki did not create *Ichiro*. In the past, he has hated Ichiro. Only rarely do his private feelings become public. When Ichiro finished his second season with the Mariners and returned home, the writer Robert Whiting was granted an interview. He was escorted to a private floor of a Tokyo hotel overlooking the flashing neon *Blade Runner* world below. Whiting is a best-selling author and Japanese baseball expert and among the world's most sophisticated translators of the two cultures. He asked Ichiro about a passage in his father's book describing their training sessions as fun for both father and son. For the only time in the interview, Ichiro switched to English.

"He's a liar," he said.

Everyone laughed, but Whiting didn't think he was joking at all. The next day, Ichiro's manager successfully petitioned Whiting not to run that quote because of the importance of filial reverence in Japan. Whiting left in what Ichiro said next in Japanese. Ichiro said his dad's behavior "bordered on child abuse."

There are other issues widening the gap between Nobuyuki and Ichiro. Rumors occasionally find their way into Japanese papers about problems between Nobuyuki and Yumiko. Nobuyuki once ran all of Ichiro's business concerns but got in trouble in Japan over an enormous unpaid tax bill, which caused Ichiro great embarrassment and cost him perhaps as much as $168,000. That seems to have cemented the split: Yumiko now oversees Ichiro's finances. There's a hometown sushi restaurant where Nobuyuki and Ichiro once ate together. The owner feels sad because they come separately now. Nobuyuki has become a teacher without a student, except for the old artifacts he keeps behind glass.

Ichiro appears to be searching for people and stories to fill the place once occupied by his father. He loves old baseball players and their histories. He formed a relationship with former Negro Leagues star Buck O'Neil, and when the Mariners played the Royals in Kansas City, Ichiro took himself to the Negro Leagues Baseball Museum. He didn't tell anyone, and they wouldn't have known except for someone in the business office noticing his name on a credit card receipt. When Buck died, Ichiro sent flowers to the funeral and wrote a personal check to the museum in his memory. He's visited the graves of old players whose records he's broken, George Sisler in suburban St. Louis and Wee Willie Keeler in Queens, and in Japan he visits the grave of the scout who discovered him. He remains connected to his own history. The alternate address on the filing forms of his personal holding company is the old Orix dorm, which has since been torn down. He has visited the Hall of Fame in Cooperstown more than any other current major league player, sneaking in and out under the radar. (He's promised all his collection to Cooperstown and not his father's museum.) The tiny village with its glowing lights and happy baseball spirit captivates him nearly as much as the museum. Ichiro likes to hold the gloves and bats of other great players and commune with them. "It's not looking at Lou Gehrig's glove," says Hall president Jeff Idelson. "It's wondering what he might have been thinking when wearing that glove."

Nobuyuki sits in his museum today and wonders how Ichiro might be feeling. He's been having recurring dreams recently about his son. In them, Ichiro is in elementary school and none of the reckoning has begun. They are close still in these dreams.

Nobuyuki cries again.

Ichiro has broken away from his father—the man who invented Ichiro, the wellspring of all that's good and bad in his life—but he cannot break away from the man his father created. He cannot escape the patterns burned into him as a boy. His American teammates all talk about how he still polishes his gloves and spikes, as he was taught. He works out every day without break, forsaking even a family, wearing shorts in the freezing Kobe winter. He's made a $160 million fortune and can't enjoy it. He's earned his rest but can't take it. He's won his freedom but doesn't want it. The kid in the essay who wrote of a life away from baseball no longer exists.

Ichiro now does to himself all the things he resents his father for having made him do.

Day 5: February 8, 2018

He's gone.

Today at the Hotel Okura, 11:46 a.m. comes and goes and he doesn't pass through the lobby. His Mercedes out front doesn't move. Over the mountain at the baseball stadium, he and his friends don't take the field, and he doesn't hit 50 soft-toss pitches or swing until he's happy. Heavy rains are coming soon. Maybe snow if the temperature stays low. A thick soupy fog covers the city when weather rolls in and it's impossible to see, a gray blanket stretched between the peak of Mount Rokko and the cargo ships floating in Osaka Bay. The cherry blossoms are at least six weeks away. Winter maintains its grip on the islands. In the hotel lobby, an enormous painting of a forest by artist Ikuo Hirayama matches the ethereal, melancholy vibe. It's Japanese baseball weather.

His American agent is still a month away from any hint of interest from the Mariners.

His Japanese manager isn't returning phone calls.

Yumiko says the timing is bad for her to talk.

Few people can ghost like Ichiro. There are no sightings of him on social media, or mention of his whereabouts in the Japanese or American press. He's not at Japanese spring training in the southern prefecture of Miyazaki or at American spring training in Florida or Arizona. He could be in Tokyo, fulfilling some of his many promotional responsibilities. The bravest thing he could do is make good on his desire to disappear. Maybe, just maybe, he found the will to put down his bat and won't emerge for five years, wandering the earth until Cooperstown calls.

Of course, that's not what he's doing. He's somewhere out there —hungry for a chance to keep his routines in motion. It's a circle Ikuo Hirayama would find typically Japanese. Ichiro's American journey will continue where it began: Seattle. He needs five more winters until he reaches 50. There are goals to reach. There are patterns he can't abandon, scars he won't let heal, and the people who run the batting cage by the Nagoya airport know about them both. They've seen the boy whose father dreamed of something and the man who lives with the reality of those dreams. The cage is open today, 11 to 11, and there's a photo of him hanging near Lane No. 8, where his father sharpened Ichiro Suzuki into *Ichiro*. The old man working the counter in the small office says that Ichiro has come back to the cages to hit perhaps five times in the past two decades. The last time was five or six years ago.

Each visit has played out the same. Around 10:15 or 10:20 at night, the staff says, a luxury car turns into the small parking lot lined with Japanese pine trees. If the cages are empty, Ichiro gets out and carries his black bat to Lane 8. He pays his bill like everyone else, $2 for every 22 balls. The staff members don't bother him, but they do watch, understanding that they're seeing something intimate. The old man behind the counter thinks Ichiro is looking for something, coming back to the place where he split in two. He swings for about 20 minutes, and only he knows what is on his mind during this trip through his past. Soon the communion is over. He pulls out of the parking lot, carrying his private burdens into the night.

SAM MILLER

The Aging Curve

FROM ESPN THE MAGAZINE

23

THERE ARE TWO outs, the bases are empty, and the batter is 23.

He is, as he steps into the batter's box, the most exciting player in baseball. As a rookie, he has hit a ball 513 feet in batting practice, thrown a pitch 102.5 miles per hour from the mound, and reached a top sprint speed—nearly 30 feet per second—faster than three-quarters of his peers can touch. These are the highlight years, and it feels like just the beginning.

But an athlete's physical decline begins before most of us notice it, and even the 23-year-old body can do things today that it might not be able to do tomorrow. Fastball speed starts going down in a player's early twenties, and spin rate drops with it. Exit velocity begins to decline at 23 or 24. An average runner slows a little more than one inch per second every year, beginning pretty much immediately upon his debut. It takes a little over four seconds for most runners to reach first base, which means with each birthday, it's as if the bases were pulled four inches farther apart. Triples peak in a player's early twenties, as does batting average on balls put into play. A 23-year-old in the majors is twice as likely to play center field as left field; by 33, the opposite is true.

Thirty-three feels so far away, but it's already happening. The 23-year-old's lean body mass peaked sometime in the preceding five years. His bone-mineral density too. He's at the age when the body begins producing less testosterone and growth hormone. His body, knowing it won't need to build any more bone, will produce less energy. Male fertility peaks in the early twenties, the same time as pitch speed and exit velocity. Athleticism is, crudely speaking, about showcasing what a body looks like when it's ready to propagate a species. The 23-year-old's machine works as it was designed to. It is undamaged, unsmudged, and every circuit in it is trained to carry on his family's tradition of survival. When you're 23, the 32-year-old Mark Trumbo says wistfully, "performance is the only thing holding you back." To watch a 23-year-old athlete is to see the perfect machine running perfectly.

The batter grounds a pitch back up the middle, inches past the reach of the lunging infielders. It appears to be a routine single, but in the fraction of a second that the center fielder leans back on his heels to gather it, Shohei Ohtani tears around first and slides into second base for a breathtaking hustle double. His team is ahead by six runs in the ninth inning. It is something that only a 23-year-old could do, and that only a 23-year-old would want to do.

Two weeks later, Ohtani's season is interrupted by a sprain in his elbow ligament. The perfect machine has broken. They will try to fix it, and he will certainly return, but when he does, you can expect him to run an inch slower per second. They stop being young sooner than you think.

26

It's late May, and the runner on third base is 26.

He's the best player in baseball, but he has, technically speaking, lost a step: When he was a 20-year-old rookie, he might have been the fastest runner in the sport. Now he's merely fast. As a rookie, he made four home-run-robbing catches; now, at 26, he hasn't made one in almost a season and a half.

Yet he has not yet begun to decline as a baseball player. He's having, by most measures, the best season of his career, and he's the easy front-runner for American League MVP. It's an odd quirk of aging patterns that ability declines before performance does: Exit velocity declines years before home runs do; speed declines years before stolen bases do. Bone density might peak around 20, but ballplayers, most aging curve studies have concluded, peak in their mid- to late twenties.

Typists' fingers slow down with age, but their typing doesn't. Older typists are "more sensitive to characters farther in advance of the currently typed character than young typists," according to research published in the *Journal of Experimental Psychology*. In other words, they type smarter.

But at the same time—and here's the real trip—they *aren't* smarter. Researchers in British Columbia studied decision-making speeds of thousands of StarCraft 2 players and found that cognitive abilities peak at 24. Other research has found that perceptual speed drops continuously after 25. The brain is changing: the ratios of N-acetylaspartate to choline, the integrity of myelin sheathing, the connectivity of hippocampal neurons—you know, baseball stuff.

But the runner on third doesn't notice. Indeed, this is what differentiates the relatively young and the relatively old: they decline at the same rate, but younger adults just don't notice. For a while, they just figure out how to type faster. This is the miracle of sports: the product of mental decline and physical decline isn't necessarily decline.

The missing variable is, of course, experience. A 23-year-old begins to decline at the same time that he learns how to play baseball better. The race between age and expertise is what determines whether a baseball player can have the best season of his career years after his body begins to fail.

The 26-year-old runner is a few steps off third base as the pitch is delivered, and the batter pops it 230 feet to right field—too shallow, it seems, to get him home. To this point in the season, only one sacrifice fly has been shallower, and that one came with the right fielder running and off balance. This one is a lazy can of corn with an outfielder squared up under it. But the catch is made with a slight reach back, and Mike Trout bolts home, diving head-first to get under a high throw.

He has lost a step, technically, but he virtually never makes an out on the bases anymore. (One this year. Twelve as a rookie, not counting five times caught stealing.) He knows what's too shallow and what's deep enough and when the right fielder has to reach *juuust* back to make the catch. He's the best player in baseball, and it feels like he will be forever.

"He's gonna understand it in a few years," says Adam Jones, a

32-year-old center fielder. "He's a tremendous athlete—as am I—
and we keep ourselves in great shape. But one thing you can't stop
is time."

But Trout probably has never even heard of N-acetylaspartate.
Maybe it's not even real. Maybe I just made it up. When you're 26
and the best player in the world, you believe decline is a problem
for another day.

30

There are two outs in the fifth inning in Los Angeles, and the
pitcher is 30.

A year ago, he was considered, more or less unanimously, the
best starting pitcher in the world, with a stretch of more than
1,300 innings—the equivalent of six full seasons!—with an ERA
below 2.00. Now he's probably not, and he might rank as low as
fifth or sixth. He allows too many home runs; his velocity has been
dropping; and he keeps missing time with lower back issues. (Early
by-product of aging: loss of water content in the spongy lower back
disks, leading to herniation and other problems.)

There's a lot of debate in the study of aging about what aging actually *is*—when it starts, how to define it, why it happens.
One thread goes like this: Through natural selection, our genes
have evolved to do certain things meant to help us reach the age
of sexual maturity, and they expend a lot of energy simply holding us together until then. After that point, though, selection is
either much weaker or irrelevant. The genes don't give the cells
instructions for how to age, and we become something more like
inanimate objects, our cells degrading thoughtlessly as we come
apart. Microbiologist Leonard Hayflick, a titan in the field, has
argued that aging is explained by entropy—the tendency for con-
centrated energy to disperse when unhindered. When the forces
of our animacy quit holding us together, we just kind of break,
haphazardly.

Or, as Hayflick has put it: A car has to be engineered to run. It
doesn't have to be engineered to fall apart.

The early part of breaking down is still mysterious, because
the physical differences at that age are mostly too small to reli-
ably detect in a lab. "We know what's happening to a 60-year-old

versus a 30-year-old, but 30 to 33—especially somebody who is a physical freak like a major league ballplayer—it's really tough to make detailed scientific statements," says Dr. Michael J. Joyner, an expert on human performance at the Mayo Clinic. "Just like people get better through marginal gains, and all of a sudden things click for them on the way up? People fail the same way. Marginal de-gains."

Ballplayers first notice it in the short, explosive moments. "To get to a 97 mile per hour fastball that's up in the zone, you *know* you can get it there," 31-year-old veteran catcher Caleb Joseph says. "It just isn't as readily available anymore. When you're 22, it's always on. You're like, 'Do I need to get a lighter bat? Is this how it's gonna be?'"

He laughs, then pauses, deciding which kind of story he's telling. "I went down an inch this year. I'm still hitting .150."

Is it that he's not as strong? That his brain doesn't pick up the pitch as fast? It could be, but it could also be that the nervous system moves slightly slower as we age, says Corey Dawkins of Baseball Injury Consultants. Joseph could identify the pitch just as quickly, decide to swing just as confidently, swing just as powerfully as he ever did—but the signal from brain to muscles takes a fraction of a microsecond longer to travel.

The simplest reading of sports is that we want to see the extremes: how fast a human can throw it, how far a human can hit it. But that's not quite true. If that's what we wanted to see, we'd let the pitcher get a running start, we'd let the hitters use aluminum bats, we'd let them all drink Deca-Durabolin, and we'd only make them play one game a week. We want to see the extremes *when limitations are put on them*. We want to see what they do when we make it hard. Age is the ultimate make-it-hard.

The 30-year-old pitcher throws a curveball for strike one, then he throws a fastball for strike two. It's 87.9 miles per hour. In a start just 363 days earlier, his fastball averaged 94 miles per hour, but today the average is 89. Less than 24 hours after this game, in fact, he will return to the disabled list, the lower back again.

But first, Clayton Kershaw throws a changeup for strike three. He throws maybe 20 changeups a year, but he sneaks one in here and it works. He strikes out the side, lowers his ERA for the season to 2.76, and leaves the game having allowed only one run. He's still very good, but baseball has become, for this pitcher, hard.

35

It's the seventh inning, the score is 4–0, and the pitcher throwing the shutout is 35.

He's been an ace for most of this decade, but in the past few years, his peers have been disappearing. Jered Weaver and Matt Cain retired last year, at 34 and 32, respectively. Tim Lincecum, 34, was in Triple A this year until he got released. Felix Hernandez, at 32, now throws in the high 80s and carries an ERA in the mid-fives.

There was a point a few years ago when the man on the mound feared he might be approaching such a fate. He'd thrown an 88 mile per hour fastball in a game, and he thought his career was ending. Now, though, at 35, he might once again be the best pitcher in the game. "Rather than stability, we have lifelong flux," wrote the authors of the StarCraft study. "Our day-to-day performance is, at every age, the result of the constant interplay between change and adaptation."

We know, or can speculate on, some things about this pitcher's body: His mitochondria—the little factories in the cells that produce energy—probably don't work as well as they used to. His muscles are probably losing elasticity; his tendons and ligaments are stiffer from having less water content; his bones are more prone to fractures or stress injuries. He doesn't produce as much testosterone or growth hormone as he did in his early twenties, and it's therefore harder for him to add muscle mass. "I could continue to squat the house," 36-year-old second baseman Ian Kinsler says, "but I'm not going to get any stronger anymore. The older you get, it's just about feeling good." Which sounds a lot like a description of hospice.

But we know that despite all of this, some guys get better. The numbers on the left side of the equation don't add up to the number on the right, which strongly suggests we're capable of far more than we think. There is some extra potential that exists, and if this pitcher can tap into it, why not any of us?

"We can identify with the decline because we all experience it," Joyner says. "But the outliers! They make us feel like we're immortal!"

The pitcher throws: 99.24 miles per hour. It is Justin Verlander's 79th pitch of the day, and he records the second out of the seventh inning with it. Not long ago, Verlander had gone years without throwing a pitch so hard. He was asked this year when he thinks he'll retire, and he said he's now thinking 45. "I don't know if that's realistic," he told MLB. com, but we don't want realistic. We want to see realistic get toppled, over and over, so that we aren't burdened by the tyranny of "realistic" in our own aging lives.

38

The game is in Seattle, there are 41,705 fans in attendance and the batter is 38.

He was once 23, once 26, once 30—in fact, he finished second in the MVP voting each of those years and won the award three times in between. But for the past seven seasons, he has played for a team whose fans have never idolized him—have sometimes resented him as an expensive burden—and today he is in a city that has virtually no connection to the greatness his next hit will codify.

"Complex systems—power plants, say—have to survive and function despite having thousands of critical, potentially fragile components," writes Atul Gawande in *Being Mortal.* "Engineers therefore design these machines with multiple layers of redundancy: with backup systems, and backup systems for the backup systems. The backups may not be as efficient as the first-line components, but they allow the machine to keep going even as damage accumulates."

The 38-year-old at the plate used to do everything: one of the best defensive first basemen ever, a valuable baserunner, and a multidimensional hitter who mastered the strike zone and homered nearly as often as he struck out. One by one, the systems have broken down: he's a DH more often than he plays the field; it hurts to watch him run; he almost never walks; and he sets career highs in strikeouts and career lows in almost everything else. His career survives mostly on the basis of one home run per week.

Catchers' framing skills peak in the mid-twenties, research has found. Batters' contact rates peak at 28 or 29. Batters swing at the fewest pitches out of the zone in their early thirties. Batters draw the most walks in their late twenties, and pitchers issue the fewest walks at about 26. Ground ball pitchers' ground ball rates peak at about the same time. The only thing that peaks with age is maturity.

Surviving in baseball is a years-long process of learning to *get through this*. It takes skill to believe, in the middle of the worst periods, that this too will pass. As Kinsler puts it, the advantage of being old is that you've learned how to handle even the longest stretches of failure because "you know it's going to change. Just from past experiences."

You master the delusion just about in time for it to cease to be true.

The pitch is a little outside, but the 38-year-old reaches out and hits a soft flare into right field. It sounds like his bat breaks. The hit—the 3,000th of Albert Pujols's career—has been, directly and indirectly, a long time coming. The 26-year-old Mike Trout leads his teammates out of the dugout and gives the 38-year-old Pujols a long, textured hug. Then the 23-year-old Shohei Ohtani reaches into a scrum of teammates and, with a big smile, pats him on the back. The fans in Seattle give a sincere standing ovation to a man whose greatness is long gone.

There's a way of looking at the data to conclude we will all die— 100 percent of the people who came before us did. But there's also a way of looking at the data to conclude that, in fact, *I* never will. *I've* been alive for a billion data points and I haven't died once.

To watch the 38-year-old these days is to see these two arguments smash into each other. It is to watch a dignified man walking alongside, but not yet into, the end. It's to see an athlete who was once the very best in the world fail, repeatedly, in public, and to see that it's okay—not at all shameful—to get worse. It's to see the smiles and the ovations among it all. It's to see that, ultimately, this isn't life and death. Just a metaphor for it.

JACKIE MacMULLAN

When Making the NBA Isn't a Cure-All: Mental Health and Black Athletes

FROM ESPN.COM

THEY LEARNED FROM an early age to keep their heads bowed and their voices low. Around the Erie Avenue row house where Marcus and Markieff Morris grew up in North Philadelphia, eye contact with the wrong person could be misconstrued as a sign of disrespect or, worse, a challenge. "Then, next thing you know, the guns are coming out," Marcus says. "I've seen guys get shot just for sitting on the wrong front step. We were surrounded by violence, gangs. You wake up every day thinking, 'How am I going to protect myself?'"

The Morris brothers were exceptional athletes, providing them with an occasional escape from an environment Marcus says felt like a tinderbox: light a match, and the whole thing will blow. Like many boys their age, the Morris twins dreamed of playing in the NBA or the NFL. "But," Marcus says, "we were living somewhere where you never saw anybody do that."

When the twins were in high school, their house burned down with their family cat trapped inside. Their mother, Angel, moved them and their brother Blake into a small home in Hunting Park with their maternal grandparents, a tight squeeze for teenage boys who would grow to be nearly 6-foot-10. They lived in the basement and slept on a mattress, with no heat and a ceiling that was only 6½ feet high, which made it impossible for them to fully stand up.

Yet they were grateful, because at least they had family who cared. Only one in 20 of their friends had a father around—the twins' dad was nowhere to be seen either—and their mother worked long hours so she could pay for their basketball shoes and something to eat at supper. The twins leaned on each other for companionship, solace, and courage.

"We were just trying to survive every day," Marcus says. "As a kid, it's fun for a minute. You don't see yourself in any danger. Once you become a teenager, you're unprotected. Now you're a target. If you're wearing some Jordans, they're coming for you. There were plenty of times I had to protect myself. You walk out the door every day looking around, watching your back, just trying to stay out of the line of fire.

"You see shootings, pistol whippings. One wrong decision, one wrong word, and it escalates so quickly into a full-blown war. It's like that in Philly. You're trapped in a box. Your opportunity is so small, so once a person gets ahold of something, they protect it with their life. It's hard to explain if you haven't lived it.

"You got respect in our neighborhood by killing someone. That's how messed up it was."

The brothers were so close that they finished each other's sentences. They liked the same foods, ran with the same friends. They were, in many ways, one person—except Marcus was more outward, talkative, and Markieff more reserved, protective. Marcus played quarterback, and Markieff lined up at center to make sure nobody messed with his brother. They were rarely apart, which made it harder for someone to jump them or rob them.

"Markieff was my lifeline," Marcus says. "We needed each other to make it out of there. Without him, we wouldn't be having this conversation."

"Whatever my brother was feeling," Markieff says, "I was feeling it too."

Perhaps, then, it's not surprising that both Morris brothers revealed to ESPN in unison that they have been living with depression. Both initially agreed to be interviewed, but when it came time to share their story, only Marcus felt comfortable enough to be quoted about his mental health issues. Confidentiality remains a major concern of NBA players who are dealing with mental health issues, and each operates on his own timetable when, if ever, he decides to share.

Marcus says his and Markieff's depression stems from demons of a fractured childhood that began with two strikes against them: poor and black.

"We grew up where there were no white people," Marcus says. "None. You just didn't see that in our neighborhood.

"At that time, I didn't trust any white people because I didn't know any white people. Honestly, I didn't feel like I could trust anybody—not even the people in my neighborhood, who I knew my whole life.

"We just walked out stressed all the time. I said to my brother once, 'You know, this is no way to live.'"

Last season, the NBA was 74.2 percent African-American and 80.7 percent people of color. That demographic presents unique issues outlined in a 2001 study by the surgeon general, which found that historic social and economic inequality, racism, discrimination, violence, and poverty make African-Americans more prone to encounter mental health challenges.

They can also be more likely to have an inherent mistrust of people who are trying to help them. When you consider that only 30 percent of coaches and 20 percent of general managers in the NBA are people of color, it's not a stretch to conclude that conflicts will occasionally arise between an African-American player and a front-office member who looks nothing like him and, as far as the player is concerned, can't possibly understand where he is coming from.

"There's some truth to that," Marcus says.

DeMar DeRozan, who has talked openly about his depression, says he developed a false persona of "invincibility" to protect himself from the volatility in urban Compton, California, where he grew up. That aura of invincibility paired nicely with his athletic endeavors, as coaches crave confident players.

"If you grow up in the inner city, you have to walk a certain way, and you have to talk a certain way," DeRozan says. "If a guy walks past you, you gotta make sure you don't show any type of weakness, so they won't mess with you.

"That's something that carries over to everything you do as you grow older. It's constant. And it's draining. For me, it just got to a point where I decided, 'There's nothing I need to hide behind no more. I'm not going to worry about someone calling me weak or soft. At the end of the day, I know what I'm made of.'"

Hall of Famer Charles Barkley says most young African-Americans understand that their path will be pocked with roadblocks, simply because racism and discrimination are still a daily fact of life. Barkley says he's treated with respect most of the time, but "it's the one a—h— that calls you some kind of slur that sticks with you the rest of the day."

"One of the biggest problems in the African-American community is none of us have fathers, so we don't have that strong male figure to guide us," Barkley says. "When I was growing up, I thought it was normal not to have a mom and dad around. Nobody I knew had both parents. And everybody I knew was poor.

"I thought it was normal for every black girl to be pregnant in high school, because in my small hometown of [Leeds], Alabama, that's how it was. It wasn't until I got to the NBA that I realized, 'Wait, that's really f—ed up.' It's a miracle any African-American player turns out okay based on where we come from."

Former San Antonio Spurs defensive stopper Bruce Bowen was a rousing success story, carving out a 13-season career in the NBA after going undrafted in 1993. He was held in such high esteem by Spurs coach Gregg Popovich that the team retired his number 12 in 2012. (Bowen has since given his blessing to have his number reissued to LaMarcus Aldridge.) Bowen was easily identifiable by his thoughtful dissertations on the game and his trademark bowtie, leading many to draw erroneous conclusions.

"People thought I was raised in a middle-class family," he says, laughing.

Bowen was actually born in Merced, California, and raised in a home in the Fresno area where he says his father pilfered his pocket money to buy booze and his mother sold off the family television to feed her crack cocaine habit. His family situation was so unstable that Bowen changed homes multiple times, often living with friends and relatives. His father was not a presence in his life —until Bowen displayed some athletic prowess.

"My mom was strung out on drugs, and my dad was an alcoholic and a womanizer," Bowen tells ESPN. "That was my reality. Even as a child I could see through all their bulls—, but what was I going to do? I didn't even know how to begin to ask for help."

Bowen says that as he grew older, he learned to suppress the fear and the rage that churned inside him.

"In the African-American culture, there's this tendency to believe if we hide our problems, we'll be better off," Bowen says. "We are brought up to believe if you talk to people about those things, that's a sign of weakness. But it's not a sign of weakness. It's actually a sign of courage because you are taking the first step towards conquering your problems.

"But the other problem we have is this deep-seated mistrust of the actual people who can help you. We are raised not to trust anybody."

A survey conducted for the Kaiser Family Foundation in 1999 found that 12 percent of African-Americans, in comparison to 1 percent of whites, felt that a doctor or health provider judged them unfairly or treated them with disrespect because of their race or ethnic background. A subsequent study by the Commonwealth Fund Minority Health Survey found that 43 percent of African-Americans, compared to 5 percent of whites, felt that a health care provider treated them poorly because of their race or ethnic background.

Bowen considers himself fortunate that he landed with the Spurs, an organization, he says, that focuses on growing not only the basketball player but also the person. He says he played with "countless" teammates, both black and white, who had mental health issues, and doesn't expect numbers to dwindle.

"Most of these kids only went to college for a year, so what did they learn in that time? Not a lot," Bowen says. "So now you come to the NBA where you are expected to be professional, responsible, and develop character.

"If you have a great organization who is willing to stick with an individual and provide them with the guidance they need, that's fantastic. But if you don't have an organization that's willing to exhibit that patience, that empathy, then that player is going to struggle. The fans might not see it, maybe not even his teammates, but he's going to struggle."

Bowen resisted talking to a mental health professional throughout his career, a decision he regrets. "I would have been a better player and a better man," he says.

His struggles, he says, had to do with issues of control. He felt compelled to micromanage every facet of his life, both on and off the floor, which increasingly became a stressful, counterproductive exercise. He was estranged from his biological parents, yet remained under tremendous pressure from other relatives to offer them financial assistance. Bowen married and had two sons, determined to be a dutiful and doting father, but when the marriage ended in divorce seven years ago, Bowen says, he knew something had to change.

"I was in a dark place," Bowen says. "I didn't want to be like my biological parents. I wanted to be a better father to my boys, and I needed some help figuring out how I could do that."

He asked a friend for a referral and began seeing a therapist, unearthing the pain of the past and learning how to reconcile and accept his future.

"So now I'm present, I'm invested, and when I feel some anxiety regarding something going on with my boys that I can't control, I can identify that," he says. "I'm more at peace. I've finally been able to realize, 'I want to control that and I can't, but you know what? That's okay.'"

Bowen, DeRozan, and Marcus Morris say that confronting the past and determining how it should fit into their lives going forward is one of the most difficult yet effective parts of their mental health treatment. But that doesn't mean you can simply walk away from where you came. In fact, most players prefer not to do that.

"People don't understand what these guys in the African-American community go through," longtime agent Aaron Goodwin says. "It's so hard for them to separate themselves from the people they grew up with. It leads to withdrawal, anxiety. There's guilt about turning their backs on people they care about but who aren't good influences in their lives. There's this pressure of, 'I have to succeed because so many people are counting on me.' And then there's all the people with their hands out because everyone wants money."

Barkley remembers those days well. As a rookie with the Sixers, he felt compelled to assist his family and his boys from Leeds financially. But as the years went on, accommodating everyone who had a hand out became a burden, a distraction—and a trigger for stress.

"Money ruins all your relationships," Barkley says. "No matter what you do for your family, it's never enough. All your friends think because you're rich, you should bail them out of every situation.

"The only time I had any peace and quiet was on the basketball court."

*

Basketball was the reason the Morris twins were able to go to college. They couldn't afford it otherwise. They signed together with Kansas, a world away from the urban Philly streets that shaped them. Lawrence was an idyllic college town with stately buildings, green lawns, and leafy trees bursting with color.

"I couldn't wrap my head around how different it was," Marcus says. "People genuinely cared how your day was going. For the first time, I didn't have to look over my shoulder every five minutes. I could walk miles and miles without worrying."

And yet, the Morris twins occasionally felt their past tugging at them unexpectedly. One night, when they were walking back from practice around 9 p.m., a car started slowly following them down the street. Instinctively, both Marcus and Markieff began looking around for a stick, a rock, anything that could be used as a weapon of self-defense.

"I'm thinking, 'Do I run? Should I protect myself?'" Marcus recalls. "In Philadelphia, when it's nine o'clock, when it's dark, and a car pulls up, you take off. I don't care if it's my mom in the car. You know something bad is gonna happen."

The Morris twins picked up their pace, trying to ignore the oncoming vehicle. The man driving accelerated to catch up with them, then pulled down his window.

"You guys need a ride?" he asked pleasantly. "I'd be happy to drop you."

"We told him, 'No, we're good,'" Marcus says. "I looked at my brother and said, 'Damn, maybe this is different. Maybe we can relax a little bit.'"

Marcus says he and his brother spent three years basking in the kindness and the calmness of their Kansas bubble. When they went home to Philly during the summer, the contrast in environments made them more determined than ever to find a way out.

Their ticket was the NBA Draft. On June 23, 2011, Markieff was selected with the 13th pick by the Phoenix Suns. Five minutes later, Marcus was taken with the 14th pick by Houston. While Markieff averaged 7.4 points and nearly 20 minutes a game in his rookie season, Marcus played only 17 games in the NBA and was shipped off to the Rockets' D-League affiliate.

"I was heartbroken," Marcus says. "I'm thinking, 'Am I not good enough? Did I do something wrong?' Then I got hurt. The way I dealt with stuff was to bottle it up, hold it in. It's my first year in the NBA, and it's all falling apart. I didn't have any veterans telling me, 'It's okay, it will get better.' I felt really alone."

Morris dealt with the disappointment by shutting down. That summer, he refused to go to Houston for offseason workouts and wouldn't answer calls from the Rockets' staff. "[Rockets general manager] Daryl Morey is telling me, 'You're hurting your career,' but I was thinking, 'Well, you guys are hurting my career,'" Morris recalls. "I didn't trust them. I didn't trust anybody."

Midway through his second season, in February 2013, Morris was traded to Phoenix and reunited with his brother. Almost immediately, his symptoms of anxiety and depression subsided. He played there for two and a half seasons, and the brothers negotiated an unusual joint contract paying Markieff $8 million a season and Marcus $5 million. The money didn't matter to Marcus. He was where he wanted to be. "I put my own career on the back burner," Marcus says. "I wanted to play with my brother. They wanted to keep him happy. It wasn't about me. As far as my career, they didn't really care about me."

In July 2015, Marcus was shocked to learn he had been traded to Detroit. The brothers were hurt and angry, and they felt betrayed.

"That's when I really went to a dark place," he says. "It was so cold what they did. After that, I made up my mind. I wasn't having no more relationships with any front-office people. I wasn't getting close to any more guys on the team. I was done. The team was over there, and I was going to be over here."

For most of his young life, basketball had been his sanctuary. But at that point, Morris says, it felt like the source of all his angst.

"I start asking myself, 'Is this for me?'" Morris says. "Growing up, I loved the game so much—it was the only thing that made me happy. But now it's stressing me out. It's all negative. It's all business, and I'm having trouble with that. So you start flipping back and forth. The money is great, but is it good for me as a human? Shouldn't that matter more than anything?"

Morris couldn't sleep because his mind was racing all the time. The Pistons tried to make him feel welcome, but he wasn't very responsive. He was often up all night replaying a missed shot or a mistake on the floor, and his play was suffering. He seriously considered quitting, but what would he do? Go back to Philly? That notion led to more anxiety, more stress. He tried sleeping pills. He smoked marijuana. Nothing granted him peace.

He was traded again on July 7, 2017, this time to Boston. By then, both he and Markieff were facing an aggravated assault charge from a 2015 incident in Phoenix, and the trial would keep him away from the Celtics' preseason workouts. It was a difficult way to join a new team, but the Celtics surprised him by assuring him his place on the team was safe. He was acquitted in October, joined his teammates in Boston, and discovered that both GM Danny Ainge and coach Brad Stevens were incredibly open about encouraging players to seek help with their mental health struggles. They introduced him to psychologist Dr. Stephanie Pinder-Amaker, whose husband, Tommy Amaker, coached the Harvard basketball team just up the street.

"When I first got to Boston, I had all these negative vibes around me from the trial," Morris says. "I spent too much time worrying about what people thought of me. I didn't want to make any friends. I wanted to be coached and go home."

Instead, Morris sat in on a mandatory informational session on mental health, with Pinder-Amaker as the featured speaker. As she discussed the unique pressures facing NBA players, he found himself nodding along. She characterized depression and anxiety as common, manageable issues that exist in all walks of life. She left behind informational pamphlets and promised their sessions would be confidential—from Ainge, Stevens, even owner Wyc Grousbeck. Morris scribbled down her number but didn't call. When she returned again for another group session, he decided to reach out.

Pinder-Amaker, he says, coaxed him into identifying his triggers for anxiety. They talked about transforming his negative thinking into positive self-talk. Eventually, that led to discussions about his upbringing and depression in his family. Pinder-Amaker urged Morris to try meditation and other relaxation techniques to lower his stress level.

"She has helped me so much," Morris says. "It may sound silly, but just closing my eyes in a dark room and breathing for 10 minutes a day helps me. I know lots of guys who are dealing with some kind of anxiety and depression—not knowing if they have a job

next season, not knowing if they're going to get traded. It's so
stressful. Everyone is pulling at you. They want your time, your
money, a piece of your fame.

"If you have depression, you should be trying to get rid of it
instead of bottling it up and letting it weigh on you and weigh on
you and weigh on you. Talking to Stephanie released so much of
that stress for me."

Identifying what triggers symptoms can become easier with input from a player's immediate circle, whether it's a partner, girlfriend, or parent. Pinder-Amaker will ask the player to determine
whether those relationships are healthy and whether those people
might also be struggling. But looping in family members continues be a challenge because many do not want to acknowledge
their shortcomings or their own mental health challenges.

Marcus Morris no longer has such misgivings. He cannot speak
for his brother Markieff, he says, but seeing a mental health therapist has made Marcus a calmer, happier, more productive member
of the NBA family. He knows the gang members hanging on the
stoop near Erie Avenue would scoff at him, deride him for being
"soft," but he no longer cares.

"We need to forget about the criticism we might hear," Marcus
says. "We need to search and find out what makes us better. This
isn't even about basketball. It's about my life."

CHRISTOPHER SOLOMON

A Terror Way Beyond Falling

FROM OUTSIDE

EARLY ONE MORNING in 2016, a few days after Christmas, the phone rang in the office of the Northwest Avalanche Center in Seattle. Scott Schell answered. Schell is the center's executive director, and he was anticipating a busy day. The night before, at a dinner party, he was informed that Washington's first avalanche death of the winter had happened. A man who'd gone out of bounds at the White Pass Ski Area, southeast of Mount Rainier, was buried in a slide.

Schell wasn't surprised that he recognized the victim's name. About two dozen ski areas dot the mountains of Washington and Oregon, and hundreds of thousands of skiers visit them annually. But the universe of intensely passionate Pacific Northwest skiers and snowboarders is a curiously small one. On discussion boards with names like Ski Sickness and Famous Internet Skiers, men and women gossip, argue, and swap snapshots of their latest descents. If they don't know each other, they usually know about each other.

Schell had often heard of the dead man. At 31, Adam Roberts was one of the most aggressive freeskiers in the Northwest. A ski model and an aspiring professional who'd attracted the interest of gear companies, Adam seemed to be everywhere in the mountains, the graceful sine wave of his turns interrupted only by long drops from tall cliffs. He was of modest height, with a weight-room torso and a voice so gentle it could sound feminine. Mutton chops thick enough for gray jays to nest in bracketed a wide smile. He frequently wore nail polish, sometimes dyed his brown hair, and rarely pursued money. People who met him often came away using the word "charismatic." Some thought him reckless.

The caller that morning told Schell he was a friend of Adam's who'd heard about his death. "I know you can't tell me detailed information," the man said. "But I'd just like to ask one question."

"What's your question?"

"I want to know if Adam was skiing alone, or if he had a partner with him."

"It's my understanding that he was with a partner," Schell said.

The caller sighed, then said something that struck Schell as odd. "I feel a lot better hearing that." He was worried Adam had gone into the mountains alone, in the hope that he would be swept away.

More than a decade before Adam was born, Steve and Judy Roberts bought 35 acres of a steep mountain clear-cut above the logging town of Randle, south of Mount Rainier. It was the mid-1970s. The couple saw themselves as back-to-the-landers, eager to live closer to nature. "They called us the hippies on the hill," Judy remembers of their initial reception by locals.

The place was heaven. Hiking trails were everywhere. So was easy access to deep powder, 35 miles up the highway at the family-friendly White Pass Ski Area. In time a small wooden sign would appear above an out-of-bounds powder shot to mark Steve's passion: ROBERTS' RUN. The couple adopted their first son in early 1983. Two years later they adopted Adam.

The parents wasted no time introducing their boys to the natural world. They took Adam on his first overnighter when he was five months old, a burro carrying the diapers. Soon there were weeklong pack trips into north-central Washington's Pasayten Wilderness. At 13, Adam climbed Mount Adams, a 12,276-foot stratovolcano, with his father and brother.

Adam thrived in Randle. He got good grades, ran cross-country, was elected student body vice president. He was a Tom Sawyer type who, when excited about pursuing a goal or a hobby, was relentless in cajoling others to help him. When he was about eight, in need of more room for his expansive Lego collection, Adam convinced his brother to sell him the "air rights" to his room. Then he convinced his dad, a contractor, to build him a loft. "He could talk me into building constantly for him," Steve says.

When Adam was seven, his parents enrolled him in the school district's learn-to-ski program, which involved night skiing at White Pass. Decades later, Adam could still recall his first night on skis —the sugar-spill of stars, the crunch of snow underfoot, the intimidating rope tow. He practiced and practiced. For a ninth-grade science project on acceleration, he decided to ski off a rock while a friend filmed him. The snow was thick and the landing poor. "Knocked out his two front teeth," Judy says.

In the fall of 2003, Adam headed 200 miles up Interstate 5, to Western Washington University in Bellingham. The city sits on a bay of north Puget Sound, so close to Canada that French-speaking voices from Vancouver occasionally invade the car radio. It's a mossy Brigadoon of 87,000 college kids, graying hippies, and people who have fled Seattle. The town's unofficial motto, "City of Subdued Excitement," fades from a mural on Prospect Street. Adding to its appeal is the Mount Baker Ski Area, 55 miles east, which holds world bragging rights for the deepest snowfall ever recorded in a ski season—1,140 inches in the winter of 1998–1999.

The university suited a creative kid who loved to ski. Adam took environmental classes at the school's Fairhaven College of Interdisciplinary Studies, where students design their own major and receive "narrative evaluations" instead of grades. Even in an unconventional setting, Adam stood apart. He was the boy with the atomic smile who rode around on a dual-axis swing bike that invited double takes.

"One of the coolest things about Adam was that you didn't need to know his phone number. He was everywhere," says Rylan Schoen, a friend and fellow skier. By night, Adam went dumpster diving behind the local Trader Joe's for discarded flowers to hand out on campus. Women who could look past his aversion to showering, which was considerable, often found his smile irresistible. He made friends at every turn. One day at the library, Adam struck up a conversation with a cyclist who was crossing the country. He invited the man home to stay the night.

"Adam had a timelessness to him," says another acquaintance from those days. "He could've been the oldest soul, or the youngest guy, at once."

People agreed that you really didn't know Adam until you'd spent a day with him in the mountains. A few years ago, a local skier named Chris Farias was at a high camp with some of her friends above Mount Rainier's Flett Glacier, toasting the summer solstice with a round of drinks. Adam skied past with a friend, and then stopped to join them. Farias was struck by the guy with a Pigpen appearance who laughed and joked and complimented people lavishly. "He was sparkling," says Farias, an attorney who now lives in the mountain town of Leavenworth.

Farias and others couldn't help but notice that Adam had his share of oddities. "The concept of boundaries just wasn't part of his operating system," says Russell Cunningham, who met Adam when Roberts was a sophomore at Fairhaven. His few possessions spilled away from him in an ever-widening circle. "The Adam Bomb," someone dubbed him. If he encountered a locked door, he might use a window. Once, unable to reach Schoen to ask if he was skiing the next day, he called Schoen's girlfriend 14 times. "He just didn't get that that was weird," says Amy Schoen, who is now Rylan's wife.

Not long after Adam and Cunningham met, they started going to the mountains together and became best friends. Both had spent a lot of time in alpine terrain but were novices in terms of doing big backcountry efforts on skis or boards.

Together they would scare themselves at Table Mountain and other peaks near Baker. On a few occasions, Adam would walk in the front door of Cunningham's house, climb the stairs, and crawl into his bed. "I'm just kind of bumming," he'd say. "Hey, you want to go skiing?"

They went even if it was raining, making turns in manky snow for five hours. They got high together and ran through Bellingham in the middle of the night, chasing the trains that rattled through town. They promised to be each other's best man someday. "Most guys, at least in the Western world, suffer from this disease that I like to call tough-guy syndrome," Cunningham says. "Adam just didn't have that. He and I had a relationship that, I think, is very, very rare between male peers. I'd never loved a girlfriend as much as I loved Adam Roberts."

Mount Adams is the second-highest peak in Washington after Mount Rainier. In summer a fit person can walk to the volcano's summit on the south side without a climbing rope. The north side is a different place—steep, glaciated, lonesome. Extreme skiers

Doug Coombs and Glen Plake first descended the north face of the northwest ridge in the 1990s, and at the time Adam did it, it had rarely been repeated. This is the route Adam had in mind when, on a summer day in 2010, he called Cunningham and asked if he wanted to do something scary.

At first the face is no more difficult than a challenging pitch at a ski resort. But as a skier descends, the mountain becomes convex, as if you're dropping over the side of a bowling ball. Ahead, all that's visible is the Adams Glacier, about 3,000 feet below. The mountain steepens dramatically, to more than 50 degrees; the face widens and grows enormous. Landmarks that the mind and body use to navigate space disappear. The world starts to spin, but falling is not an option.

"At any point in that route, if you fall you almost certainly die, because there's zigzagging 500-foot cliffs and seracs and crevasses," Cunningham says. "It might be the best line in the lower 48."

After completing his descent of the run with Cunningham, Adam's confidence skyrocketed. The next year, with alpinist and snowboarder Liz Daley—who died in an avalanche in Argentina in 2014—Adam skied the Coleman Headwall on Mount Baker, which Cunningham declined to attempt. "It was bulletproof ice and 50, 60 degrees for 2,000 feet," he told me.

That year, Adam also made a first descent of Mount Adams's Klickitat Headwall. Then he turned to Mount Shuksan, the 9,131-foot peak that stands guard above Mount Baker Ski Area. Broad-shouldered, regal, robed with glaciers, Shuksan is often said to be the most photographed peak in the nation. A tongue of ice pours down the western flank of the mountain until it's forced over a 500-foot cliff by a steep face: the headwall of Hanging Glacier. At some points the headwall tilts at nearly 55 degrees. A mistake would toss a skier toward the void. Adam skied that too.

He also started to get somewhere with his dream of becoming a professional athlete: A full-page photo in *Freeskier* in 2010 of him skiing Hollywood Spine on Mount Baker. A full page in *Skiing*. The cover of *Red Bulletin,* Red Bull's adventure magazine. He appeared in a Patagonia catalog and on the side of city buses in Seattle. He got free gear from smaller companies that made ski packs, goggles, and bamboo poles.

"Adam perfected the photo turn more than any other skier I know," says Schoen, referring to a shot in which the skier's body is frozen in action, the powder a bow wave breaking against their goggles. "He didn't have any tricks in his back pocket. But he went big." Sixty, seventy, eighty feet of air.

In videos that Adam's friends sent me, he's unmistakable. His electric green pants and tangerine helmet stand out against winter's monochrome. He punches through a hedge of trees and accelerates toward a row of cliffs. Then he's airborne. With his legs tucked neatly beneath him, his upper body quiet, he's a missile flying true.

After the camera shutter clicks, the missile veers. He doesn't crash, exactly. Instead he hip-checks the earth, an intentional move designed to save his knees. This often resulted in Adam embedding deep in a crater of his own making—hot-tubbing, as skiers put it.

People who saw Adam ski were amazed and sometimes worried. On Mount Shuksan, Adam caught an edge on both the northwest couloir and the line above Hanging Glacier, his body tomahawking through space. In each instance he managed to self-arrest in forgiving snow before hurtling over cliffs.

"If it had been corn snow, firm, he'd have been dead," says Cunningham. Another time, Cunningham descended the north face of the northwest ridge of Mount Adams one day after Adam had been there and was horrified to see the sweeping turns his friend had laid down, the signature of a skier moving at more than 30 miles an hour. "To free ride that face," Cunningham says, "is to tickle the dragon's testicles."

Not infrequently in the videos I saw of Adam—skiing out of bounds at White Pass, on Pelton Peak in the North Cascades, and on the island of Hokkaido, Japan—he's pursued by "the big guy in the white suit," as avalanche professionals call the rush of tumbling snow. "He told friends he loved to set off avalanches and outrun them," says his friend Jeff Rich. "He said it was fun."

In pictures, Adam leaps seracs and skis at the lip of dark crevasses. He hangs by his fingertips from a bridge in the Olympic Mountains, his grin broad and serene, even with 40 feet of air beneath his feet. "He stood on edges," Judy says. "He skied edges. He climbed edges."

Some people wondered if Adam had a death wish. What they didn't understand was that the mountains were helping to keep him alive.

*

During the winter quarter of Adam's sophomore year, 2004–2005, something changed. He began to obsess over exercise and food. He would eat with the vigor of a young, powerful athlete and then, despairing, run for two hours and then go to the weight room for two more. Tortured, self-flagellating ideas looped in his head. He became convinced he was a bad person—the reasons why were always changing, but to him the evidence was everywhere. He tried to purge his thoughts by writing them down in dozens of journals. Resolution eluded him. The sentences, scrawled in his crabbed, indecipherable script, bend back on themselves, going nowhere.

His parents struggled to find answers. A therapist who helped Adam end his exercise bulimia around 2006 told them, "There's something more here than just an eating disorder." Over the years they would get other diagnoses: depressive disorder with anxious distress, schizo-affective disorder, obsessive-compulsive disorder. Nothing fully explained him. They began a years-long march through medications: Lexapro, Abilify, Risperdal, Quetiapine. "None of them really ever did much," Judy says.

Steve and Judy realized that Adam's exercise obsession had earlier precedents—events they thought he'd put behind him. When Adam was a boy, a dentist told him to brush his teeth thoroughly. He brushed them so thoroughly that he scrubbed off portions of his gums and had to have a transplant. One day, when Adam was around ten, he told his mother, "I want to be dead." Eventually, with counseling, such comments subsided.

They wondered: Were Adam's adult troubles caused by the same demons, reemerged? The boy with the welcoming smile now struggled to live normally. Within a few years, to remain in Bellingham, he paid $50 a month to pitch a tent in a friend's backyard during a Pacific Northwest winter. Slugs moved in with him. Mold grew on his pillow. At one point he slept in his mother's car.

In his early twenties, he began to move around almost constantly—from Bellingham to the mountains to Randle and back again. Somewhere else was always better, more fun. One day he called Judy from Seattle. "I'm on the freeway. I'm pulled over. I can't do anything," Adam said, distraught. "I can't decide if I want to go to Bellingham or come home."

"You have to get off the freeway," she said. Eventually he was able to calm down and pick a direction.

During this time, Adam began to ski obsessively. He headed into the mountains 200 days a year, going alone if necessary, thumbing in the rain by six in the morning. He had discovered something that he not only liked but needed.

"Adam, in normal life, felt like he couldn't feel," Cunningham says. "He'd see two people walking down the street holding hands and kissing, and be like, 'God, I wonder what that feels like, to actually be in love?'" Adam had intense feelings—a Tuesday morning bowl of cereal could be the best bowl of cereal he had ever tasted, friends said. "But for him," Cunningham says, "when he got into some really serious shit that he knows is dangerous, that he damn well knows could kill him, and eventually will kill him, he's—for the first time in hours, days, weeks, months—feeling alive again. For him, skiing a 60-degree section of icy gnar way up on Mount Shuksan, above a 3,500-foot fall where most people are freaking out, Adam is laser-sharp focused and calm. Perfect. He clicks into his element. That's what he's designed to do."

To survive in such places, Adam no longer had the luxury of a noisy mind. All else had to fall away. For a few minutes the freight trains that banged through his head grew quiet. The silence was a form of freedom.

"He wasn't a poor homeless guy anymore; now he's wealthy," Cunningham says. "The beautiful thing about mountains is they're the great equalizer."

In the summer of 2012, Adam met a striking graduate student named Eliza Andrews at a bluegrass concert. They danced and shared a few kisses. That night, Adam wrote his number on her hand. She didn't call. A few days later, Adam showed up at her apartment building. Andrews was surprised and also hesitant. He was so handsome, though, and so flattering and persistent, despite his quirks. "Then I sort of felt like, Oh my God, he's just misunderstood," she told me. "Now it's my mission to help people understand."

They dated for nearly three years. They hiked and skied and kayaked. He started taking his medication again and went back to seeing a therapist, which he'd never stuck with. Andrews accompanied him. Their relationship steadied him somewhat.

Adam was a challenging boyfriend—complimentary and generous but also deeply self-absorbed. "He took, took, took and never gave back, I would say mostly emotionally," Andrews says. Adam would call her or Cunningham and talk for long stretches about his tangle of worries, then show no interest in theirs. "Just fix me. Just fix me," he told the therapist. Andrews broke off the relationship several times, but Adam wouldn't give up. "He kept finding ways to get back in," she says.

One spring evening in 2015, when Andrews had returned from a ski race to the house they'd begun to share with others, Adam confessed that he'd cheated on her. Andrews asked him for distance. "My ego needed to heal from the fact that he left me, after I've given this guy so much," she says. "It hurt even more, to try and push somebody away who was hurting so bad." Adam wrote her dozens of emails and texts over the next few weeks, pleading for another chance. "Whatever is wrong with me destroyed us," he said in one. "It destroys me every day."

In July of 2015, Andrews came home one night and found Adam asleep in her bed. She screamed and he left the bedroom. The housemates found him on the back porch and told him to leave. Adam exploded, shoving one woman and striking a guy who intervened. The police were called. Andrews went to court and got a temporary protection order.

Adam began to slide downhill. He moved around Bellingham in a slow shuffle—the city walk, friends called it. He was never a great self-promoter, and his ski career stalled. He would sell the goggles and skis that companies gave him in order to keep going in the mountains. He stuck with jobs long enough to put gas in his gypsy wagon, a one-room, green-roofed hobbit house he cajoled Steve to build for him on the bed of a pickup truck. Inside was a mailbox-size woodstove. Adam lived for days on end in the parking lot of Mount Baker.

Meanwhile, he obsessed over his ex-girlfriend. In Adam's mind, everything would be better if he could only get her back. By the end of June 2016, he'd violated the protection order at least five times—turning up at a bar and a farm where she worked, and near her home. Prosecutors filed felony stalking charges against him.

In July, Andrews went to Whatcom County District Court, where she had asked for a renewal of the protection order. Adam appeared as she waited. Violating the no-contact order in the courtroom, he knelt beside her, sighing, trying to speak to her. "Adam, what are you doing?" Andrews said.

"I don't care," he replied. When a five-year renewal was granted,

Adam cried out. He was removed from the courtroom in hand-cuffs.

The week before Mother's Day that year, Adam and Judy went to an appointment with a psychiatric health professional near his parents' home. "You've got to control your behaviors," the therapist told Adam.

"I am trying," he insisted.

"No, you're not trying enough," she said, then left the room to make his next appointment. Adam grabbed a snow globe and threw it through a framed picture. He swept a computer off a desk. Three policemen arrived. Adam resisted. An officer pressed a Taser to his rib cage and fired, then fired again. Adam fell at his mother's feet. He was booked into the Lewis County Jail.

Another blow had come a few months earlier. In February of 2016, Adam was helping prepare Mount Baker Ski Area for the Legendary Banked Slalom, the mountain's marquee event and the longest-running snowboarding race in the world.

The North Cascades typically show off on race weekend by dumping snow, and that year the weather didn't disappoint—more than a foot of powder fell, landing on a slick, precarious surface. Adam dodged his duties and was cruising around the resort with Corey Warren, a friend and photographer. Adam was feeling antsy.

"We gotta get out to the Arm, it's looking pretty good," he said, referring to the Shuksan Arm, a long ridgeline that connects the west flank of Mount Shuksan to the uppermost reaches of the ski area. The Arm is a dramatic sight, striped with steep lines that show up regularly in ski magazines.

Warren got swept up in Adam's excitement. They made their way to a gate that leads to the backcountry and outpaced two dozen other skiers to get fresh tracks near a ski line that locals call the Beast, which has a steep entry. Adam made a quick turn for the camera and stopped. Behind him, a small slide raced downhill. He smiled.

As Warren skied down to set up the second shot, another avalanche cut loose. It grabbed Warren and carried him at least 50 yards downhill, burying him waist-deep and leaving him rattled. He composed himself and the two continued on. They set up for a final shot.

"This is gonna rip," Adam said. "I'm gonna arc to the right, make two turns, then I'm gonna arc out."

The Shuksan Arm is such a prominent feature above Mount Baker that a crowd of racers, spectators, and staff saw what happened next. Adam pushed off. The snow cracked open above him. "He could not outrun it," Warren says. "He didn't even get his one turn. It was like ball bearings. It just funneled him."

When the snow settled, Adam wasn't visible. The slide had carried him over a rockfall. Warren hurried to the edge. Adam —stripped of poles and goggles—was walking uphill, a nervous smile on his face.

"Dude, are you okay?"

"That wasn't what I expected. I rallied my back on that cliff."

Warren skied away to find help. At a spot where backcountry skiers reenter the ski area, a patroller was waiting for him.

"Hey, is that Adam Roberts up there?" the patroller asked.

"Yeah, it is," Warren said. "We just skied off a slide. He's fine, but he hurt his back and lost his skis. Can you send up a sled?"

"We're not calling anyone for Adam," the patroller replied, according to Warren. "He's on his own."

If Adam had been severely injured, ski patrol would've likely sent aid, even though he was out-of-bounds, but there wasn't much interest in giving him a lift after this near-miss. Adam had annoyed patrollers by ducking ropes and launching off big cliffs without regard to the consequences for people below him. He'd gotten warnings and had his pass pulled for the day. This slide was just the latest personal foul.

When Adam reached the lodge, he was met by a Whatcom County sheriff's deputy and by Duncan Howat, Mount Baker's general manager. The deputy issued a no-trespass order that forbade Adam from coming back for the rest of the season. Adam adored Mount Baker, and he deeply respected the Howat family, who had run the place for half a century. The ban devastated him.

"The most challenging and heartbreaking part of working with Adam was that there was never anything malicious, or intent to do any harm," says Gwyn Howat, Mount Baker's executive vice president and operations manager. Yet his pursuit of whatever he needed "straight-up jeopardized people's lives. The paradox of that was very difficult to navigate."

Friends noticed that Adam's decision-making was getting worse —and as more experienced skiers second-guessed skiing with him, there were fewer people around to check his riskier impulses. Rylan Schoen had gotten engaged to Amy recently, and they both decided he shouldn't ski with Adam anymore. Jeff Rich begged off when Adam called to ski; privately, he told friends he didn't want to be there when the inevitable happened.

After the incident at Mount Baker, Cunningham cornered his friend. "Are you doing this on purpose?"

"Kind of," Adam told him. "I'm kind of out of control of myself. I keep making bad decisions. I know they're bad decisions. But I just don't care about my life anymore, because I'm so fucking depressed every single day."

He filled Cunningham's voice mail. "I don't want to die," he said in one, "but I don't have a future."

The writer David Foster Wallace, who took his own life in 2008, wrote a passage in *Infinite Jest* that captures the agony experienced by someone who's in enough despair to consider suicide. Wallace said that no one leaps to his death from a burning building by choice. The person jumps because the flames are worse, "a terror way beyond falling."

The house that Steve and Judy Roberts built, and where they raised their sons, is snug, made of timber, south-facing to welcome the afternoon sun. The living-room window frames the white bulk of Mount Adams as it noses above a rumple of green peaks. Behind the living room sits a bedroom. On the bed there's a box made from local maple and yellow cedar, its lid inlaid with an image of the mountain. Steve made it. Now 68, he has a ragged woodsman's beard and the vise handshake of a lifelong carpenter. The handshake comes later, though, because when you show up to talk about Adam, Steve will meet you at the car door with wet eyes and a bear hug, even if you're a stranger. Inside the box are the ashes of his son.

Judy, 69, places a plate of homemade cookies on the kitchen table, not far from a book, *Healing After Loss*. She's observant, kind, yet direct. "The most incredibly sad thing to me is that he had it all," she says. "He had the perfect girlfriend. He had a ski career that was developing nicely. But he torpedoed it. He torpedoed it all."

For five hours one spring day we talk about Adam. Judy says her son was one of the strongest people she's ever met. A therapist once told her that if she took as much medicine as Adam was taking, she wouldn't be able to get up in the morning.

Talking to Judy and Steve, you realize how large the blast zone of mental illness can be. Years ago, Judy says, when Adam was wracked by his eating disorder, "almost every day he'd call and say, 'I want to kill myself.'" Do you have any idea, she says, what it's like for a mother to write the memorial service for her son—not once, or twice, but many times? Later, Adam routinely sent her as many as 400 texts per day. One time he sent 753. The messages were often brutal, self-hating. "You can't read stuff like that all day long and have it not affect you horribly," Judy says. "Mostly I would just delete everything as fast as I could, and he knew that. Still it came in."

Near the end, Judy wondered if she should fear her own son. One night in Randle, she and Adam stood at a window together at home. "Oh, it's such a beautiful sunset," she said. Adam punched the wall next to the glass and fell to the ground, holding his hand. "I can't feel anything," he moaned. "I can't feel anything."

Judy is strong, but when she speaks of these things she dabs her eyes. She doesn't share them because she wants your pity. She wants you to understand, all of it.

They tried everything. When Judy retired and Adam fell off her insurance, they paid out of pocket for mental health treatment. They got Adam on federal disability and also secured state help. "It was really hard to explain to someone why this person is on disability when he goes out and skis these things, but we were out of resources," she says. "We put out so much money for this kid."

Five months after Adam's death, his parents found themselves still sorting through many emotions. There was grief, of course, and regret at not finding a way to help him. Judy is frustrated that the last few years had darkened the memory of Adam, her favorite hiking partner. She pauses, considering how to word something else that she and Steve have also felt: relief. When I visited, they had just returned from a vacation. For the first time in years, a ringing phone didn't scare them. "The last ten years, we haven't been able to do anything without having continual fear and worry about Adam," Judy says.

By the autumn of 2016, Adam seemed exhausted. Ahead lay

possible criminal trials for stalking and for trashing the therapist's office, which could result in prison time. Adam's actions
had stripped him even of the solace of skiing: during the summer of 2016, he was required to wear a GPS ankle bracelet, so he
couldn't wear a ski boot. Some friends, like Cunningham, exasper-
ated, pulled back in hopes that Adam would finally help himself.
It didn't work. Friends tried to keep him cheered up, but the spark
was gone.

That fall, people told Judy about another therapy they might try
for borderline personality disorder. Her son waved her off.

A friend asked Adam if he could help.

"Everyone has helped me," Adam said.

In the Pacific Northwest, winter arrives with the subtlety of an
overdue freight train. Storms gather in the North Pacific and spin
south until they smash into the first solid thing they encounter,
which is often the South Cascades. By Christmas of 2016, more
than 10 feet of snow had fallen at White Pass.

Thanks to the mountains' low elevation and proximity to the
sea, it's not uncommon for storms to arrive accompanied by warm
temperature spikes. On December 20, the day before the winter
solstice, it rained in the mountains, then grew cold and sunny for
days. Ice formed. Such rain crusts create a slick bed upon which
newer layers of snow can easily slide.

On the day after Christmas, photographer Jason Hummel and
Adam skied together at White Pass, a snowy, uncrowded, and fun
mountain for the expert who knows where to look. For some locals, this means heading out of bounds for a "road run." Just beyond one of the resort's boundaries, off a snowcat route called the
Plank, lie ungroomed and unpatrolled tree-flecked trails. This is
classic Northwest skiing, rarely tracked out by others. The runs
end at Highway 12; from there it's a short hitchhike back to the
ski resort.

That day the skiing was terrible. "While we were sidestepping
ice, we talked about how bad the avalanche conditions were going
to be when it snowed a foot," Hummel told me.

That night snow began to fall. By morning nearly a foot of
new powder covered the ground at White Pass, but the wind collected it much deeper in sheltered places. In its daily bulletin, the
Northwest Avalanche Center warned: "The safest plan is to avoid

avalanche terrain of consequence." Adam said good-bye to his mother and headed to the ski hill. On his bed he left three books. One was a popular manual for telemarkers. The second was *Staying Alive in Avalanche Terrain*. The third was a self-help title called *Love Is Letting Go of Fear.*

At the mountain, Adam flagged down Wesley Martin, an assistant supervisor at the ski school, and invited him along. Martin was excited. Adam was a celebrity at White Pass. His picture had been on the trail map.

Martin, 26, was working that day, and the two set up a plan: when Martin could shake free, they would meet behind the ticket booth to spin a lap. Several times that day they met for a road run.

"The day was midthigh deep, just blower pow," Martin recalls. He couldn't stop smiling, but Adam was struggling to enjoy himself. "Every time we got done, he'd say, 'I wish the run was longer. I'll bet it's better at Baker.'" Even so, Adam ghosted through the trees so quickly that Martin, though a very good skier, had trouble keeping up. Martin tried to lift his spirits. He quoted song lyrics by the John Butler Trio, about someone chasing what they can't obtain: *And if you just look around man / You see you got magic.*

At two o'clock, Martin got another window from work. He and Adam headed out for another road run, working a popular backcountry zone that locals call the Grand Couloir. Grand is a misnomer. While the walls of the steep, narrowing gully quickly rise to more than 100 feet on either side and the couloir is large enough to be rippled with a few ski lines, a snowball tossed from the top can nearly reach the bottom of the gully and the creek that drains it in winter. It's a classic terrain trap—anything caught in a slide will be funneled into the creek and likely buried.

On the descent, a large slough of snow caught Adam and ripped off one of his skis. It took 15 minutes to find it. Even so, the men decided to take one more run.

Throughout the day, Adam had been sending Judy texts, the same litany of self-recrimination and regret that had become numbingly familiar.

> 11:56 a.m.
> *I was driven..ski at baker and then school..why*
> *Why did it kill me..I killed me*

12:57 p.m.
White pass nothing

2:45 p.m.
But I coolant [sic] *work..never been able to live on,own..never been able to work and live and make life..it's so so sick..its so sad*

At 4:15 p.m., after riding the chairlift, Adam sent her a last round of texts. One read:

I feel so so dead..skiing feels so sick..i, know nothing.. Why why am i here..why

The skiers walked the Plank and headed out of bounds. It was still snowing; the oyster light of a December afternoon was failing. Somewhere, under the deep snow, lay the old sign: ROBERTS' RUN. They stood at the Grand Couloir again, but this time Adam had led them higher, to an entry of the gully that was steeper than anything they'd skied together that day, perhaps 45 or 50 degrees.

"This looks sketchy," Adam said.

"I don't like this one," Martin replied. His legs wobbled with exhaustion from chasing Adam all day.

The Grand Couloir is not a single open funnel; it's punctuated by small islands of trees that break up the terrain. Martin told Adam he would ski the adjacent line that the two had skied last time. He took a few steps uphill and looked back. Adam had already dropped in and was gone.

Martin hiked about 40 yards and skied his short alley. At the bottom, Adam wasn't waiting. Martin yelled. No response. Ascending the gully Adam had skied, above he saw a fracture line on the slope that signaled the crown of an avalanche. It was a large slide, more than 100 yards wide, reaching down to the rain crust. Martin was not as experienced as Adam in the backcountry and he carried no avalanche beacon or rescue gear. Though Adam routinely carried such equipment, that day he had carried only a beacon. He had not switched it on.

Martin skied to the road and hitchhiked to the ski area for help. Ski patrollers located Adam at 5:53 p.m., a little more than halfway down the gully. He was in perfect position—upright, hand gripping a ski pole, the other pole inches from his outstretched hand. He looked as if he was about to make a slashing right-hand turn and pull off one last escape. His orange helmet, still on his head, was beneath four feet of snow.

It's hard not to wonder what Adam wanted when he stepped onto the slope for his last run. Did he hope to die? Perhaps he was trying to find a way to live, in the only way he knew. Or perhaps, in his exhaustion, he had ceased to choose. He would let the mountains decide for him.

"It would be inaccurate to say that Adam took his own life," Cunningham says. "It would also be inaccurate to say that he didn't."

Many of us head to the high peaks in search of something we hope to find there. "Nature's peace will flow into you as sunshine flows into trees," John Muir wrote, urging others into the hills. Perhaps Adam's story differs from yours and mine mainly by degree. All of us seek a quiet mind, a glimpse of sunshine through the trees. The difference is how far some of us will go in pursuit of it.

About two weeks later, a couple hundred people braved a snowy Saturday to come to Randle. In a church that Steve had designed, they laughed and cried and sang and told stories about Adam. They burned some of his journals, sending the words skyward. That night several of his friends stayed together, drinking and remembering. The next day they all went skiing.

More than a year later, Cunningham still misses his friend terribly, but he sees the world differently these days. Heading into challenging backcountry is no longer like crossing into hostile terrain. It's a homecoming. Adam taught him this. "Home is everywhere," he says. "Home is in the mountains."

Adam's many friends have rallied behind Judy and Steve. Judy posts videos and pictures on Adam's Facebook page, including pictures of her own hikes. Everyone comments. The couple has dozens of children now.

On a warm cloudless weekend last August, Judy and Steve removed some of the last of their son's ashes from the wooden box. They headed to Mount Adams, accompanied by a few of his friends, just as former girlfriend Andrews, Hummel, and others had accompanied them to other peaks earlier in the summer. They hiked to a spot where the family had camped when Adam was a boy. There in the mountains, the parents put their son to rest where he had always felt most at ease.

JOHN BRANCH

Children of the Cube

FROM THE NEW YORK TIMES

THERE WERE THREE worthwhile vantage points for "Max Park vs. the World," an exhibition featuring seven of the globe's fastest speedcubers. That's the moniker for the growing faction of people who solve Rubik's Cube–style puzzles at mind-bending speeds. Six of them formed a relay against Park, an autistic 16-year-old from California who is breaking most of their records.

One good spot was from the audience, joining hundreds of (mostly) young people gazing up at the celebrities of speedcubing the way NBA fans crowd sidelines to watch Stephen Curry warm up.

Eyes and phones were up. Mouths were open. My son was in the crowd, somewhere.

On stage was Feliks Zemdegs, a 22-year-old Australian who holds the world record in the 3 by 3, the six-sided, three-layer configuration of the original Rubik's Cube, which bestows an illusion of brilliance on those who can solve it. Zemdegs has done it in 4.22 seconds. Earlier in the day, hundreds lined up for his autograph.

Around him were other record-setters, all famous in this world, each smiling behind a mixed-up cube of a different size—a 2 by 2, a 3 by 3, all the way up to a 7 by 7.

"The team assembled by Feliks to take down Max Park!" an MC said through microphone.

Park sat at a nearby table alone, with cubes of all sizes in front of him. He owned world records in the 4 by 4 (18.42 second), 5 by 5 (37.28), 6 by 6 (1:14.86), and 7 by 7 (1:47.89).

I wondered if a better vantage point was behind the stage, the same view that the competitors had, directly into the awed faces of their fans. Most of those in the audience had qualified to compete at CubingUSA's nationals too, alongside their fast-fingered heroes, over three summer days inside a convention center.

But I settled for the third spot to watch—off to the side, neither competitor nor fan, but merely a parent trying to make sense of it all. Among the spectators, expressions of wonder tilted like sunflowers atop the craned stalks of their necks, aimed toward the bright light of speedcubing's stars, was that of my son, Joe, competing at his first nationals.

He is 16, straddling the moat between childhood and adulthood. He has spent most of his years trying to fit in but usually being pushed out. We learned he had attention deficit hyperactivity disorder in kindergarten, and some symptoms often associated with autism continue to vex doctors and psychologists as he approaches his junior year of high school.

His biggest issue remains socialization. Joe's a smart and tenderhearted kid, but like the cubes he carries everywhere, he can be hard to decipher and solve. Most don't give him the time.

When not at the skate park, he's usually home at the piano, practicing the Mozart pieces he learned on YouTube, or studiously putting together jigsaw puzzles, or practicing his cubes with a timer. I forget the last time he was invited somewhere.

Yet there he was, fitting in as never before. Like everyone else, he held a plastic cube, both a security blanket and a badge. He had a lanyard around his neck, identifying him as one of about 600 competitors, a special collective.

He had found acceptance by doing nothing more than being himself. Funny that it would come in a place where he could leave all the reinvention to the familiar 3 by 3 object in his hands, the one that has 43 quintillion possible configurations but that he and all the others could solve in seconds.

The crowd hushed. The race began. In little more than five minutes, Max Park solved all six of the puzzles, leaving the world behind.

"A valiant effort from the dream team," the MC said.

I walked away with no doubt about the best view—that of a parent, watching a child find his place.

Max Park vs. the World

Max Park's parents, Schwan and Miki, knew something was different with their son when he was a baby. He seemed to live in his
own world. For a time they wondered if he was deaf.

Doctors told them it was autism, the developmental disorder
that can show itself in a range of symptoms from a young age—
among them, the delayed use of spoken language, a lack of eye
contact or interest in engaging with others, repetitive sounds or
mannerisms, a hyperfocus on certain activities.

Another issue can be fine-motor skills. Max's therapists and parents put the boy through all kinds of exercises to improve his dex-
terity—picking up coins and placing them in a slot of a bank, for
example. When he was seven or eight, Max was handed a Rubik's
Cube.

"He fell in love with it," Schwan Park said at a competition in
Berkeley, California, a couple of months ago. "And he practiced
all the time."

The Parks were just glad to find therapy that did not feel like
a chore. Soon, Max could solve a 3 by 3 cube in about the time it
takes to read this sentence aloud.

Just about everyone knows what a Rubik's Cube is. Invented in
1974 by a Hungarian architect named Erno Rubik, it had its first
big moment in 1980 and 1981, when it was named toy of the year
by people who confer such awards.

But fads fade, and by the end of 1982, even the *New York Times*
declared it dead. The cube remained famous, in a nostalgic way,
but as a fascination it lay mostly dormant for 20 years.

These days, most people fall into two camps. One is filled with
those who remember Rubik's Cube as a pop-culture relic, as evoca-
tive of the 1980s as leg warmers and Duran Duran. They have no
idea that cubing is having another moment.

The second camp is filled with speedcubers.

The World Cube Association, formed in 2004 to approve events,
track times, and provide order to all the high-speed twisting, says
more than 100,000 people have competed officially. Popularity has
grown exponentially in recent years. The number of first-time competitors in 2017 was about 24,000, five times more than in 2012.

Cubing's resurrection began slowly about 15 years ago. The

2003 world championship was the first since 1982. Cubing clubs cropped up at college campuses, from Cal-Berkeley to Rutgers, spreading the gospel by holding open competitions.

The internet, particularly YouTube, slingshotted the rebirth. A puzzle that once seemed impossible was demystified in how-to videos. Cubers long ago figured out that the clunky Rubik's Cube was not built for speed, so other manufacturers jumped in, mostly Chinese companies like MoYu and Gan, engineering slick-moving variations of all conceivable shapes and sizes.

They show up in packages on my porch with startling regularity, in exchange for my son's allowance and savings account.

Joe gets them for birthdays and Christmas too—polyhedrons of all sizes, including an 11 by 11 cube, tetrahedrons (pyramids), do-decahedrons (12 sides), and some with so many sides that I can't figure out how to count them, never mind turn their parts. There are single-color cubes where the moving parts are not square; they shift into incomprehensible shapes when they are scrambled, and back to a cube when solved.

Besides the puzzles in his backpack (usually a dozen) or scattered around the house (who knows), they are displayed on an Ikea bookcase in his room, bought specifically for that purpose. He tells people that he has 200 puzzles in his collection. I'm scared to count, lest my brain compute the dollars spent.

Sometimes a new cube will arrive that looks just like a dozen others he already has, but Joe assures me that it's way better. I long ago got past the horror of entering his room to find his latest puzzle shattered into a pile of hundreds of plastic parts. He puts them back together after lubing them and inspecting the inner workings—usually. He could create a cubing junkyard with spare parts in his desk.

The persistent clicking of cubes being solved is a soundtrack of our family. I worry when I don't hear it coming from behind his bedroom door.

The puzzles are sold at online customization shops and retailers like the Cubicle, which has emerged as the sport's cultural trend-setter. It sponsors most of the world's top cubers, putting them in team jackets and paying travel expenses to competitions. It supplies contest purses, including the $23,200 at stake during last month's nationals. Top cubers are on the verge of making full-time livings solving puzzles.

That is the growing world that Park, speedcubing's latest star, now inhabits and dominates.

Like a lot of parents of modern-day cubers (including me), the Parks didn't know that cubing competitions were a real thing until their child asked to go to one. Max was 11, without many friends at home. They went.

"He knew everybody," Schwan Park said. "He knew all the other cubers, their names, their times. We thought: Oh, this will be a great place for him to socialize."

The Parks used cubing to reinforce other lessons—how to sit down correctly, how to make eye contact with a judge and say, "I'm ready." His cubing times weren't the point.

"To us, it felt like free therapy," Schwan Park said.

At his second contest, Max won the 6 by 6 event. These days, he holds the world records in 4 by 4, 5 by 5, 6 by 6, and 7 by 7. He won the 3 by 3 and the one-handed 3 by 3 events at last year's world championships in Paris, but does not hold those records —not yet anyway.

"He is breaking cubing," said Phil Yu, 28, chief executive of the Cubicle and still a world-class competitor. "He is physically really strong. And his turning speed is out of control."

Part of what the Parks practice with their son now is how to handle the fame and attention—the autograph hounds and photo-seekers, the glad-handers and back-slappers, the people who may misread Park's autism as aloofness and walk away disappointed in their hero.

Yet Max Park fits in too. He's adored by the cubers who want to be more like him, and liked and respected by the older cubers whose records he's now breaking.

"This group is really accepting," Schwan Park said. "A lot come from the same situations, people looking to fit in. We meet a lot of parents, and we all want the same thing for our kids."

"800 People Just Like You"

At my son's first cubing competition, in Berkeley nearly two years ago, he averaged 48.43 seconds per solve in his attempts at the 3 by 3, still cubing's glamour event. Now at nationals, he averaged

19.91—a "sub-20," considered an elusive breakthrough just a couple of years ago, speedcubing's four-minute mile.

His average would have put him in the top 10 in the world in 2004. Now it didn't crack the top 500 at nationals.

But his goal was personal bests, and he got them in 3 by 3, Pyraminx (a pyramid), and Skewb (a cube with pyramid-shaped corner pieces).

The highlight, though, was just being there.

"It's the story I hear nonstop," said Kit Clement, the executive director of CubingUSA. "Cubing initially can feel antisocial—you do it alone, no one understands you. Then you come to a competition and suddenly there are 800 other people just like you."

Cubing competitions are mostly a quiet parade of competitors unscrambling puzzles against an automated timer (40 of them at nationals) in front of a judge. They are more about data collection than spectacle.

Most time is spent waiting. At nationals, competitors sat at large, round banquet tables. They practiced their own puzzles and borrowed others and spun them constantly in their fidgety fingers. Even if there was no conversation, there was the comfort of someone clicking and clacking alongside.

It felt like a never-ending lunch in a school cafeteria, where every table was the cool kids' table.

"We're all on the same wavelength here—we all speak the same language," said Brandon Harnish, a longtime competitor who, now 22, oversees competitions as a World Cube Association delegate.

He looked around. Round tables were filled with children.

"All these people sitting together, hanging out, feeling comfortable?" Harnish said. "That's not a goal. It's a result."

My son has been to 11 competitions now, and I've talked to children and parents at most of them. Not all speedcubers come from the same mold, of course, but most seem to have interests in computers, science and math, often music. (A few even mentioned origami.)

Not all are shy, but a lot of them are, at least at home, where their fascination with cubes is a quirky curiosity, not a binding trait. I am far from the only parent in awe of how much my son comes out of his shell when he enters a room about to hold a cubing competition.

The trickiest puzzle is figuring out why only about 10 percent of speedcubers are female. (At nationals, where the median age was 16, 41 of 634 competitors were female.) Some suggest that the issue is a self-fulfilling one; girls see few other girls and stay away. The World Cube Association wants to add female delegates, who run sanctioned competitions, to provide role models to younger girls.

At the airport gate in San Francisco, while waiting to board the plane to Salt Lake City, my son excused himself. Maybe he heard the clack of cubes the way a dog picks up a scent, but he sat down next to Sameer Aggarwal, a slight, bespectacled 13-year-old from Bellevue, Washington, playing with a cube. He was on his way to his first nationals too.

The boys struck up a conversation and fidgeted with puzzles as strangers nearby watched in wonder. Sameer's parents and I shared smiles and shrugs.

Manish and Rakhi Aggarwal later described their son as a studious middle-schooler, excelling in math, science, Spanish, violin, and piano—and now cubing. He qualified for nine events at nationals, and did so well that he made the semifinals in three of them.

"We're on top of the world, actually," Rakhi Aggarwal said on the last day.

Adults tend to be most amazed by speedcubing—I can tell by the reaction of strangers watching my son twiddle away in public. It's probably a generational perspective, one ingrained from the original era of Rubik's Cube, when solving it felt virtually impossible.

I never came close to solving a Rubik's Cube as a child. But alone in the hotel one night during nationals, excited that my son was out to dinner with new friends, I followed an online tutorial narrated by Yu, the Cubicle chief executive, that has been viewed nearly 10 million times. In an hour, after some hiccups and playbacks, one of my son's 3 by 3s went from chaos to order.

"What makes you and me different," Yu told me, "is thousands and thousands of practice hours."

I haven't practiced since. But my son rarely puts the cubes down. On the plane ride home, he tried solving a 3 by 3 cube blindfolded, one of the many hard-to-fathom variations of speedcubing. He stared at a scrambled cube and examined the pattern of the colors. After a couple of minutes, he covered his face with his hat and took a deep breath.

I watched as my son's fingers rotated the layers at an incomprehensible speed. They paused sometimes as his brain tried to conjure the current position of the colors, to tell his fingers what to do next. I quietly recorded with my phone.

In a minute, the six sides of the cube went from kaleidoscope to nearly solid. He opened his eyes. Only a couple of pieces were in the wrong spot.

So close, I said, amazed and proud.

He smiled. "We can go again next year, right?" he said.

BONNIE D. FORD

Holding Her Own

FROM ESPN.COM

CONSIDER HER GRIP. It is the most unseen element of her skill set, yet the essence of her game flows from its control and precision. The shifting configuration of her palm and fingers on the rounded octagonal handle determined the angle of the racket face, which in turn dictates the pace, spin, and trajectory of a shot. The fan's eye naturally tracks elsewhere: the ball, her feet, her outstretched arm, her expression. But Petra Kvitova's dominant hand, armored with calluses and trained like a trellised vine around the same shape since childhood, is at the root of her strength.

And now imagine that grip closing over the cutting edge of a knife with all the adrenaline of self-defense and the force of a two-time Wimbledon champion and yanking it away from her throat, where an intruder had held it. The blade bit deeply into the fingers of Kvitova's left hand.

She flexes the hand in late April, almost a year and a half later, to demonstrate that she can't clench her fist in celebration quite as tightly as before. Her long fingers curl into her palm, leaving a small space at the center, as if she's cupping something fragile. The scars are thin and faint, but residual clumsiness still causes her to fumble with objects sometimes.

"I'm happy that I have all my fingers, at the end of the day," Kvitova says.

She's feeling light and grateful on the day before her opening match at the WTA tournament in Prague, an event she watched from the stands last year, not yet ready to test her hand in a match. A jazz recording croons softly in the lounge of the downtown In-

terContinental Hotel, where Kvitova has permitted herself a slice
of chocolate cake and a cappuccino with soy milk.

"Being in the top 10, it's a little bit weird for me," says Kvitova,
28. "In a year? I couldn't really expect that. But when the last season finished, I was already feeling more normal. To have the same
start of the season as the other girls, same offseason preparation,
everything. So, I feel normal."

At the behest of investigators, Kvitova has never divulged the
details of what happened in her apartment on December 20, 2016.
She would rather not return to that moment anyway. It's what she
did with it that matters and explains how she has created an extraordinary new normal.

Kvitova wins her opening match in Prague the next morning
before a full house as fans who were turned away peer through a
hedge and a windscreen in hopes of catching a glimpse of her on
the tidy center court. She wins the next four matches and the tournament. She moves on to Madrid and runs the table, then travels
to Paris and wins her first two French Open matches before finally
yielding after 13 straight victories on clay.

Three weeks later, she defends her 2017 title on grass in Birmingham, England. It is Kvitova's sixth tournament win since her
comeback from the attack and her fifth this season. Now ranked
seventh in the world, she has vaulted firmly into contention for a
third Wimbledon championship.

The rectangular green jewel box of Centre Court is never far
from her mind. The first thing she asks Radek Kebrle, the surgeon
who operated on her hand, when he visits her bedside the day
after her four-hour surgery, is: Pane Doktore, pojedu na Wimbledon?

Doctor, will I go to Wimbledon?

"At the moment, I thought, 'You are crazy,'" Kebrle says later, almost whispering the word. "Your injury is so difficult. We're talking
about if I will be able to brush my teeth and do all my things and
use my hand, and you want to ask . . . of course, I understood the
question. And I told her, 'We'll do everything to get you there.'"

But Kebrle doesn't sugarcoat it. Ten percent, he tells her: that is
his estimate of her chances to come back at the elite level. Rehab
will be slow and hard, and he will need her full concentration and
cooperation.

She waits until he leaves before she allows herself to cry. And then she grabs the slim lifeline he has cast in her direction and refuses to let go.

Kvitova seems to have emerged from nowhere, fully formed, when she is named WTA Newcomer of the Year in 2010. Mere months later, she upsets Maria Sharapova to win the 2011 Wimbledon championship as her childhood idol, Czech-born icon and fellow lefty Martina Navratilova, applauds from the stands.

In fact, Kvitova's early career is less observed than many. Western reporters wrestle with the consonants in her last name—pronounced KFIT-oh-VAH, three syllables, please, not Kah-VIH-toe-vah—and her unlikely, uncommonly quiet backstory.

It takes more than three hours to get from Prague to Kvitova's hometown of Fulnek (population 6,000) on the country's perpetually congested highway system. A castle perches in the hills above a small commercial district that includes a household appliance company where her mother, Pavla, once worked in the purchasing department. Her father, Jiri, a retired teacher, spent his spare time hitting with his sons, Jiri and Libor, and their much younger sister on the town's clay tennis courts.

It's easy to see how her father's passion and her mother's composure merged in Kvitova as her parents sit in the kitchen area of a new, two-story clubhouse completed last year, overlooking four clay tennis courts. Petra donated the money to build the clubhouse, and her junior trophies sit atop the cabinet that holds cups and saucers.

Petra sprouts early and slender and gifted, but her parents don't have the money or the inclination to send her away to hone her talent. School is the priority, and there are days when she has time to play for only an hour. By age 16, she stands out enough to be spotted by a scout from the regional tennis center in Prostejov, about an hour away.

Jiri Kvita, a big-framed man with salt-and-pepper hair who shares his daughter's penchant for self-deprecating humor, does most of the talking through an interpreter while his wife takes in the scene with her steady, brown eyes and adds an occasional detail.

"It's hard when your child leaves," Jiri says. "It wasn't until she was 16 that she went [to Prostejov] occasionally, and it wasn't until she was 17 that she stayed." They insist that she finish her last year of high school via independent study even as she begins to travel.

Years later, at the most uncertain point of her post-attack recovery, she taps into an old habit and enrolls in a university course.

Kvitova thrives in Prostejov, where many prominent Czech players have come of age. The complex includes a stadium with a retractable roof, multiple outdoor courts, a gym, dorms, and a restaurant. It is one of many arms of the Czech tennis industry presided over by Kvitova's early patron and Czech business manager, Miroslav Cernosek, whose company also owns the Prague tournament.

At age 21, after uncorking an ace to put away Sharapova at Wimbledon, Kvitova is still unaccustomed to the spotlight, especially when it includes a microphone. Her voice shakes as she speaks on court during the trophy ceremony. At the champions' ball, pressed to say a few words, she tries to describe her thoughts on match point: "I have a chance now, and you never know if it will be more or no. Okay, you have to do it, and I did it."

Katie Spellman, then working in communications for the WTA, watches and listens. She has seen Kvitova interact with the Czech press and knows she loves to banter. Once she becomes Kvitova's public relations manager in 2012, they work at bridging the language gap. Spellman gives Kvitova a copy of the children's book *The Secret Garden* to broaden her vocabulary and shows her transcripts of postmatch interviews by Sharapova and Roger Federer.

By the time Kvitova wins Wimbledon again in 2014, she is able to speak with far more fluidity and nuance. She now routinely laces answers with idiomatic English. "What is the key to playing well on clay?" she repeats in response to a question this spring. "Tough to say. If I know the key, I would already use it."

She wears her fame more easily now as she walks through public spaces, unmistakable at six feet tall, with stylishly tousled blond hair that she pulls back into a thick braid when she plays and a pale, blue-eyed gaze that can be almost disconcertingly direct.

Her father asks the reporters who have come to Fulnek to let the world know that he and his wife are "not haughty, greater-than-thou types." He is the one who cannot contain his tears when Petra wins Wimbledon for the first time, his face working with failed effort, while Pavla smiles serenely at her daughter.

His face crumples briefly with a different emotion at the memory of the morning they learned Petra had been attacked. "Horrible," he says hoarsely. "When we say, 'Happy Birthday—I wish you a lot of luck and a lot of health,' it's no longer a cliché for us."

Her family's small-town humility remains at Kvitova's core. As the coffee break at the InterContinental winds down, she offers to pay (and is rebuffed), then won't leave the table until the check is signed, not wanting to strand the interviewer by herself.

Following the attack, Kvitova's fellow WTA players—who voted her winner of the circuit's sportsmanship award for grace on and off the court six out of the past seven years—fill Twitter with paeans and blow up her phone with supportive messages. When world number-one Simona Halep breaks through to win in June at Roland Garros after falling short in three previous major finals, she reveals that Kvitova had sent her private notes of encouragement: "She said it's gonna come. I just have to keep working."

The goodwill that envelops Kvitova makes the events of 18 months ago even more unfathomable.

Alone in the backseat of a hired car on that December morning, facing a tedious, 145-mile ride to a specialized hospital north of Prague where Kebrle, one of the foremost hand surgeons in the country, is expecting her, Kvitova doesn't dwell on "why me?" There is only "what now?"

Her wounds have been disinfected and swaddled in a cooling wrap at a local hospital in Prostejov. She and her brother Jiri have gone back to the flat where she was attacked to gather a few personal items and the Christmas gifts she bought for her family. When they close the door, she is resolved never to return.

Kvitova's mind tunnels into a place where she is in control. She has obligations. She has already contacted Cernosek, whom she was supposed to join at a charity event that day. He arranges for the car she is in now and the security guard who will be posted by her room after the surgery. There are other people who need to know. She is a celebrity, and the news will leak fast. One-handed, she hits contacts on her phone, taps out texts, and records voice messages. A part of her is in shreds, but her mind is clear.

She reaches Marijn Bal, her agent at IMG, at 4:59 a.m. ET and tells him, through tears, that she is not going to be able to play in the Australian Open next month. Bal thinks she is referring to a previously diagnosed stress fracture in her right foot. It's okay, he says, let's get healthy. No, she says, something just happened.

She confers with Bal in Florida, Spellman in Toronto, and Czech tennis press officer Karel Tejkal in Prague. She tells them what she wants. They will post statements she helps shape, saying she is "shaken" but determined. She wants to speak to the media as soon as she's released so she can spend the holiday in peace with her family. Her fitness trainer, David Vydra, will meet her at the hospital, along with her good friend, doubles specialist Lucie Hradecka. She tells everyone else to stay home, that she will be fine.

"I've seen Petra cope with nerves that would put anyone else in a dark room trembling in a corner," Spellman says. "She was so nervous before the 2014 [Wimbledon] final with Genie Bouchard, and then she won in two sets, and everyone saw what she did with those nerves.

"I guess when you're a champion, and you're able to cope with all those emotions on the court and stick to your processes—that's a big part of what players are taught to do—she was able to apply that. She was the protagonist, and everyone else followed her lead."

Twenty minutes after Kvitova arrives, Kebrle surveys the damage in the operating room. The knife has done its worst on her left index finger, which is slashed to the bone and hanging loose at the last knuckle. Seven flexor tendons, which give the hand its prehensile grasping ability, are severed in her fingers and thumb, their ends separated like snapped rubber bands. The ulnar digital nerves of her thumb and index finger will have to be repaired. There is no guarantee that she will ever regain feeling there.

Kebrle takes his time with the multiple incisions and uses suturing material that will dissolve. He inserts a pin in the finger that was nearly amputated. Because Kebrle treats other tennis players for various hand and wrist ailments, he is hyperaware of where they develop blisters and calluses and where scar tissue will be most problematic. He tries not to leave any more than he has to.

He does not sleep well that night.

"I knew who I am treating, I knew her needs, and I knew she is in a very big danger of not coming back," says the shaggy-haired Kebrle, a 20-year veteran in his field with a kindly face and a frank manner. "I said I was afraid of my own ass because at the end if she does not come back, everybody will connect me: I was the one who finished the career of Petra Kvitova.

"The trouble with this injury is you have to treat it, and then you have to mobilize it from day two, day three. You have to try to move the tendon, but you cannot pull on it, so it doesn't rupture.

And the wound—it wants to have rest for healing, but you must mobilize it. So it's a kind of slalom in between."

On the second day after her surgery, Kvitova places her right fingertips on her left fingers and gently, incrementally, begins to press.

The physical aspect of rehabilitation comes easily to Kvitova, even when it's painful. She amasses a collection of splints, some to extend her damaged fingers, others to help them bend. She has a ravenous desire to hold a racket again, even if she can't fully feel it, even though she will have to start out by hitting foam balls, like a kid in a beginner's class.

Intermittent flashbacks and anxiety are more problematic. She works with a mental coach who urges her to channel her mind toward the small accomplishments of each day and week, to steer her mind's eye toward cheerful images of her nieces and nephew.

But there are some situations she has to confront by herself. Three weeks after surgery, she walks into an empty shower stall at the Sparta Prague club after working out on a stationary bike, hyperaware of her surroundings. "I didn't think too much about the past," she says with remembered enthusiasm. "I was very happy about that." It will be a couple of months before she's willing to rent her own flat in Prague.

It isn't the reboot Kvitova once envisioned for the 2017 season, when she'd intended to rebuild momentum and mount a campaign for another major.

Kvitova's serve, powerful forehand, variety, and timing are among the best in tennis, but her high-risk game requires an intensity that she has sometimes struggled to maintain in the seasons following her second Wimbledon title. Her nickname of "P3tra," referring to her tendency to play three-set matches, encapsulates her ability to dig herself out of competitive trouble she would rather avoid.

She changes coaches early in the 2016 season and splits up with her fiancé, pro hockey player Radek Meidl, the latest in a string of high-profile companions including fellow tennis players Adam Pavlasek and Radek Stepanek. Weeks before the attack, she makes another shift, hiring former ATP pro Jiri Vanek and telling him, "I want to be number one, I want to win one more Grand Slam, I want to do it, I feel it inside," Vanek recalls. He is impressed by her ambition, but then a stress fracture sidelines her. The violent knife attack catapults them into crisis before they've had a single formal practice together.

"I couldn't stay by myself," Kvitova says. Her voice wobbles slightly. "I needed help, to be honest. I am independent, and suddenly I couldn't do anything."

Kvitova is afraid to go out alone. She can't drive with her hand immobilized, and she doesn't want to hire a bodyguard. "I'm a private, quiet person," she says. "It would be terrible to ask someone to go with me to the dinner and stay three tables away." Instead, her coaches become her de facto security detail. She moves in with Vanek and his family in Prague. Her coach and fitness trainer take turns ferrying her to Kebrle's office.

The muscular, animated Vydra, a former pro triathlete, chokes up when he talks about that time. "The first question was, will she ever play tennis again?" he says through an interpreter. "I said I am 100 percent sure that she will. She trusted me, so she then put all into it, that she would return." He tells her he spoke from authority, having survived a brain aneurysm: "I know even if you are totally dead and you are feeling like you can't do this, if you have a strong head, you can force yourself to get up and to do it."

After three months, Kvitova is allowed to pick up a racket. Her grip closes around its familiar contours over the next few weeks in a gradual handshake, reacquainting itself.

A French hand specialist, Dominique Thomas, treats her twice at his clinic in Grenoble with aggressive electro-stimulation therapy. It accelerates her healing, and as Kvitova's optimism grows, she is diligent to a fault. She overworks the hand, and it swells up again. Kebrle is concerned about the index finger. If it remains inflexible because of scar tissue, he might have to perform another surgery that will set her back weeks.

One day, she hears the finger click and finds she can bend it. Kebrle tells her the worst of the adhesions has freed up at last, confirming that holding the racket is actually the best therapy of all. "Once she started playing tennis, you could see it from week to week, that her function has increased, and it started to work as a normal hand," he says.

Her progress is kept strictly under wraps as she trains in the

Canary Islands and Monaco. She sends video clips of practice to her doctors and her agents, and one day, she sends a photo with a caption noting a small off-court victory: "I'm holding a wine glass."

"All the way through, she was saying, 'This is gonna be a challenge, but I love challenges,'" Spellman says. "Maybe nothing else would have given her that motivation—if it had just been an injury. It gave her the inner strength to want to prove she could do it."

By mid-April 2017, Kvitova decides she will try to play at Roland Garros, a month before the doctors initially thought was possible. Her public comeback begins in the interview room in Paris, a session she rehearses with Spellman, trying to anticipate the questions reporters will ask, strategizing what to do if she cries. The lights over the dais make her sweat, but she doesn't wilt or break down. "I felt like the tennis was taken away from me, and it wasn't my decision," she says. "Suddenly I couldn't do what I love. I see a little bit from the different angle. So I'm happy that I'm here."

Tennis people are welcoming and kind, but they are also unsure how to react, casting covert glances at her hand. She understands why. "I saw people very happy to see me back," she says. "Then I felt sometimes they were curious how my hand was, but they didn't ask. Uncomfortable. But I think I will be the same as they were."

Only Boris Becker, on site as a Eurosport television analyst, asks her about it directly. Kvitova does a credible impersonation of his voice: "Petra, show me your hand." She turns it over to display her palm. He exhales and says, "Okay." She walks onto center court with her fingernails painted bright red and wins her first match. She loses in the next round, but she has cleared the most important hurdle.

Kvitova defies the odds again the next month, knitting together a week's worth of matches on grass to win the Birmingham title in late June. She doesn't even look surprised when she beats Ashleigh Barty in the final, though she will later say she was awash in disbelief. She turns to Vanek and Vydra in the stands after receiving the trophy and says, in Czech, "Is this normal?" It's an inside joke in her camp, an acknowledgment that they are on uncharted ground.

She loses in the second round at Wimbledon but feels encouraged when she reaches the U.S. Open quarterfinals and plays Venus Williams toe-to-toe through three sets.

In December 2017, a year after the attack, a Czech publication includes Kvitova and her surgeon in an annual "Czechs of the

Year" photo spread. She is resplendent in a red dress; he is gallantly kissing the left hand he repaired. The image reflects a story moving toward a happy ending, but there's still one critical piece missing.

Based on Kvitova's description, police quickly release a sketch of a suspect in his thirties. A few confirmed details make their way into Czech media reports. Kvitova's name was not on the exterior buzzer panel of the five-story building, whose modest appearance betrayed no hint of a millionaire tennis player in residence. The intruder gained access by posing as a utility worker. She was attacked in her bathroom. He made off with a few hundred dollars.

The authorities characterize the crime as random, but a month later, a police spokesperson uses the term *vydírání*—translated as "extortion" or "blackmail" in English-language reports. Under the Czech penal code, the word can simply mean a forcible, violent act, and it carries a higher possible sentence when grievous bodily harm is inflicted.

In the semantic swirl and the absence of hard information, theories flourish, some fueled by Kvitova's early and successful comeback. Was it really possible that one of the most celebrated athletes in the country could have been an arbitrary target? Were her wounds really that serious? Did police bungle the investigation?

Kebrle gets calls from colleagues asking if the whole thing is an insurance scam. He is unequivocal about the nature of her wounds: "The way it's done, it shows it was a defens[ive] injury. That's the biological reaction of the body. Less for more. I lose my hand, but I will save my life." In August 2017, a frustrated Kvitova decides to release the surgeon's graphic before-and-after photos of her hand, shortly before the U.S. Open.

Radio silence persists until November, when another police briefing is held to announce that despite hundreds of interviews, tips, and a sizable reward for information, there are no new leads, and the case has been shelved.

Police spokesmen stonewall ESPN's inquiries this spring. A harried but polite receptionist at the Prostejov police station makes phone calls, comes out from behind her desk, and explains there is an embargo. Emailed requests to regional authorities in nearby Olomouc get the same answer.

But there is movement behind the scenes. According to recent

Czech media accounts, a cold-case unit tackles the case early in the year. On the eve of Roland Garros in late May, an unidentified man is taken into custody. News outlets in the Czech Republic report that he had a criminal past, including being a member of a gang that preyed on elderly people. Kvitova initially identifies him through a photo, and then, after she's finished playing in Paris, returns home and picks him out of a lineup.

"I think I [will] feel relief when everything is done," she says after the arrest becomes public knowledge. "Obviously, it's great news so far, but—when you play, and for example, you have one game to serve for the match, or you have match point—it's close, but it's still far away. So that's how I feel it."

Czech law gives authorities wide latitude in holding suspects during investigations, closing hearings and withholding information. Specific charges could come in late July, according to the latest police statement.

Kvitova, who continues to refrain from detailing specifics of the attack or discussing legal aspects of the case, says she will not be afraid if and when the time comes to open up. "I think I will, I can, but I just can't now because of the police," she says in Prague this spring. "But I think I am okay to tell it. I don't have anything to hide."

The numbness the knife left might never completely dissipate. Kvitova has learned to make a celebratory fist with her other hand. She sometimes kneads the fingers of her left hand with her right while she's at rest, trying to coax a little bit more flexibility from them.

"From my view, it's not really improving much, but I think I'm pretty happy with the way it is anyway," she says after one of her matches at Roland Garros in May. This is Kvitova's new ordinary. It can be traced back to that long car ride when, with her career in limbo, she seized on what she could do rather than what might be lost.

Wimbledon is almost upon her again. Simply making the trip will not suffice this year, not after a 38-7 season that includes titles on hardcourts, clay, and grass, raising her own expectations as high as they've ever been.

"I'm kind of surprised how I handled everything," she says. "Obviously, I'm a pretty positive person, but to be positive in this kind of case was just so different. When you lose the match, you can be positive that you have a chance next week. But when I'm going to the hospital without knowing if I can ever have all my fingers back —of course, I didn't want to think too much how bad it can be."

Kvitova would not wish what happened to her on anyone, yet the scar tissue that temporarily bound her also led to a profound discovery. The surgeon's skill salvaged her grip, but it was her own handiwork that mattered most in loosening the physical adhesions and conquering the fears that could have held her back. Consider the strength that led her to fight with her dominant hand and then fight for that hand, in the service of an obstinate and ardent notion: no one was going to pry her away from what she loves.

LOUISA THOMAS

Game Plan

FROM THE NEW YORKER

IT WAS AUGUST 2012, and Becky Hammon, the point guard of
the Silver Stars, San Antonio's franchise in the WNBA, was on her
way home from the London Olympics. While waiting to board a
connecting flight in Atlanta, she spotted the craggy face of Gregg
Popovich, the head coach of the NBA's San Antonio Spurs. Popovich is widely considered one of the greatest coaches of all time,
and is known for a capacity to inspire selfless team play even among
players of colossal ego. One of his many fans, Barack Obama, has
said that if he were a free agent in the NBA he'd sign with Popovich. Hammon was far less famous, but Popovich was an admirer,
and he recognized her too. He had been watching her play since
2007, the year before she led the Silver Stars to the WNBA Finals.
From time to time during the next few seasons, Popovich would
call or text Dan Hughes, the Silver Stars' coach, with comments
about her performance.

Though only five feet six, Hammon was a commanding presence on the court: gum-snapping, energetic, her quick cuts and
jab steps to the basket punctuated by a swishing ponytail. She
could slip through a narrow space between two defenders and
drive to the hoop, scooping a shot that would skim the rim and
slide through the net. Like Magic Johnson, she flipped no-look
passes over her shoulder, and, like Stephen Curry, she hit shots
from half-court. But Popovich was most struck by her prowess as
a court general: she had an uncanny ability to direct her teammates around the floor. "I'd watch the game, and the only thing

I could see—it's an exaggeration, I mean, but—was Becky's aura, her leadership, her effect on teammates, her effect on the crowd, the way she handled herself," Popovich told me. "She was, like, the ultimate leader. Energy, juice, vitality. At the same time, she was doing intelligent things on the court, making decisions that mattered." In the NBA, a woman in charge was almost unthinkable, but he was considering hiring her.

Hammon and Popovich managed to sit together on the flight to San Antonio. They talked until the plane touched down, but not about basketball. He wasn't interested in whether she could diagram a play. Popovich has a more character-driven view of coaching—and of coaches. "I wanted to find out who she was," he said. "What did she think? How intelligent is she? How worldly? What goes through her mind? My ulterior motive, if that's the way to put it, was that I wanted to find out whether she had the interest and the tools to be a leader, to run a team."

Rebecca Lynn Hammon, who is now 41, was born in Rapid City, South Dakota. She has a heart-shaped face framed by chestnut hair that falls below her shoulders, and she speaks in a cheerful, sincere voice with a Midwestern accent. She was raised, and remains, a devout Christian. She is unapologetically American. And yet at the London Olympics, she told Popovich, she had played in a red uniform for the Russian Federation. Four years earlier, she'd been passed over for the U.S. team's first round of tryouts for the Beijing Olympics, and Russia had offered her a spot on its national team; she also played in a Russian league. Popovich, who had been a Soviet-studies major at the Air Force Academy, was fascinated. He told Hammon about touring the Soviet Union with the U.S. Armed Forces basketball team in the seventies, and, as she drank a beer, she told him what it was like to live in Moscow and to lead players who were, at first, wary of an American teammate. "I was a proud, arrogant American," she later recounted. "But, at the end of the day, you live in the world with billions of people, and everyone has a unique upbringing and experience." Hammon had become a naturalized Russian citizen in order to play in Moscow —a difficult decision. Some Americans called her a traitor. Even the U.S. head coach, Anne Donovan, said that she was unpatriotic, though later she backed off, saying, "I hold no grudge, and more power to her."

As their flight neared its end, Popovich could barely conceal his interest. He said, "So, if I ever hired you and I asked you something, you'd tell me the truth?"

Hammon found the question curious. "I don't know why else you'd ask if you didn't want me to tell the truth," she said.

"Good," he said. "I don't want a bunch of yes-men."

The following year, Hammon suffered a torn ACL, a season-ending injury. While she recovered, she asked Popovich whether she could sit in on a few Spurs practices. The team is famously reluctant to grant access to outsiders, but he agreed. Soon, she was attending coaches' meetings and film sessions, analyzing games and discussing strategy. To the untutored eye, basketball seems infinitely more improvisational than football, in which each play is conveyed in a kind of committee meeting, the huddle. And yet both the offensive and the defensive sides of basketball involve extensive planning and preparation. The most gifted coaches, like Popovich —or, in their time, Red Auerbach, of the Celtics; Red Holzman, of the Knicks; and Phil Jackson, of the Lakers and the Bulls—can make even the greatest soloists harmonize with their teammates. By the end of the season, in the spring of 2014, Popovich noticed that Hammon was confident enough to argue with him about the finer points of, say, offensive ball movement and floor spacing. "That's when I knew, if I had an opportunity, I wanted to put her on staff," Popovich said.

That summer, Hammon retired from the WNBA, and the Spurs announced that they had hired her as an assistant coach, making her the first full-time female coach in big-time American men's sports. Popovich and his general manager, R. C. Buford, insist that they had no intention of making a political statement. "It has nothing to do with her being a woman. She *happens* to be a woman," Popovich said.

But professional sports are the last major area of American culture in which the segregation of the sexes is not only tolerated but sanctioned. On the field, the ice, and the court, the reasons are obvious: differences in size and strength can make it difficult for female athletes to compete against their male counterparts. In the famed Battle of the Sexes, in 1973, Billie Jean King caused a sensation when she crushed Bobby Riggs, but King, at 29, was in her prime, while Riggs was 55. Few, if any, tennis fans believe that

King could have defeated Jimmy Connors or Arthur Ashe. But sex discrimination on the sidelines is also taken as a matter of course —at least when it comes to women coaching men. (Men coaching women is common in the professional and the college ranks.) On social media and sports talk radio, the reasons that women could never coach men are presented as if they were as inevitable as differences in testosterone levels: women won't tolerate the locker-room culture; men's teams are "more athletic" than women's, making them incomprehensible to the female imagination; and women simply cannot command young men. Mike Francesa, one of the most popular sports-radio hosts in the country, once said of Hammon, "What would qualify her to be a coach, on a professional level, of a men's team?" He added, "It's not even something that would make sense to aspire to." Nearly half a century after Title IX, the belief persists: women cannot coach men, particularly at the professional level.

By hiring Hammon, Popovich challenged the idea that the best male athletes in the world would be diminished by the leadership of a woman. "I was, like, Hallelujah," Julie Foudy, a former captain of the U.S. women's national soccer team and an ESPN analyst, told me. Also among those who cheered the decision was Adam Silver, the slender, savvy lawyer who has been the commissioner of the NBA since 2014. While the NFL struggles to position itself between its activist players and its more conservative fans, Silver has expressed a desire to make the NBA progressive and inclusive—a league of the woke. Silver first made his political mark by forcing out the owner of the LA Clippers, who had been caught on tape making racist remarks. Silver has supported star players like LeBron James and Stephen Curry in criticizing Donald Trump. Two years ago, Popovich attended New York's gay-pride parade and saw Silver riding an NBA float. In October, Silver hired a retired Air Force lieutenant general named Michelle D. Johnson as the head of referee operations. "It's not inclusion for its own sake, or diversity for its own sake," he told me. "It's the consequence of expanding the pool of candidates." Last year, he said that he expected to see a female head coach "sooner rather than later."

James said last week that he and his teammates on the Cleveland Cavaliers would welcome a female head coach. "If she knows what she's doing, we'll love it," he said. "I mean, listen, at the end of the day, basketball, it's not about male or female. If you know the game, you know the game." Many people speculate that Hammon will be the NBA's first female head coach, not least because she has Popovich's support. Talking to Hammon, though, I was struck by her ambivalence about her role as a pioneer. She recognizes that she is an inspiration for many young women, and a target for many wary men. At the same time, she resists the attention to her gender. "If you don't want a female coach, don't hire one!" she said, with some exasperation. But, she continued, if "you want to hire somebody who's qualified and will do a good job, then maybe you should consider me." Like Popovich, Hammon believes that coaching involves more than drawing up plays or breaking down defensive schemes. "You shouldn't get into coaching unless you care about the people you're leading," she said. That doesn't fit the popular image of a successful coach—your Belichicks and Lombardis. But it is, as it happens, the philosophy of the Spurs.

As a kid growing up in South Dakota, Becky Hammon had two great passions. One was basketball. When she was a toddler, she learned to dribble. She later played for hours with a Nerf ball and a small hoop nailed to a door, battling her older brother and her father, who played on his knees. When she was older, the games moved to the driveway, where there was a hoop mounted to the deck. Her parents installed floodlights so that games could go into the night. From the age of 10, she took hundreds of shots a day. "Playing basketball for me is like breathing," she said.

Her other passion was her faith. Every Sunday morning, Sunday evening, and Wednesday night, the family attended services at an evangelical church. When Hammon was seven, the church showed a movie based on the Rapture, called *A Thief in the Night*. She thought of being separated from her family, and she was terrified. Soon after, she went to the front of the church and declared that she had accepted Christ into her heart.

Becky's mother was convinced that she would become a minister or a missionary. Becky wanted to play in the NBA. Her father had to tell her, gently, that it wouldn't happen—but she might aim for a college scholarship. Even that seemed unlikely. Hammon was under five feet until around eighth grade, and a growth spurt sputtered out at five feet six. "I'll never be able to compete athletically," she remembers realizing, "so I have to learn how to beat people with my mind."

She told me that Christianity gave her "courage and comfort," a sense that there was a purpose to her life. "You can't separate the two," she said, of her faith and basketball, as we sat in the kitchen of the Spurs' training facility, in San Antonio. "It would be like trying to strain my white blood cells from my red blood cells. It would be like trying to separate my personality from my soul."

At Stevens High School in Rapid City, Hammon became the school's all-time leader in scoring, assists, and steals, and she was voted South Dakota's Player of the Year. There was no clear road from Rapid City to a top college program, but, after Hammon's junior year, she got a break. She was invited to an elite training camp in Terre Haute, Indiana. Soon, it was clear to everyone there that the diminutive guard with the long ponytail could shoot.

One of the people watching was an assistant coach at Colorado State, who reported back to the head coach, Greg Williams. Williams went to Rapid City to watch Hammon play; he then offered her a full scholarship. "Though she was not arrogant, she believed in herself," he told me. In 1995, when Hammon started her freshman year at Colorado State, the team had rarely finished a season with a winning record. During her senior year, the team finished 33-3 and made the Sweet 16 in the NCAA tournament. "Nothing bothered her," Williams said. "Becky always wanted to take the tough shot." She became the school's all-time leader in points, assists, and threes, and the leading scorer, male or female, in Western Athletic Conference history.

When Hammon graduated, the WNBA was in its third season. It was not the first women's professional basketball league, but it was the starriest, with NCAA and Olympic legends like Lisa Leslie, Rebecca Lobo, and Sheryl Swoopes, and it had the full backing of the NBA. On the WNBA's draft day, Hammon was in Fort Collins, waiting for her agent to call; the phone didn't ring. There had been an influx of established players as a rival league folded, but the real problem was that Hammon was considered too small to compete. Though she wasn't drafted, the New York Liberty offered her a spot at its training camp, where not every player would make the team. She survived the cuts and signed a contract for $25,000.

The Liberty had some of the best players in the league, like Teresa Weatherspoon, an energetic ball handler, and Vickie Johnson, a silky-smooth scorer. Hammon challenged herself to match up against them in practice. Before long, she had made herself indispensable as a substitute player, coming off the bench to score and to guide the team. In 2003, she became the starting point guard. "Her size never mattered," the Liberty's head coach, Richie Adubato, said. "When she drove to the basket, it didn't matter who was in there. She had one shot blocked, I think, in four years."

In 2007, the San Antonio Silver Stars traded for her. Dan Hughes, the coach, would watch her take on multiple opponents and think, *She's in trouble—we're in trouble.* Then he came to appreciate how "she'd hang in the air longer, create spin, and hit the corner on the backboard," and he began looking forward to seeing how she got out of such situations. "I became a fan," he said.

Hammon became one of the most popular players in the WNBA, but the league struggled financially. Since its promising first years, many teams have lost money; several have been moved or shuttered. In the WNBA, players' annual salaries max out at just over $100,000; in the NBA, the minimum is more than $500,000, and stars make tens of millions, never mind endorsement money. WNBA players routinely spend about half the year overseas, where private patrons or wealthy corporations back teams as vanity projects. In 2007, Hammon was making about $95,000 a year, then the WNBA's maximum salary, when CSKA, a Russian team, offered her a four-year deal worth around $2 million. As part of the deal, Hammon would become a Russian citizen; the rules of the Russian Premier League prevent teams from fielding more than two American players.

While Hammon was negotiating her contract with CSKA, she learned that the U.S. Olympic team had not invited her to its first round of tryouts. The exclusion reinforced the idea she had about herself. "I've always been on the outside looking in," she said. "The kid not picked." The Russian national team asked her to play for them, and she accepted the offer. She wanted to play in the Olympics, and Washington's political relations with Moscow were not nearly as fraught as they are now. "This is basketball, it isn't the Cold War," she said at the time.

She moved to Moscow for the CSKA season in 2007, and began training with the national team in 2008. She spent seven months a year abroad for the next six years, until she started working with the Spurs. "I was an outsider," Hammon told me. "They looked at me with one eyebrow"—she cocked hers. Anna Petraková, who played with Hammon on CSKA and the national team, told me, "When people come to Russia, they always seem a little standoffish. They don't always integrate in the culture." Hammon was different. "She just came with an open heart." Hammon learned a little Russian, and at games she enthusiastically fumbled her way through the national anthem.

Many people thought that Hammon was naive, or worse. Some American players called her disloyal. Far more painful for Hammon was the reaction at home, in South Dakota. "I come from a red state, where it's God, country, family," she told me. "I got my mom calling me on the phone saying, 'You don't understand people of my generation,'" and crying every time they spoke. Before that, she'd been the spirited point guard, the all-star everyone loved. Now everyone was questioning her. "I took a beating," she said.

At the Summer Games in Beijing, in August 2008, the U.S. beat Russia in the semifinals. After the game, Lisa Leslie, one of the most decorated Olympic basketball players, refused to shake Hammon's hand. The U.S. went on to win the finals. At the medal ceremony, Hammon stood on the lowest step of the podium, in her Russian uniform, a bronze medal around her neck. When the American national anthem played, she placed her hand on her heart. Still, she was proud of the Russian national team, and of her ability to integrate with the players. Hammon told me, "I'm Russian to them, and it has nothing to do with the passport I'm holding.

"I think that journey helped prepare me to do things that people hadn't done," she said. "It helped me take a lot of crap. It helped build something inside me."

When Hammon began observing Spurs practices, she assumed that it would help her get a job with a college team or in the WNBA. "Coaching women, that's where my mind-set was the whole time," she said. Then, one night at dinner, Tony Parker, the Spurs' point guard, who is a close friend of Hammon—"She's sort of like my big sister," he told me—said that he thought Popovich might hire her. "Really?" she replied.

"It was almost like a perfect match, because Pop likes to try stuff," Parker recalled. "I thought it would be perfect for those two to get together—great basketball minds." He had no doubt that she would be accepted by the other players. "She had the support of the point guard, so she's good," he added with a smile.

Popovich and Buford, the Spurs' general manager, watched how she behaved in meetings and interacted with players on the floor. Tim Duncan, one of the game's greatest power forwards, is known to be exceptionally reticent. Parker once said that, during his first season, Duncan didn't even speak to him. Hammon realized that she would have to break through with Duncan over time, and off the court. "Let's be real," she said, and laughed. "I was not sitting there trying to give Timmy extra tips."

"With a new job, when you go, you shut up," Popovich said. "You don't try to prove to people how smart you are, or that you have better ideas. She was cognizant of that sort of managerial thing." In August 2014, the Spurs offered Hammon the job as an assistant coach.

The announcement was greeted with fanfare. President Obama tweeted his congratulations. The mainstream media ran complimentary coverage. "No one is going to come up and say, 'I'm so pissed you got that job, I can't believe it,'" Hammon said. "There's certain noise that I know goes on, but no one ever says it, because it's not the politically correct thing to say." Players and opposing coaches were, for the most part, encouraging. Stars like LeBron James and Chris Paul told her that they were happy she was hired. Last week, James told reporters, "You guys know how fond I am of Coach Pop, so for him to bring Becky in there, to be able to be an assistant and give her input—I don't quite know how much input she has, I'm not there on a day-to-day basis—but just having her face there, it means a lot."

Jeff Van Gundy, the former coach of the New York Knicks and the Houston Rockets and a commentator on ESPN, told me, "I'm not the social conscience of the NBA. I'm also not the most enlightened. Twenty years ago, I would have laughed at the notion of a female assistant or head coach. But I think we are becoming a more enlightened league. I think coaches are. But you know who doesn't get enough credit? Players. I think they have really made incredible progress."

Most of the criticism came from the noisiest and nastiest corners of talk radio and social media. At Hammon's first press conference after her hiring, a reporter read her an anonymous email that called it a publicity stunt, and suggested that the only thing the players had to learn from her was advice on baking cookies. "People are, like, 'What do you say to that?'" Hammon said. "At the end of the day, you have to say, 'So what's the truth in that? Is that true? No, it's not.' So I have no comment to that—other than, I make good chocolate-chip cookies. That's a fact."

This has not been an easy year for the Spurs. The team's longtime stars are aging or retired, and its MVP candidate, Kawhi Leonard, has been out with a quadriceps injury for all but nine games. Still, throughout the regular season, the Spurs remained on track to make the playoffs for the 21st straight time. Since Popovich became coach, in 1996, they have won five championships, and from 2000 to 2017 they had 18 consecutive 50-win seasons—a stretch of excellence that is nearly unparalleled in sports. There are plenty of factors that explain their success: a keen eye for talent abroad, a famed analytics department, and the good fortune of drafting Duncan. But there is something more: the team ethos—selfless play above all—instilled by Popovich and known around San Antonio as "the Spurs way."

Because of their success, the Spurs have not been eligible for the highest picks in the draft. Instead of relying on college superstars, they have built their team through some crafty trades and by pushing their young players to the limit. They scout top international players—like Parker, from France, and Manu Ginóbili, from Argentina—and sign NBA veterans like Pau Gasol, from Spain, who is 37 but can anchor a defense and move in a way that creates space on the floor; they also, as in the case of Leonard, hone the raw athletic talent of less experienced players. When the Spurs are at their best, the ball moves fluidly and freely. Duncan, who retired in 2016 and was perhaps the least flashy major star in the NBA, was emblematic of the team's unselfish style. On a given night, almost anyone on the roster can be the leading scorer.

Popovich rejects the idea of winning at all costs. "We want to win the right way, we want to lose the right way," he told me. At the team's first film session after losing to the Miami Heat in the NBA Finals in 2013, Popovich reviewed the team's mistakes and then said, "Gentlemen, if this is the worst thing that ever happens to you in your life, your life is going to be a breeze." During games, he'll call a quick time-out to shout at a player, or bench someone

for playing badly. But off the court he does not talk about staying focused or decry "distractions." To the contrary, he tends to
talk politics with his players, his coaches, and reporters. He once
brought in John Carlos, the sprinter who gave a Black Power salute
from the Olympic podium, to speak to the team. Two days before
the 2014 NBA Finals, when the team gathered in the video room,
he displayed a photograph of Eddie Mabo, an Australian indige-
nous-land-rights activist. A few weeks ago, the Spurs traveled to DC
to play the Washington Wizards, in a game that had implications
for the playoffs. While they were in town, Popovich took them to
visit the Supreme Court.

   "Everybody talks about everything ad nauseam," Popovich told
me. "I'm sure the coaches are, like, 'Oh, my God, can't we just play
basketball?' I think it's a huge part of what we do, because it helps
them love each other, it helps them feel responsible to each other,
it helps them want to work for and with each other—and it helps
them understand that when they're 32 or 35 or 37 their life starts
all over again, and it's probably not going to have anything to do
with basketball. They need to know what they're walking into, and
what kind of social system we have, and what kind of world we live
in, because they're going to be raising kids by then too. And it's
important to have your self-image be much more, and hopefully
have basketball be a small part of who they are when they're done
with this."

   Popovich's rules include: don't skip steps, have a sense of humor, and get over yourself. These rules are another way of reaching the equilibrium between humility and self-confidence which
Hammon first found through faith. Popovich said, "She knows
what she knows and she knows what she doesn't, and, what she
doesn't know, she gets her ass in the film room, or nails down one
of the other coaches." He added, "I think she's a star."

When Becky Hammon played basketball, she was known as a
shooter, but she loved passing. It was her way of dictating the game
while getting others involved. Now she charts the Spurs' passes
in order to see which ones lead to scoring. It isn't her primary
responsibility—like other assistants, she is responsible for scouting
and for helping to game-plan for a list of opposing teams—but it
calls on her experience as a point guard.

   At first, the aim was to get a picture of the pace of the game:

Hammon would note each time the team pushed the ball down the court. Then the project evolved. How many times did they kick it out of the post? How often did wheeling it around the perimeter lead to an open shot? These days, all the top teams emphasize passing. But, with Leonard out, it has been especially important for the Spurs. So the coaches focus on reading defenses and baiting opposing players, trying to set up an open shot. They have heated debates about spacing on the court.

Popovich and Buford told me that Hammon is an effective coach because of her "basketball IQ." But she is also adept at the human elements of the game. When she started working with the Spurs, she noticed how Duncan communicated with his teammates nonverbally. "His leadership — if you go back, you see Tim is touching people all the time," she said. She talked about the impact of Ginóbili, who is 40: "Even if Manu never steps onto the court this year, the way he understands culture and brings people together — it's always about the team." This year, the Spurs have been tested by Leonard's absence and by tensions over when and whether he might return. But part of a coach's job is to deal with the unexpected, and to fix relationships when they break down. Lately, the team has been carried by 32-year-old LaMarcus Aldridge. By the end of last season, Aldridge was so frustrated that he asked for a trade. Instead, he and Popovich talked through their differences. "Maybe what worked for Tim Duncan wasn't working for LaMarcus," Hammon said.

Hammon fits in with the Spurs' cooperative mentality. "She's committed, she's passionate, she's smart, she's worldly," Ginóbili said. Some of her reputation comes from her accomplishments as a player. The WNBA has had trouble getting traction with NBA fans, but many NBA players follow the league with respect. Jonathon Simmons, who left the Spurs last year, for the Orlando Magic, said in 2015 that Hammon is a "players' coach." He told me that he meant it literally: "She once was a player, so she understands, she relates."

Of course, players talking to a female reporter about the first female coach are unlikely to offer skepticism, and it is easy to find examples of sexism and even alleged sexual violence within the NBA. In October 2016, the former Chicago Bulls point guard Derrick Rose, now with the Minnesota Timberwolves, was tried and cleared in a rape case. Rose testified that, at a 2008 NBA rookie-

orientation program, he was told not to leave behind used condoms, reportedly saying, "You never know what women are up to
nowadays." (A spokesperson for the NBA said that players were
instructed on how to dispose of condoms, but not because of concerns about exploitation by women.) In February, more than a
dozen current and former Dallas Mavericks employees told *Sports
Illustrated* that it was an "open secret" that the team's former president sexually harassed employees and that the management tolerated sexual harassment and domestic violence. (The former
president has denied the allegations.) In response to the article,
the Mavericks announced that they had suspended one employee,
terminated another, and hired outside counsel to investigate the
allegations.

When I asked Hammon about the Mavericks allegations, she
said, "The culture of sports has been 'He's acting like a boy.' What
does that mean? You're acting like an animal? There needs to be
boundaries. There needs to be an environment where everyone
can succeed."

Some people talk about Hammon's career as though it were a quick
fix for sexism in the NBA. Instead of calling for more women to
be hired, they focus on the advancement of this particular woman.
It's a little like assuming that Barack Obama's presidency would
end American racism. In fact, Hammon's success has not yet led
to many more coaching opportunities for women. In 2015, the
Sacramento Kings hired Nancy Lieberman, a former head coach
in the WNBA and in the NBA's development league, as a full-time
assistant. (She was recently named a head coach in Ice Cube's Big3
league, featuring retired NBA players.) Last October, the Kings
also hired Jenny Boucek, another former WNBA head coach, as
an assistant. But no other franchises have followed suit. "When 10
other teams have a Becky Hammon, that will tell me the culture is
changing," Popovich said.

The big question for Hammon, Popovich told me, is "Is this
going to end up being something? Is she going to be able to ma-
triculate and get into a head-coaching position?" Hammon is still
early in her career, and it could take some time. "Some people are
in the league 15, 20 years before they get into a head-coaching
position, if they do at all," Popovich said. "I tell her, very straight-

forwardly, I don't know. Because I look at our country, and I have all kinds of doubts about all kinds of things, let alone whether she's going to be a head coach." Steve Kerr, the head coach of the Golden State Warriors, said last week, about the possibility of a female head coach, "I don't know if it's going to happen soon. Becky Hammon would be the one you'd say right away who could possibly get an interview."

In 2015, Hammon served as the Spurs' head coach in the NBA's summer league, in Las Vegas, and won the championship. It was not a rare accomplishment for an assistant coach, but it was a significant one. Afterward, a former NBA executive indicated in a tweet that if he were a general manager he would want to hire Hammon as head coach. Jeff Van Gundy told me, "I called him up and said, 'Bullshit you would. Because you don't know her, and that would be your one shot. I would like to think you would, but no way.' I think it's going to take someone like Pop—who's entrenched, who has great job security—to pull that trigger. You're not going to see someone who has his job on the line. Is that fair? No. Is that reality for Becky? Yeah."

For Hammon to be hired as a head coach, Popovich said, "it's going to take somebody who has some guts, some imagination, and is not driven by old standards and old forms." He went on, "If somebody is smart, it's actually a pretty good marketing deal —but it's not about that. It's got to be that she's competent, that she's ready."

Last spring, Hammon turned down an offer to become the head coach of the women's basketball team at the University of Florida, after considering it seriously. She was also invited to interview for the Milwaukee Bucks' general-manager position—an unusual occurrence for an assistant coach who has been on the job only three years. Hammon said that, when she asked why she was being considered, she was told that "ownership had asked them to reach out." (The Bucks declined to comment.) More recently, she interviewed to be the head coach of the men's team at Colorado State, before withdrawing her name from contention.

When I asked Hammon why she turned down the University of Florida job, she said that Popovich and the Spurs had more to teach her. "If you're interested in cars, it's like Henry Ford coming and saying, 'Hey, why don't I teach you about the Model T?'"

Her goal is not to save the sport from itself, or to prove that women can thrive in male-dominated professions. She doesn't have time to worry about taking on doubters. "My motives shouldn't be to change people's minds," she said. "My job is to be the best that I can be, and if that changes your mind then great, but I can't be consumed with how you feel about me."

KERRY HOWLEY

Everyone Believed Larry Nassar

FROM NEW YORK

I

LARISSA BOYCE was 10 when her coach, John Geddert, forced
her legs into a split so hard she cried. He pulled her right leg
up toward his torso, sending shooting pains through her groin
and hamstrings, and he kept pulling. "Racking," as it's called, was
common practice at the gym, but it was evidently too much for
Larissa's mother, who marched onto the mats and told Geddert
to take his hands off her daughter. From then on, Larissa would
train under Kathie Klages, a relatively low-key coach with unruly
red hair and glasses at Michigan State University's Spartan youth
gymnastics team. Klages, like Geddert, considered herself a dear
friend of an athletic trainer named Larry Nassar and sent her gymnasts to him.

When, six years later, Larissa felt ready to talk about the fact
that Larry had penetrated her with his hand without warning, she
approached Klages. Larissa remembers her office as a small room
with a desk, a window, and green carpet. "'I have known Larry for
years and years,'" Larissa recalls Klages saying. "'He would never
do anything inappropriate.'"

Larissa named another gymnast who had been touched, and
when Klages called her into the office, she told her the same story.
Klages countered by bringing in college gymnasts, who said that
Larry had touched "around" the area but that it was never "inappropriate."

"That's not what happened to me," Larissa said. Klages, who has been indicted for allegedly lying to police about this and another such instance, maintains that no one ever came to her with complaints of sexual abuse.

According to Larissa, Klages said she could report the allegations but doing so would have "very serious consequences" for both Larry and Larissa. Larissa couldn't look at Klages, so she stared out the window. She didn't want to get anyone in trouble. Afterward, she cried in the bathroom and resolved never to tell anyone again. She worried that Klages would tell Larry.

The next time she went to visit Larry, he closed the door, pulled up a stool, sat down, and looked at her. "So," he said, "I talked to Kathie."

"I'm so sorry," Larissa said. "I misunderstood. It's all my fault."

It was 1997. Most of Larry Nassar's victims had not yet been born.

II

It has by the fall of 2018 become commonplace to describe the 499 known victims of Larry Nassar as "breaking their silence," though in fact they were never, as a group, particularly silent. Over the course of at least 20 years of consistent abuse, women and girls reported to every proximate authority. They told their parents. They told gymnastics coaches, running coaches, softball coaches. They told Michigan State University police and Meridian Township police. They told physicians and psychologists. They told university administrators. They told, repeatedly, USA Gymnastics. They told one another. Athletes were interviewed, reports were written up, charges recommended. The story of Larry Nassar is not a story of silence. The story of Larry Nassar is that of an edifice of trust so resilient, so impermeable to common sense, that it endured for decades against the allegations of so many women.

If this is a story of institutional failure, it is also a story of astonishing individual ingenuity. Larry Nassar was good at this. His continued success depended on deceiving parents, fellow doctors, elite coaches, Olympic gatekeepers, athletes, and, with some regularity, law enforcement. Before getting caught, he managed to abuse women and girls whose names you know—Simone Biles,

Aly Raisman, McKayla Maroney—and hundreds whose names you don't.

As of November 5, it looks likely that Nassar has destroyed the sport's governing body, USA Gymnastics. In an open letter citing the "struggle to change its culture," the U.S. Olympic Committee began the process of decertifying USAG, which withheld knowledge about Nassar from its members for over a year and whose former president was recently arrested by U.S. Marshals for disappearing Nassar-related documents. The organization is being sued by hundreds of accusers represented by "37 or 38" law firms, according to the lawyer charged with organizing them; it's hard to keep count.

Nassar has pleaded guilty in three separate trials and been sentenced to a collective minimum of 100 years. Michigan State University has settled with 332 women for half a billion dollars. Karolyi Ranch, the dated, isolated training camp where Olympians were required to see Nassar, has been shut down. Yet strangely little has been said about the man, his strategies, his undeniable and persistent success in serving his own needs. One can read news reports for hours about athletes and judicial process and, inescapably, the triumph of "finding a voice" without being informed of what, precisely, this man had done to any of the athletes whose voices required finding. News broadcasts are hard to parse: a dozen medalwinning gymnasts, of three different generations, "speaking out" about what was typically and unspecifically called "abuse" but that many of them had understood to be "treatment." There are logistical questions. How had he molested girls who were never alone with him? What, precisely, motivated coaches and administrators to protect him—at great risk to themselves? With what rhetorical magic had he argued himself out of complaint after complaint?

Nassar is neither charismatic nor smooth; he is nerdy, a little awkward, a little "Inspector Gadget," as one gymnast put it. He is a man who laughs a lot and snorts when he laughs. He tells dad jokes and never dirty ones; his voice is nasal and his patter never-ending. His talkativeness, particularly on technical matters relating to the body's response to injury, can verge on excessive, even logorrheic. "Sometimes," says a former colleague, "it was like, 'Okay, Larry, that's enough, got it.'" Yet he projects such kindness, such determined, tireless selflessness, that people around him are rendered inarticulate when they attempt to express his essential benevolence. "He was such a kind man," says the father of a girl Nassar abused many times, his voice bright with incredulity. "I really cannot say enough good about Larry, because he is just a wonderful man," Nassar's neighbor Jody Rosebush told the *Detroit News* last year after the allegations emerged. He had helped shovel snow; he had rushed across the street in bare feet when she'd had a sudden medical issue. "He will do anything in the world for anybody. We all love Larry. We really, really love Larry." Jessica O'Beirne, the host of a podcast called *GymCastic* and perhaps the most biting editorialist about Nassar and his myriad enablers, had him on the show before the allegations were made public. "I just love Larry Nassar," she said by way of introduction. "He's totally amazing . . . He's just amazing. I think he's awesome. And that's from personal experience. He's just . . . he's great."

Much-loved Larry placed himself in a position of authority in the least-monitored space full of children and proceeded to become the most successful pedophile in sports history. Beyond the choice of medical school, the apparent research interest in the sacrotuberous ligament, the intense focus on a world populated by 11-year-old girls, the useful belief in alternative therapies, there was also this: his incredible brazenness. Nassar molested young girls in his office while their fathers watched. He molested elite athletes under blankets in busy gyms teeming with people. Even a paranoid parent would not have perceived a meeting with a doctor in an open gym, a few feet away, to be an encounter requiring vigilance. Your daughter was safe because you never left her side. When mothers might have a moment of pause, a flicker of suspicion, there was the reassuring thought that no man would try something right in front of them.

"It's like that story," the mother of a gymnast tells me, "'The Emperor's New Clothes'? It's been a while since I've read it, but I believe it was a little child who finally says, 'Doesn't anybody know that the emperor has no clothes on?'"

It was a little child who alerted the townspeople in Hans Christian Andersen's story, but upon reflection, "The Emperor's New Clothes" demonstrates precisely the opposite lesson of that learned through the decades-long saga of Larry Nassar. In order to be heard, the little child does not need to age 20 years, join a chorus of other adults telling the same story, and be corroborated by digital evidence of the king's depravity. The king, in Andersen's story, is immediately exposed. The story of Larry Nassar is that of a man more skilled at deception and a world more credulous.

III

Trinea Gonczar, now 37, is the oldest of three in an athletic family and the most intense. At six years old, just starting out at Twistars —the gym owned by John Geddert, who had forced Larissa into a split—she looked at her mother and demanded to know why she hadn't been put in gymnastics earlier. Three years later, the gym was her entire existence outside school and the only social life that mattered. "Those girls just melted into one another and became one," says Dawn Homer, Trinea's mother, a tall, soft-spoken woman and founder of a medical-billing company. "They were one another's best lives. It was like a cult, and I don't say that in a bad way." Trinea's sisters excelled at volleyball and basketball; Dawn noted that there was less cultlike intimacy on these teams. When Trinea was selected for Geddert's team at nine years old, Dawn was required to attend a meeting. "One hundred percent of the girls will be injured," she recalls a coach saying. "But we have a trainer right here."

Larry was, in Trinea's words, the "dorky escape from John," John being a man you'd need to escape from because he might, in a rage, twist your arm, shove you against a wall, and call it, as he did five years ago in conversation with police, a "discipline meeting." (A prosecutor later ordered Geddert to undergo counseling.)

"I don't have a good reference to compare him to," Trinea says. "I don't know another coaching style. We won. We were good. John made a good product. We were hand-selected. You were picked. Measured. Your toe point was measured, your muscles were measured, your splits were measured."

Gymnasts were afraid to disappoint Geddert, afraid to admit to injury lest they be accused of lying. By contrast, Larry was unfailingly reassuring: He had a plan to make you better, a series of discrete steps to get you back on the mat. He knew what was wrong, had likely "attended a conference" or "given a lecture" on precisely the injury in question, and knew how to fix you. You might feel hopeless, but your career as a gymnast was not over. He pushed girls to talk about their goals, their dreams of gymnastic greatness. Dawn Homer and other parents recall being moved to tears as Larry promised their worried girls that they'd continue to be the athletes they were meant to be.

In 1990, when Trinea was nine, her hip began popping out of its socket whenever she was on bars. Larry suggested that she needed more work than he could provide in the gym and asked if she might come over to his apartment with her mother. Trinea knew this invitation was considered an honor among the other nine-year-olds with whom she spent all her time, and she was proud.

When she arrived with her mother, another girl was leaving. Larry had filled his bath with ice water, and he left the room while Trinea undressed and lowered her shivering body into it. On the toilet, an egg timer ticked through 14 minutes. She flipped through a USA Gymnastics magazine he'd left by the tub. When she came out, in shorts and a T-shirt, he gestured toward a table in the living room.

There was a chair a few feet away, by the television, where Dawn sat that day and many, many days afterward. It was angled such that she could see only Trinea's head and shoulders. Larry maintained a steady, quick patter with Dawn through the treatment. He asked about her other girls. He told them about his plans to move beyond athletic training and go to medical school; he wanted to be a doctor like his grandfather.

Trinea—60-odd pounds, curly brown hair (it was 1990, and it was a perm), hands ripped from bar work—was all muscle. When she showed the neighborhood boys her six-pack, they told her she looked like a Teenage Mutant Ninja Turtle, which she did not take as a compliment. Like Nassar, she was a talker; at the mall, she greeted every single person until her mother told her to stop talking to strangers. Nassar bent her knees, placed her leg over her hip, turned her over, and placed her on her stomach. He moved the table, with her on it, while he worked. While she was on her stomach, out of her mother's view but without breaking the flow of conversation with her, he penetrated Trinea with his ungloved hand.

"Anytime she is in pain," Larry said to Dawn, "no matter what time, what day, you call me and I will get her in for treatment."

It was true; he always did. Larry spent hours teaching Dawn how to tape Trinea's shins. He came over to the house for dinner.

"Larry fixed my ankles," Trinea says. "He fixed my shins. He fixed my knees. He fixed my shoulders. He fixed my wrists. We called it 'the magic of Larry'—he could fix you so you could compete. And I always wanted to compete."

"We had the best clinic available to us for gymnastics injuries that anyone in the world could have. We had the best," says Dawn. "We were so lucky."

At Twistars, the idea of family was more than notional: Larry proposed to another athletic trainer at the gym and asked Geddert to be a groomsman. Trinea attended the wedding and thought Nassar's bride the luckiest woman in the world. When Trinea was 15, a cyst ruptured on her ovary and she required surgery; it was the Nassars standing over her as she opened her eyes.

In the late '90s, another gymnast came to Trinea and said Larry had penetrated her with his fingers. She was looking for corroboration, support for her intuition that something was not right. It's a scene Trinea plays over and over in her head. "He does that to me all the time!" she said lightly, happy to be in the position to comfort someone. "You're fine." Trinea's lawyer estimates that she was molested 856 times.

IV

Nassar's interest in women's gymnastics extends deep into his history, which matters because there are two stories one can tell about Larry Nassar: a man who drifted slowly into darkness and a man whose career goals were structured by desire. In high school and college, Nassar was an athletic trainer, essentially an on-site EMT for athletes, taping and icing and bandaging. By the late 1980s, he was working with USA Gymnastics, Michigan State University, and John Geddert. He worked regional and national meets, shook hands, and dealt with injuries as they arose.

"He was tireless in taking care of the kids," says William Sands, the research scientist who has probably published the most on the sport of gymnastics in exercise medicine and someone Nassar considered a personal hero. "He was up early and went to bed late. He would do anything for an injured athlete. He was an astonishingly giving person."

Who was paying him to be at all these meets remains unclear

because the people who can elucidate these economic relationships tend to be themselves subject to ongoing legal action or are
employed by the legal quagmire that is USA Gymnastics. But a
word that emerges frequently in conversations about Nassar is volunteer. He volunteered, for instance, at Geddert's gym 20 hours a
week. He volunteered at the 1987 Pan-American Games and volunteered at the 1988 Olympic trials. According to Sands, Nassar
maxed out two credit cards working his way up, cementing a reputation as someone who could identify an injury, concoct a plan,
and get an athlete back on the floor. Liked and trusted and ever-
present, he knew the body and knew the sport. Whereas another
doctor might ban an injured athlete from competing altogether,
Nassar could tell her which tricks were still safe to perform. He
was, by almost all accounts, good at what he did.

By the late '80s, Nassar had decided to become an osteopathic
physician, which entails being trained in osteopathic manipulative therapy, learning to move a patient's joints and muscles in
ways said to relieve pain and dysfunction. OMT is based on the
intuitively appealing but largely unsupported idea that a wide ar-
ray of diseases spring from musculoskeletal irregularities, and one
therefore expects to be touched differently by an osteopath than
by an MD; one expects to be folded and bent and cracked. Ma-
nipulated. He chose, too, to practice alongside athletes in contexts
that lacked the intermediary structures of a traditional doctor's
office—receptionists, insurance companies, medical records. After
his residency, he was named the national medical coordinator for
USA Gymnastics, the organization responsible for selecting and
training Olympians.

If you're old enough, you remember watching Kerri Strug hurl
herself in the air, land hard on a badly injured ankle, collapse, and
guarantee all-around gold for the American team. This was taken
at the time to be evidence of athletic heroism and American grit,
fodder for sponsorships and presidential photo ops and write-ups
in which it was not mentioned that her vault had been, in the end,
unnecessary; the team had the scores to win. But stick with the
camera a bit, beyond memory, and watch coach Martha Karolyi
carry a crying Strug toward a young, dark-haired physician. This is
the moment Nassar becomes "the Olympics doctor," the man who
cares for the athletes millions of children aspire to be, and his ac-

cess to girls widens inexorably, constrained only by the number of minutes in the day.

The prestige conferred on Nassar by his volunteer position at the Olympics, by both the parents of gymnasts and clinical sports medicine in general, is hard to overstate and hard, from the outside, to understand. That Nassar was an inexperienced physician who had just finished his residency in '96 did not seem to matter, because in sports medicine the caliber of athlete one treats is taken to be correlated with curative power. Hospitals pay millions of dollars for the privilege of treating sports teams; UC–San Diego Health, for example, pays $1 million to treat the Padres.

Nassar covered the walls of his office with signed pictures of Olympians and gave girls he favored Olympics patches, pins, and jackets. Parents interviewed for this article come from diverse backgrounds and have daughters at very different levels of gymnastics competition, but they all once shared an astonished gratitude that Nassar would even see their kids. The circular quality of this claim to competence became clear in the testimony of parents of actual Olympians; they too were told their kids were lucky to see Larry, who wouldn't be in his position if he didn't know what he was doing. Whether they believed this or not, they were required to leave their kids for weeks in Huntsville, Texas, at Karolyi Ranch, where the showers were moldy and the blankets stained and the food so bad the kids were always hungry; where there were no parents, and cell-phone service was spotty, and Nassar would knock on their doors at night, bearing candy, to treat them in their beds. If this was drift, it was drift straight into the least-monitored space full of young girls, into a position of authority requiring a decade of career building, in a specialty that allowed him particular latitude.

V

The trick was to establish traditional medical credibility and then get weird. A mother we'll call Jane began bringing her gymnast daughter, Kate, to Nassar when Kate was eight and suffering from back pain. Larry diagnosed her with spondylolisthesis, a spinal disorder. When a pediatric spine specialist confirmed the diagnosis, Jane, who has some medical training, was impressed that Larry, a

generalist, had caught it. When he started using cupping—a practice in which suction is said to release muscles—she went with it.
When he invited them over to his house to administer manipula-
tions to Kate in his basement, she went with that too.

William Sands, the scientist Larry idolized, was at Karolyi Ranch
doing research when he walked in on Larry inserting acupuncture
needles into a gymnast's back. "I rolled my eyes and walked out,"
he said. "This is such a crock of pseudoscientific bullshit that I
don't want anything to do with it. And cupping? Give me a freaking break." Sands was so offended he cut off contact.

Alternative treatments, along with frequent references to presentations given and conferences attended, lent Nassar a useful air
of the creative scientist. Who knew what he would try next? But his
best cover—the story that would get him out of police stations and
back into exam rooms—was not in fact pseudoscientific bullshit.
As his career progressed, he began to develop a research interest
in the musculature of the pelvis: the sacrotuberous ligament in
particular. He developed, for instance, two PowerPoint presentations called "Pelvic Floor: Where No Man Has Gone Before" and
"Pelvic Floor: The Final Frontier." He was associating himself with
evidence that back and hip problems can be addressed through
pelvic-floor physical therapy, which is, according to J. Welles Hen-
derson, an OB/GYN and clinical professor specializing in pelvic
disorders at University Hospitals in Cleveland, "mainstream medicine," "a first-line treatment," and "backed by 30 years of well-es-
tablished research" on patients with weak or spastic pelvic floors.
(Sands, for his part, still considers it a "crock of shit.")

There is, according to Rhonda Kotarinos, a pelvic-floor physical therapist and the author of several studies on the subject, a
correlation between pelvic-floor dysfunction and strenuous exercise in young female athletes for reasons that remain speculative
but may have something to do with the way developing the glutes
over-recruits the pelvis, leading those muscles to shorten. Pelvic
pain not uncommonly presents as lower-back pain. It would not be
out of the ordinary for a trusted, almost always female specialist in
pelvic disorders to enter the vagina, palpate the levator ani against
the grain of the muscle fiber, and look for painful trigger points
that suggest the muscle has lost the capacity to fully elongate or
shorten. Opinions vary on whether PFPT is an appropriate treatment for young women, but unambiguously damning was the fact

that Nassar hardly ever explained what he was doing, never gained consent, never used gloves, and found it necessary for ankle and knee injuries. He did not use the phrase "pelvic-floor physical therapy"; when he did explain himself, which was rare, he called it "myofascial release" or "intravaginal adjustment."

He didn't call it anything when he molested Chloe Myers, another young woman who was suffering from debilitating back pain with a bent coccyx and facet-joint syndrome. He covered Chloe in a blanket and positioned himself between her and her chatty, outgoing mother, Kristen, a few feet away. It wasn't until he stopped and washed his hands that Kristen wondered where his hands had been. It occurred to her that he wouldn't have to wash his hands if he had merely been touching her daughter's leg. It occurred to her that if he had done an internal exam, she would have expected him to wear gloves. In the car on the way home, Chloe said that his hands had been "way up in there" and that it had been uncomfortable. Kristen was alarmed. But Chloe also said she felt much better. She continued to feel better every time she went back.

Like many women and many parents of female athletes, Kristen knew of treatments that involve vaginal penetration; Chloe's chiropractor had mentioned something. "I did know there was a legitimate treatment that could help, internally, like an internal adjustment," she says. "I was aware of it. And this was Larry. So it was no big surprise that he was trying some kind of alternative treatment."

Some women were surprised. Directly after Nassar touched her in 2004, 17-year-old Brianne Randall filed a complaint with Meridian Township police and had a rape kit administered at the local hospital. Detective Andrew McCready called Nassar and asked him to come in for questioning, which he did. Nassar told McCready that he had indeed touched Brianne's perineum, that it was part of a treatment called "sacro-tuberous-ligament release," and that the treatment was "published in medical journals and training tapes." He also gave McCready his PowerPoint presentation on said ligament, in which he is pictured cupping a girl's buttocks and pressing near a girl's vulva. McCready then called Brianne's mother to tell her the case would be closed and that "no crime was committed."

When, in 2014, cheerleader Amanda Thomashow reported an assault to one of MSU's Title IX investigators and university police, the latter launched an investigation and referred the case to prosecutors for review. The office of Ingham County prosecutor Stuart Dunnings concluded that the prosecution "would not be able to sustain [its] burden at trial" and declined to prosecute. Dunnings was later charged, imprisoned, and disbarred for soliciting prostitutes.

MSU Title IX investigator Kristine Moore launched her own investigation. She interviewed three osteopathic physicians and one athletic trainer. All four found Nassar's conduct to be medically appropriate. All of them worked for MSU and knew Nassar personally. Dr. William Strampel, the dean of the College of Osteopathic Medicine at MSU, instructed Nassar to have a chaperone in the room and avoid skin-to-skin contact, though he never enforced these new rules and Nassar would not follow them. Strampel has since been arrested and charged with, among other things, sexually harassing and groping female medical students.

Thomashow, concluded Moore, failed to understand the "nuanced difference" between osteopathic manipulative medicine and sexual massage. "Dr. Nassar has presented on this nationally and internationally," reads the Title IX report, "has videos posted to the web that explain the procedure, and is widely known for this work . . . We cannot find that the conduct was medically inappropriate and thus cannot find it was sexual in nature." That "videos posted to the web," presentations, and PowerPoints are distinct from peer-reviewed publications seems not to have occurred to MSU, the Ingham County prosecutor's office, or Meridian Township detectives; nor does the idea that people Nassar has worked with, and in some cases mentored, are poor sources of objective testimony. This was not stellar police work, but it was the level of investigatory prowess available to the women of Michigan, and it was precisely the level of scrutiny Nassar's cover was designed to weather, right up until the day a former gymnast named Rachael Denhollander emailed the *Indianapolis Star.*

VI

When the *Star* broke the story, in September 2016, and all of elite gymnastics read it, not a single person interviewed for this piece believed that Denhollander and a second, anonymous accuser had been assaulted by Nassar. Dawn Homer asked Trinea Gonczar whether Larry could be capable of such a thing, and Trinea said, unreservedly, "No." She waited patiently for medical experts to come forward and defend the practice.

"They're describing," Chloe Myers told her parents, "the exact same treatment I was receiving." It had helped her back pain, she reasoned, and thus was legitimate. "They weren't remembering right," Chloe's father concluded. Nassar asked his colleague, fellow osteopathic physician Steven Karageanes, to lend him his support, and Karageanes said he would. Parents concluded that Nassar had, in his boundless generosity—all those extra appointments in his home, free of charge—"put himself in a bad position" and allowed his treatments to be "misconstrued." William Sands thought it would all blow over. According to the *Wall Street Journal,* Dean William Strampel had this to say to students at a meeting at MSU: "This just goes to show that none of you learned the most basic lesson in medicine, Medicine 101: Don't trust your patients. Patients lie to get doctors in trouble." Kathie Klages asked her gymnasts to sign a card that read, THINKING OF YOU.

Denhollander's allegations were backed by a growing list of accusers; there were by February 2017 at least 50 complaints to the police. If Michigan was paying attention, it was hard to tell. Parents of gymnasts continued driving their girls from Twistars to his house for treatments. Larry ran for school board, pulled out, and still got 2,700 votes. Not even Larissa Boyce, who had accused him of molesting her in 1997 and been shut down by Klages, believed Denhollander's account. "I had convinced myself," she says, "that it was a medical treatment."

"No one was buying it yet," says Karageanes. "There was no quote-unquote evidence. He had supporters lined up to defend him. It would have taken a monumental effort from the first people coming out to get the public on their side."

Although, much later, the only story line American media would be able to process was one of a "survivor" who had "found her voice" and was ready to "take on" her abuser in open court, it did not appear to be a woman at all who had persuaded those closest to this story, including most of the "survivors," to come forward. It was, rather, a set of external hard drives—tossed to the curb in the trash in the days after Denhollander went public, on a day when the garbage crew was behind schedule, and recovered by the FBI. Had the crew been on time, had the agents been late, had the warrant come through a day after Nassar decided to dump his digital history on the street, he might still have the support of most of the people he abused.

Healthy people tend not to distinguish between varieties of child pornography or think much about the habits of its consumption, but Nassar's accumulation of more than 37,000 images suggests an unusual level of deviance even among pedophiles. According to a sentencing memorandum issued by federal prosecutors for the Western District of Michigan, these images form a particularly "graphic" and "hard-core" collection, including children as young as infants and images of children being raped by adults.

Here was a fact that one simply could not integrate into the image of a dedicated doctor attacked by confused or malicious women. The story stopped making sense. Mothers struggled to find a way to ask their girls whether they'd been digitally penetrated at the gym. Parents awoke for the first time to the possibility that their daughters' first sexual experience had taken place at the hands of Larry Nassar, often as said parent watched from a few feet away. "Did Larry do anything to you?" Michael Weiszbrod, an affable state administrator, asked his 13-year-old daughter, Ashleigh, a few times, and she shook her head no. He and his wife took this as authoritative until one day, months later, when Weiszbrod found himself watching Nassar's sentencing hearing at work. He was thinking about another physician who worked at the gym, Brooke, whom Larry was training. When he got home, he put down his bag and turned directly to Ashleigh, who was hunched over her homework, legs crossed on the couch. "Did Larry touch you," he asked, "different than Brooke touched you?" Ashleigh was very still, and then she was crying. She had seen Larry at Twistars once a week for three years.

Jane asked Kate, 14 at the time, whether she thought Larry was guilty, and Kate said no. Jane left it alone for a while. Later, in the car, Jane's husband asked their daughter whether she knew what Nassar had been accused of, and she said yes. He asked if Nassar had done treatments to her that "fell into this category," and she said yes. He asked if there had been penetration, and she said, "Dad, this is hard to talk about."

In the light of day, parents thought about the choices they'd made, hearing them in a new and horrifying light. "All of a sudden, the stuff you think is normal coming out of somebody else's mouth doesn't sound normal," says Jane.

It did not sound normal, for instance, that every week after practice, Jane had driven her daughter to a white three-bedroom house with green shutters, next to many identical houses in a development on a quiet street in Holt, Michigan, and taken her to see a man in the basement of that house. It didn't seem normal that he never billed for these visits or that he always had hot chocolate waiting.

"I hear myself telling you this," says Jane, "and I know it sounds crazy. It sounds crazy! But when I was pulling into his driveway, someone else would be pulling out."

A detective told Trinea Gonczar that there were images of little girls in his bathtub—the bathtub in which she had waited, alongside the egg timer—but the detective could not tell her whether she was among them. "That's when I started to think back and go deep into the places I had been with him," says Trinea. "How many times I had been to his house. How many times I had been to MSU. How many times I had seen him at the gym. Realizing that there was probably never a time I didn't have this treatment."

VII

The goodwill Nassar built is so resilient that even now it cannot be wholly erased. Trinea's husband asked her to revise her testimony because it was too kind—people might get the wrong idea. "I don't hate Larry," she says. "I don't want him to be raped and beaten in prison. I feel like the parents of someone who shot up a school. You still love them today like you did yesterday."

"I'm still grateful to him," says Chloe's mother, and her father wonders aloud whether sometimes he really was just performing vaginal treatments in the interest of his daughter, who, after all, says she is "100 percent sure" the treatments she considers abusive helped her back pain every time. "I don't know," he says. "Is it 24/7? So every time he has someone in there? Are there times when he is just doing the treatment?" Says Dawn: "I really believe Larry at some point in his life thought it was the appropriate treatment. I don't know when he went to the dark side and changed it."

Is this their naïveté, or is it ours? Nassar "groomed the entire community," reads a *Lansing State Journal* piece from January on the town of Holt. At a certain level of psychological reduction, every friendly conversation, every accurate diagnosis, every accommodation was part of Larry Nassar's strategy. Did he shovel the neighbors' snow as part of a plan to gain access to ever more girls? Apart from being an implausibly simplistic picture of a single human mind, this would not even seem to be the ideal psychology for a successful pedophile. A man who takes pleasure in going out of his way for people, who thrives on simple gratitude, who finds actual satisfaction in lifting the spirits of an injured gymnast, is one you risk letting into your life. One you call, as Trinea once did, family.

"Larry," she said on the fourth day of Nassar's sentencing hearing, staring straight at him, voice deep with controlled fury. She had known how young the other accusers would be, but somehow it hadn't struck her until she walked into that room full of them. They were little girls. Her rage was such that she spoke slowly and almost in a whisper: "What. Have. You. Done." Between sobs she looked him straight in the eye, cocked her head, and raised her eyebrows, a look of profound disappointment and deep familiarity. Larry had sat emotionless, listening to other women he'd abused, for hours prior to this. Sometimes he shook his head, as if to deny their claims. During Trinea's testimony, something changed. He started to shake, and then he started to cry.

"I think his heart broke because my heart broke," she tells me later. "I was worried the other girls would hate me because of his reaction to me." There's pride in her voice, the triumph of having been the one, out of the hundreds, who actually broke through. This may be her win, or it may be his. There are a lot of ways to make a person feel special, and Larry Nassar knows all of them.

BETH DAVIES-STOFKA

Winning at the Cost of Silence

FROM BASEBALL PROSPECTUS

A YEAR AGO, WE learned that Luke Heimlich, a star pitcher for the Oregon State Beavers, was convicted of sexually molesting his six-year-old niece when he was a teenager. He confessed, was placed on probation, sent to counseling, and was required to register for five years as a sex offender. He did everything that the state of Washington required of him, and none of what it did not, including notifying his team of the crime, until the news was leaked through a bureaucratic error. Then early last month, he sat down for a series of interviews with the *New York Times*. Now 22, he wants to clear the air because he wants to play in the majors.

He told the *Times* that he is innocent; he only pleaded guilty to protect his family. He couldn't comment on the specifics of the incident, because there was no incident. "Nothing ever happened," he said. Heimlich is widely considered a top-100 draft prospect. Rumors have it that he'll be selected somewhere today, the second day of the draft. Attorney Sheryl Ring recently explained the legal status of his case, showing us how, from a legal standpoint, Heimlich cannot now re-litigate his case.

He decided to do just that, however. When he sat down with the *New York Times*, he tossed his case into the court of public opinion. There it lives, with people only too glad to accept the challenge and conjecture. Just read the comments on Ring's post. Or don't. I tried but I couldn't get far. I longed to see evidence of an overwhelming public commitment to protect the victim, but I didn't. It's all about Heimlich; is he guilty, is he innocent, should he pitch, how well could he pitch . . .

Do we only care about little girls until we want to win baseball games?

I, too, am a victim of childhood sexual abuse. I generally stay private about it; it's not a trauma I want to revisit. But there's something about the Heimlich case that is pushing me to open up. I am aware that players are human beings, which means that inescapably, some portion of them are victimizers. Some are victims. Some are both. Sometimes I know the details. I've seen more than one player receive convictions or suspensions for terrible crimes. But to my knowledge, there are no other felony sex offenders attempting to reverse their convictions in the *New York Times* before they are even drafted. If the team I rooted for drafted Heimlich, the statement would be clear: winning is more important than the safety of children, the pain of survivors, or the people who help them carry on. It will reopen one of the oldest wounds that survivors bear. *No one cares about you.*

On the weekend that the *Times* was in town, Heimlich took the mound against Arizona State. The reporter witnessed nearly 3,000 fans standing to cheer his name. How are survivors supposed to react when they see that? It makes me anxious.

We pay for what our abusers did. We spend our lives paying for it. Most of us stay silent, but Heimlich's niece told her parents what happened. Her father, Heimlich's brother, called the police, but most members of the large family sided with Heimlich. They shamed and marginalized an innocent six-year-old girl. By disbelieving her, they abandoned her. Ultimately, her parents divorced.

What if she blames herself for that? I endured a lot because I believed that if I didn't, my parents would divorce. It never occurred to me that if they had, it would not have been my fault. It never occurred to me that I was innocent. Survivors need to hear that we are innocent, that we did nothing wrong, that we were not to blame, that we are not liars, that we matter, that we are loved. I'm quite a bit older than six, and I still need to hear those things. I need them to be frequently reinforced. The legacy of self-loathing that accompanies sexual abuse is very powerful stuff, and we are endangered when abusers are showered with praise.

We're endangered anyway. Sometimes we think that we will never be safe or secure. Compare the case of Luke Heimlich to that of Junot Díaz. In his now-infamous personal essay "The Si-

lence," published in the April issue of *The New Yorker,* Díaz confessed to his own experience of sexual abuse. Raped at eight years
old, Díaz achingly describes the wounds his rapist inflicted. "I can
say, truly," he writes, "que casi me destruyó." None of the details
are the same as mine, but the suffering that Díaz describes is, in
a word, *mine.* Childhood sexual trauma, whatever the form, leaves
the same mark. It imprints itself upon you, forcibly becomes part
of who you are. It steals your life.

Díaz addresses his essay to someone he calls "X," a young
man who attended a book reading several years ago. X needed
someone to see his pain and thought Díaz could do it. Quietly,
he asked, "Did it happen to you?" But Díaz couldn't cope. He responded with what he calls "evasive bullshit." Now he's burdened
with regret as he remembers. "I wish I'd told you the truth then,"
he writes. "You looked abandoned . . . I never really did forget how
you walked out of the auditorium with your shoulders hunched."

The image of that abandoned young man pierces me. The most
crippling legacy of childhood sexual trauma is not the depression
that eats your days, weeks, and years. It's not the self-loathing, the
confusion, the fear of love, or even the suicidal ideations. The oldest, deepest root in an abuse survivor is the fear of abandonment.
It is the root that will not wither.

It has so much control of us that we remain silent. We never
share our stories, for fear that it will drive those around us even
further away. Instead, we live as if already buried—provided we
live. We become amnesiac, acting out of our pain, cutting, drug-
ging, drinking, and destroying. We shrink from intimacy. We can't
figure out how to navigate the terror.

Sometimes, we perpetuate our abuse. We abuse others. The
reactions to Díaz's painful confessional reveal him to be a survivor who harmed both himself and others. He forced himself on
women, casually dismissed them, and verbally abused them, violating their personal space, their trust, and their hearts. We aspire to
hold people responsible for their actions, and in Díaz's case, we
are doing that.

But it's confusing. In the midst of the revelations of his own
violations, for which he must be held to account, I am afraid. Díaz
openly acknowledges that his rape turned him into an abuser. He
publicly accepts his responsibility for his wrongs. The public response has not been warm. Meanwhile, Heimlich represents the

opposite. He is a convicted abuser who denies his wrongs. And thousands cheer for him, because unlike Díaz, whose job is to reflect us through art, Heimlich's identity is almost inconsequential. His purpose is to win baseball games. How can I weave these two realities together without being shoved into fearful silence?

I think back to X, shoulders hunched, looking abandoned. I long to hug him and tell him it will be okay. He could be any one of us, molested, raped, or sodomized as children, now struggling with the consequences. We are uncounted because we are too ashamed to speak. Instead we act out in self-loathing and despair. Some rage, transmitting their abuse by verbally and even physically abusing others, lovers, spouses, their own children. Others break the chain, but turn the knife inward. We self-abuse and we enter abusive relationships. How many of us are addicts? How many of us are suicides? How can we know, since survivors are too ashamed to speak?

Childhood trauma launches a cycle of trauma, whether that is ongoing self-abuse or the abuse of others. The harm that is done is permanent. However, the cycles can be broken and they need to be. We need to create an environment to make that possible. Forgiveness is closure and peace, and survivors need that. We've been hurt enough. We should not have to live out our lives, broken and unredeemed.

We can't expect victims to extend grace to their victimizers, or watch others cheer them on toward their own glory. No one has to forgive Díaz for what he did to them. Díaz does not have to forgive his rapist. Heimlich's niece does not have to forgive her family or the thousands who cheer him at baseball games. She doesn't have to forgive her ex-uncle Luke. The whole ugly web of abuse is simply unforgivable, all of it, the abuse, its legacy, the pain that divides us.

From the very center of our pain, we have one, terrifying hope. *Tell the truth.* We have to tell our stories, and to be able to tell our stories.

The reactions to Heimlich and Díaz are chilling, as are the reactions to any number of people who have dared speak out against popular and important figures. But we have to muster the strength to tell the truth. We have to help people understand the reality of what it means to live as a survivor and to struggle to reclaim our lives. We have to tell our stories if we are going to fully feel our humanness. We have to tell our stories in order to protect others. We have to start confessing, whatever truths our stories contain, so that we and others may live. Survivors can undo the cycle.

But at what price? Must we watch as young pitchers are cheered by adoring fans? Must we watch the fall from grace of a once widely adored writer after he tells his—our—story? Will we be abandoned all over again?

These are the risks we take. It could be worth it. When Heimlich's story became public last year, a nasty local discourse erupted —inevitable when sports is involved—but in the midst of it, there was also healthy discussion about childhood sexual trauma. In an opinion piece for *The Oregonian,* John Canzano wrote:

> On my radio show on Friday, we took calls from a mostly male audience that defended the victim. I was moved by the discourse. It was authentic, charged in the right direction and included some powerful moments from callers. Some called in to share their stories of abuse. Others, their anger.

He also wrote:

> Justin Myers, my colleague and friend at 102.9-FM and 750-AM, hosts a brand new show with DeVon Pouncey weekdays 9am–noon. They've only been on air for five days, but Myers delivered a haymaker on Friday. He spoke openly about his own repeated abuse at age five in what was a powerful segment of radio. There are no winners in this story. But one of the things that has come from it is the sharing of stories such as this.

There are no winners, this is true. It took some time, but I finally found a capable and caring professional to help me. One of the hardest sessions we ever had was the one in which he had to tell me that the damage done cannot be undone. We can layer joy into my life, quite a lot of it in fact, but the abuse made me. Not a day will go by, not one, when I won't have to wisely and intentionally act to make sure that I am going to be okay. Just for that day.

This is so much easier when we don't have to do it alone. That's why we have to speak up. We need people talking, sharing, and hopefully, connecting. This is how we care for ourselves and restore some life to what was lost. It's how we protect others. It's how we transform the strangely opposed realities of the Heimlich and Díaz cases into a rational, powerful discourse about protecting children in peril, and prevent those cases from multiplying.

And it's also why the simple act of accepting Heimlich into the membership of baseball, into the caste of people whose talents we root for and whose successes we celebrate, abandons those of us who have suffered in the way that Heimlich's victim has. Baseball struggles with the concept of ethics between the white lines: the occasional matter is decided by unwritten rules, and the rest are referred to the written ones. Beyond that, winning is everything, and fans are carried along by that same momentum.

But winning is not everything. We'd really like the world to be black and white, especially when it comes to morality, but it's not. We are complicated, messy creatures. If we can take each other in, with empathy and caring, then maybe healing can finally begin.

HEATHER DINICH, ADAM RITTENBERG, AND
TOM VANHAAREN

The Inside Story of a Toxic Culture at Maryland Football

FROM ESPN.COM

SEVERAL CURRENT UNIVERSITY of Maryland football players
and people close to the Terrapins program describe a toxic coaching culture under head coach D. J. Durkin before offensive lineman Jordan McNair's death in June after a football workout.

McNair, who was 19, died two weeks after being hospitalized
following a May 29 team workout. He collapsed after running 110-
yard sprints, showing signs of extreme exhaustion and difficulty
standing upright. No official cause of death has been released, but
ESPN reported Friday that he died of heatstroke suffered during
the workout and had a body temperature of 106 degrees after being taken to a hospital.

Over the past several weeks, two current Maryland players, multiple people close to the football program, and former players and
football staffers spoke to ESPN about the culture under Durkin,
particularly strength and conditioning coach Rick Court, who was
one of Durkin's first hires at Maryland in 2015. Among what they
shared about the program:

- There is a coaching environment based on fear and intimidation. In one example, a player holding a meal while in
a meeting had the meal slapped out of his hands in front of
the team. At other times, small weights and other objects were
thrown in the direction of players when Court was angry.

• The belittling, humiliation, and embarrassment of players is common. In one example, a player whom coaches wanted to lose weight was forced to eat candy bars as he was made to watch teammates working out.

• Extreme verbal abuse of players occurs often. Players are routinely the targets of obscenity-laced epithets meant to mock their masculinity when they are unable to complete a workout or weight lift, for example. One player was belittled verbally after passing out during a drill.

• Coaches have endorsed unhealthy eating habits and used food punitively; for example, a player said he was forced to overeat or eat to the point of vomiting.

After ESPN requested interviews with Maryland officials and provided details about its reporting on McNair's death and the football culture, a university spokesperson on Friday afternoon said, "The University of Maryland has placed members of our athletics staff on administrative leave pending the outcome of the external review." No further details were provided.

Although grueling workouts, expletive-laced rants, and hot-tempered coaches aren't unusual in college sports programs, those who have been at Maryland told ESPN that what they saw or experienced under Durkin has been excessive. The current players said they had talked with multiple players who described similar views about the team's culture but feared repercussions if they talked publicly. The two players spoke on the condition of anonymity.

A former Maryland staff member said: "I would never, ever, ever allow my child to be coached there."

A second former staffer said that while he has seen and heard coaches curse at players, he'd never been on another coaching staff with this kind of philosophy. "The language is profane, and it's demeaning at times," he said. "When you're characterizing people in such derogatory and demeaning terms, particularly if they don't have a skill level you think they need to aspire to, or they may never get, then it's rough to watch and see because if it was your son, you wouldn't want anybody talking to your son that way."

"The way they coach us at Maryland, tough love—it's really more tough than it is love," one former player said.

ESPN requested to interview Durkin and Court, but athletic department officials declined to make them available. The university issued an initial statement earlier Friday before announcing its personnel decision that reads: "The alleged behaviors raised in the ESPN story are troubling and not consistent with our approach to the coaching and development of our student athletes. Such allegations do not reflect the culture of our program. We are committed to swiftly examining and addressing any such reports when they are brought to our attention."

Shortly before McNair's death and while he remained hospitalized, Maryland coaches held a team meeting during which, according to sources, players criticized the methods used by Court and Durkin. Durkin was initially receptive to their concerns, sources said. Players and other team sources said voluntary workouts in late June and July, after McNair's death, lessened in intensity. But when Maryland opened preseason training camp August 3, the workouts and overall climate around the program largely returned to how they were before McNair's death, the sources said. Since the middle of this week, however, there has been more attention paid to players who show fatigue or distress.

"Now that we get to camp, it just seems like regular business," a current player said. "That's when I started to get upset because I feel like nothing's really changed. Have these guys learned their lesson?"

Exactly what happened during the May 29 workout and to McNair is being investigated by Rod Walters, a university-hired, former longtime collegiate athletic trainer. Walters's report is expected to be released September 15. McNair's parents have hired the Baltimore law firm of Murphy, Falcon & Murphy to investigate as well.

Maryland's statement Friday also addressed the Walters investigation: "We will be able to speak in greater detail when the review is complete and shared with the public. Our consultant has work to do to finish this investigation. We will take appropriate action when we have the full details. Our thoughts remain with Jordan McNair's family, friends, and teammates."

McNair's father, Martin, declined an interview request but said of his son: "As much as I miss my son, what I really miss, I miss being a father. I miss that fatherly advice of, 'How is your week going?' Ending a call with 'I love you.' . . . That's what I miss most. That's the empty void for me right now."

ESPN reported Friday that the workout in which McNair participated began at 4:15 p.m. on May 29, and he and other linemen were near the end of their sprint set when McNair started having difficulties, according to multiple sources. McNair family attorney Billy Murphy told ESPN on Thursday that McNair had a seizure at about 5 p.m., following a sprint.

"Our reading of the medical records and the 911 call Maryland made to the EMT to come to the field reveal that 45 minutes into the practice, he had convulsions and a seizure on the field," Murphy said, "and the 911 call reflects emergency personnel noted McNair had experienced a seizure."

A 911 call recording obtained by ESPN shows that at 5:58 p.m., an unidentified man described McNair as "hyperventilating after exercising and unable to control his breath."

Murphy called the one-hour time gap between McNair showing distress at about 5 p.m. and the 911 call being made "an utter disregard of the health of this player, and we are extraordinarily concerned that the coaches did not react appropriately to his injury."

McNair died at Cowley Shock Trauma Center in Baltimore on June 13.

Maryland officials said in their statement: "At no point before or during the external review has a student-athlete, athletic trainer, or coach reported a seizure occurring at 5 p.m."

Several current football players and people close to the program say that because of the program's culture, players were all but forced to try to complete whatever workout came their way.

"It shows a cultural problem that Jordan knew that if he stopped, they would challenge his manhood, he would be targeted," one of the current players said. "He had to go until he couldn't."

Several current players and people close to the program described a sustained pattern of verbal abuse and intimidation of players. A former staff member said "verbal personal attacks on kids" occurred so often that everyone became numb to them.

"We always talked about family, but whose family talks to you like that, calls you a p—y b—?" a third former staffer said. "There are so many instances."

Former Maryland defensive lineman Malik Jones, who transferred after last season from Maryland to Toledo, said he had an altercation with Durkin after Durkin took exception to Jones's smiling during a team meeting. Durkin and Jones went to another room and, according to Jones, Durkin accused him of "bad-mouthing the program" and encouraged him to leave.

"He basically got in my face, was pointing his finger in my face and calling me explicit names and things of that nature," said Jones, who appeared in six games last season for Maryland. "I'm not going to let a guy bully me . . . He called me a b— and stuff like that. I'm not going to tolerate that."

A former staff member recalled a time when one player was in a team meeting with food on a plate because he was rushing from a meal to get to the meeting, and Court smacked the plate of food out of the player's hands, yelling at him.

"It was embarrassing," the second former staffer said. "It was the ultimate of embarrassment."

He described Court as "a very aggressive, in-your-face, matter-of-fact" coach who "would use any language he deemed appropriate to get a response or move your needle."

"He's just a ball of testosterone all the time," one current player said. "He's really in your face. He'll call you [expletives], he'll challenge you in the weight room. He'll put more weight on the bar than you can do, ever done in your life, and expect you to do it multiple times. He'll single people out he doesn't like, which is a common practice here. Guys are run off. They'll have them do specific finishes at the end and do harder workouts or more workouts just to make their lives miserable here. He's kind of Durkin's tool to accomplish that. He's the guy people hate, and that way Durkin doesn't have to take the blow for it. Guys can't stand Coach Court."

Jones said he witnessed several "rants and outbursts" from Court.

"They did go by the philosophy of balls to the wall," Jones said. "Push to the extreme? That was an everyday thing. I've seen him get physical with guys sometimes, throw objects at guys sometimes, small weights, anything he had in his hand at the time. I don't think he was trying to intentionally hit them, but I know for a fact he purposely threw them in their direction."

Another former player alleged the staff made an injured player do a tug-of-war competition against the whole defensive back unit.

"They made him do it with one hand," he said. "Coach Court called him a p— after he didn't win. One [player] was doing a tug-of-war . . . and he passed out . . . I saw his body slowly giving away, and the strength coach was like, 'Keep pulling, keep pulling!' . . . He collapsed on the ground. He looked at him like, 'You quit on the team.' It was really barbaric."

J. T. Ventura, a former safety who played from 2013 to 2017 under former Maryland coach Randy Edsall and Durkin, said the workouts were particularly intense the first season under Durkin. Durkin came to Maryland from Michigan, where he was the defensive coordinator and linebackers coach. He worked under Jim Harbaugh at Michigan and Stanford, and for Ohio State coach Urban Meyer at Bowling Green and Florida.

Maryland was the first to hire Durkin as a head coach, and he immediately wanted to put his stamp on the program. Durkin's staff has gone through significant change, as only four original assistants from 2016 remain, and seven have since departed College Park. More than 20 players have left the team in the past two and a half years.

"They were trying to weed out players," Ventura said. "They actually called some players 'thieves' for being on scholarship and not being very good. During some of the workouts, there were kids who were really struggling, and Coach Court, he'd keep on yelling. He would use profanity a lot, try to push kids when they reached their limit during workouts.

"If a kid would stop or go on the ground, him and the medical staff would try to drag players up and get them to run after they'd already reached their limit. They definitely bullied us to make sure we kept on going."

Team sources said the verbal barrages from Court have continued this month in preseason camp.

Durkin made Court one of his first staff hires in December 2015, appointing him to lead Maryland's strength and conditioning program. The two first worked together at Bowling Green in the mid-2000s. The *Washington Post* reported that Court was the first call Durkin made after landing the Maryland job.

Players and other sources close to the team said Durkin and Court were aligned in all elements surrounding workouts and strength training.

"They're joined at the hip," one source said. "They're the same. They use the same language and the same classification."

Added a current player: "They usually target and pick a couple people they think are soft and go after them . . . [Durkin and

Court] feed off of each other. I would say Court is as much responsible for the culture as Durkin."

A former staff member said Court is Durkin's "confidant."

The culture criticism centers on Durkin and Court but also draws in Wes Robinson, the Terrapins' head athletic trainer. Though Durkin and Court came in together after the 2015 season, Robinson has served in his position since 2006, working with previous Maryland coaches Ralph Friedgen and Edsall. One former staff member who worked with Robinson at Maryland described him as "meek and mild-mannered."

"He was always very professional," a fourth former staffer told ESPN.

Those who have known Robinson for many years agreed, but multiple former staffers said he changed his tenor to match Durkin's and the environment that Durkin sought to create around the program.

"It did seem like he was trying to become someone he really wasn't," the third former staff member said. "I'm sure he probably felt a certain amount of pressure from D.J. I think most trainers probably do, but I think Wes may have morphed into a personality that he's really not. I thought he was excellent at his job."

Multiple sources said that after McNair finished his 10th sprint while two other players held him up, Robinson yelled, "Drag his ass across the field!"

Said the first former staffer of Robinson's apparent change in approach: "Players aren't the only ones who can be bullied."

Current and former players and other sources described a program known as the Champions Club that was created by Durkin to reward players who met expectations for workouts, academics, training table, and other areas. Players who could not complete workouts risked being removed from the Champions Club for several weeks or months. A former staff member said the club became a significant point of pride for the players.

"As soon as you sit out a run, you feel a little dizzy or lightheaded, you're not in Champions Club anymore," a former player said.

Current and former players also described several incidents where staff members targeted players because of weight issues. Sources said a former offensive lineman whom the staff deemed overweight was forced to watch workouts while eating candy bars as a form of humiliation. Another former Terrapins player said his inability to gain weight resulted in members of the strength and conditioning staff sitting with him at meals to make sure he ate.

"They were trying to make me gain weight really, really fast," said the player, who left the program. "That involved me overeating a lot, sometimes eating until I threw up. They always had me come back for extra meals. Once, I was sitting down eating with a coach, and he basically made me sit there until I threw up. He said to eat until I threw up. I was doing what they asked me to do, trying to gain the weight, but at the time, I just couldn't gain the weight, and I guess they weren't understanding that."

McNair's death has prompted players and people close to the program to speak up.

"I would've never thought a kid would pay the ultimate price," the third former staff member said. "I don't know, maybe we were all blind to what was being developed there. I don't know. I just hope it doesn't happen again."

One current player told ESPN that university leadership, including athletic director Damon Evans and president Wallace Loh, had "a lack of action" in their response to McNair's death.

"We had a kid die . . . It took all summer for us to even get a third-party investigation to meet with, and the timing [of those interviews] is absolutely horrendous," the player said. "This is a huge problem at Maryland."

ESPN requested to interview Loh, Robinson, and Evans, but university officials declined to make them available. According to a Maryland official, Evans addressed the team on multiple occasions, including a private moment of reflection on June 15 held in McNair's honor that the athletic department organized for all student-athletes and staff. Evans was also in attendance at a June 1 meeting in which the team received a medical update on McNair, a June 13 team meeting, and a June 21 meeting for parents. Loh went to the hospital and funeral and "interacted with players at both," according to officials.

The two current players who spoke with ESPN and other sources close to the program said they are concerned about how Walters's investigation is being managed.

Players had to return early from their time off to meet with investigators on August 1, two days before the first preseason workout. A sign-up sheet was posted on the office door of Jason Baisden, the team's assistant athletic director for football operations and equipment. Meetings took place in the offensive staff's meeting room in the Gossett Football Team House.

"They tried to interview players at the most inconvenient time, in Gossett, basically right in front of Durkin's office," one of the current players said.

"Basically anybody can walk by, any coach or whoever really wants to can walk by and see who signed up and see who's talking to the investigation," the other current player said. "They're singling us out even more when it's supposed to be an anonymous investigation."

The player said that each meeting was scheduled for only 15 minutes. Players were asked what they wanted to share about the May 29 workout and were advised to see counselors.

"It was a joke," the same player said.

University officials confirmed there was a sign-up sheet posted but disputed the allegation that it wasn't an anonymous process. According to a university spokesperson, players were also allowed to sign up by text message, they were verbally reminded by the coaches to participate, and had the "opportunity to walk in any time anonymously."

"There were multiple ways student-athletes could volunteer participation in the external review, including confidentially meeting with consultants to offer information without being identified," said university spokesperson Katie Lawson. "They will still have the opportunity to do so."

A source said that investigators are expected to return to campus next week to interview more football players.

VIRGINIA OTTLEY CRAIGHILL

The Lost Cause

FROM SPORT LITERATE

Disaster Artist

IT'S RAINING AND cold. The massive crowd is going nowhere fast. Mashed together like cattle in a stockyard, we are about 30 yards from the entrance. From here we can see only two security screens, like the ones at the airport. Some guys farther behind us get ugly, start pushing, and scream at the gatekeepers, "What's the fucking holdup?! You guys are idiots! We paid a lot of money to stand here in the fucking rain. Get us inside now, ASSHOLES!" People close to the entrance turn and collectively roll their eyes, although we're probably all thinking the same thing. It's 7:15 and kick-off is in an hour.

We're waiting outside the Mercedes-Benz Stadium in Atlanta, Georgia with tickets to the 2018 College Football National Championship Game between the University of Alabama and the University of Georgia. The Tide versus the Dawgs, in the vernacular. The guy behind us is right about one thing: everyone in line likely paid a lot of money to be here. My husband went to Georgia, and he loves football, so he paid some obscene amount of money, an amount I never want to know, to take us, our son and daughter and me, to this game.

The problem, I suspect, is Donald Trump. The president of the United States flew to the game earlier on Air Force One and is now ensconced in a cozy luxury box with former Georgia Governor and current U.S. Secretary of Agriculture Sonny Perdue. My suspicion is later confirmed by one of the ticket takers, who says Trump's arrival set security back hours and caused traffic gridlock and unconscionable waits at the entrances. Trump knows he has a fan base in Alabama and Georgia.

We're now 30 minutes from the coin toss and have only moved two feet. The man behind me presses his crotch into my backside. I am tempted to #MeToo him after watching the Golden Globes, but he appears to be pushed forward by the aggressive crowd behind him and probably can't help where his crotch ends up. I give him the benefit of the doubt. My husband keeps telling the people in line around him how badly he needs to use the bathroom, which is probably not what they want to hear. My son, who wears a Georgia sweatshirt and a red ribbon in his hair, points out a woman a few yards ahead of us in line. She has a whitish translucent pointy poncho over her head that we all agree looks disturbingly like either a condom on a penis or a KKK hood. But her hair will be fine once she gets inside. My husband holds up a broken and ineffectual umbrella.

The National Football Championship Game would be an excellent setting for a disaster film. Instead of a vengeful sniper (*Two-Minute Warning*) or a suicidal Vietnam vet flying an explosive blimp over the stadium (*Black Sunday*), in my version the electricity in the stadium would be cut once everyone is inside and the stadium doors locked while kidnappers with night-vision goggles hired by a secret cadre of Republican senators seek out the president. This is not as far-fetched as one would think since the electricity went out at the Atlanta International Airport two weeks before Christmas.

When I mention this to my family, my daughter, who is wearing a Georgia football hat and ear plugs, tells me to keep quiet in case the Secret Service is listening. In disaster films of the 1970s, the smart, attractive people always made it out alive, while the stupid, unappealing characters died in horrifically entertaining ways. The drunk, screaming guys behind us would definitely meet their maker in my film. Even a nice character like the one played by Shelley Winters in *The Poseidon Adventure* had to die because she was fat and somewhat old. At least she drowned sacrificing herself for one of the cuter, younger characters. At fifty-seven, I most likely would not be saved in my own film, but my children would probably make it.

Getting inside has become a matter of increasing urgency for my husband. We slowly inch closer to the security screens, jamming ourselves toward where you empty your pockets into the little bowl, raise your arms, and submit to metal detectors. Shouts of joy come from those who have finally made it through to the other side. The women in front of me have clear plastic purses with the Georgia bulldogs' insignia on them; they get through quickly. The men take longer because they have to pull everything out of their pants pockets and often forget some piece of change. That sets off the scanner, and they have to get a pat-down from the guards, who probably do not enjoy it any more than the fans do.

My husband goes first, after telling the guard, the woman scanning the electronic tickets, and everyone around him that he's going to piss himself. He does not get a pat-down. The woman points him in the direction of the nearest bathrooms, three floors up. He hands me his phone with the electronic tickets for the rest of us, and runs. Not having bathrooms on the ground floor seems like shortsighted planning for a building that costs $1.5 billion. After our son and daughter scan in, they take off for our seats. It's close to kick-off. They yell back at me to go to Section 309. I stand on the gray concrete floor and wait for my husband, though we did not communicate about where to meet, and I have his cell phone, which has the seat numbers on it. After five minutes, I get anxious and head up the first flight of stairs. The stadium is cavernous, bigger than anything I've ever been in, bigger, probably, than the ship in *The Poseidon Adventure*. It has no logic. Crowds of people who just made it through the scanner run past me to their seats; it's a blur of red and black. Someone has urinated on the second flight of stairs. I pray it's not my husband.

"Fuck Trump"

Section 309 is all the way on the other side of the stadium, about two miles away, over something called the Sky Bridge. The announcer introduces President Trump, and there are sounds of booing, hissing, and cheering. My feelings about him become more negative, if possible, because of the inconvenience he has caused the people trying to get in, and I mutter under my breath,

"Fuck you, Trump." I realize I sound like the rude people in line behind me, but their anger was misdirected at the security guards. Apparently, I am not alone in my sentiments: protesters projected "FUCK TRUMP" in giant letters onto the stadium before he arrived. At this point, people are mostly in their seats, though many are frantically buying $8 beers. We had our beer and chicken tenders from Publix earlier while sitting in our car in a vacant lot where we'd paid some guy $30 instead of $50 to park. We gave the attendant a piece of chicken, and he left to get a cup of coffee and never came back. My husband will probably spend the rest of his life trying to make up the cost of these tickets, so I hope our car is still there when we get back.

I see my children standing in the hallway outside Section 309. They don't know where the seats are, and they don't know where their parents are, who know where the seats are. I pull out my husband's cell phone and show them, but they're angry that I left him. He's a big boy and probably knows where to go, I say. We spot him a few minutes later. His pants are clean, so we all embrace for a moment before heading in. We've missed the anthem, the president, the coin toss, and the kick-off, but are otherwise on time.

o to o

There is no way to express the hugeness of the new stadium; it is huger than Trump's hands, and the crowd—over 77,000 people—is possibly bigger than his inauguration. Our seats are high up on the 25-yard line, but the field and players are clear; we can see every play. And if we can't, there are multiple jumbotrons that make it possible to see each hair on UGA quarterback Jake Fromm's scruffy beard. We're in the UGA section and the fans around us seem reasonable enough. All of them are white, though I don't correlate reasonableness with whiteness. In the first quarter, UGA makes some stunning plays, and the crowd erupts. The woman in front of me wears a black sweater, black pants, and black booties, has a red and black G painted on her cheek. She turns around and high-fives me every time something good happens for the Dawgs. The man next to me high-fives me too. Everyone's congenial and rabidly excited by Georgia's strong opening.

13–0

I should explain that I am not a football fanatic, or even a fan. I'm from Atlanta and went to graduate school at UGA but never went to a game, so my loyalty is questionable. If I watch football, it's because people in my family are watching it. I've come along with a sort of anthropological mind-set. What makes so many people spend their hard-earned money for this event? Why is it so important? What will change if Georgia wins? Or loses? Why is college football like some kind of religion? The man next to me graduated from UGA in 1997 (he looks older). He flew out to Pasadena the week before for the Rose Bowl (Georgia beat Oklahoma, which is why we're here). The woman next to my husband flew down from Washington with her husband, but left him in their hotel room because he is older, she explains, and she doesn't want him to have a stroke or a heart attack if the game gets too intense. People should not die over football games. Neither my son nor daughter went to Georgia, but my son feels some esoteric emotional connection with this team, perhaps inherited from his father. My husband and my son played football, but my daughter is the real athlete of the family, and her interest stems from a physical and intellectual understanding of what it takes to do what these players do on the field.

What they do on the field is slam into each other a lot. The Tide plays dirty. Because of the jumbotron, we can see when one Alabama player takes down the UGA ball carrier then knocks him in the head after he's on the ground. We can see another 'Bama player put a last-minute choke-hold on a UGA player that doesn't get a flag. It's beginning to make me mad, and this surge of emotion is actually helpful because now I'm standing up and screaming at the ref and cheering "sic 'em, sic 'em, sic 'em" when Georgia kicks to 'Bama after another touchdown. My husband takes a picture of me doing this to send to his friends who bet him I would be reading a book throughout the game. It suddenly seems hopeful and joyous, though there is a gnawing sense that the evil genius Nick Saban will never let Alabama lose.

At the end of the second quarter, Georgia is up 13–0 and the crowd is elated. My son notes that, curiously, Saban has benched his first-string quarterback and put in the second string "true freshman" quarterback, a guy from Hawaii named Tua who's never started a game. It interests me that Tua is from Hawaii, which is nowhere near Alabama. A "true freshman," by the way, is someone who is actually a first-year college student, not someone who's been sitting on the bench for a year. So the two quarterbacks in this game now are just around 18 years old. What would it be like to be 18 and the center of this storm of insanity and adulation? What would it be like to know that the president of the United States (whoever it is) has flown down in Air Force One to watch you? What would the rest of your life be like after this?

Kendrick

My son is excited that rapper Kendrick Lamar is the halftime entertainment. It's the first time the National Championship has had a halftime performer, and certainly the first time Donald Trump has seen Kendrick Lamar perform (it turns out Trump did not see him perform; he supposedly left before halftime). When I comment to my son that the majority of the people in the stadium are white, so Lamar's rap might be lost on them, he notes that the majority of people who go to Georgia and Alabama are white, with the exception of the players on the field. I tell him this sounds racist, but he tells me it's not racist if it's true.

Lamar appears on the jumbotron but he's not on the field. They've set the halftime show outside in Centennial Park, a free, non-ticketed venue, instead of inside the stadium, which makes sense. Why should Kendrick Lamar perform for all the rich white people in the stadium (including Trump, if he were still here), who probably only listen to Tony Bennett or Taylor Swift, when he can entertain the people of Atlanta, the majority of whom are of color (at least it appears so on the jumbotron) and have been waiting outside in the cold and rain? It seems like a very egalitarian choice, except for the fact that we're inside a warm, dry stadium, and they're outside freezing.

Most of the people working in the stadium are also of color, blacks, Latinos, immigrants: the servers, bathroom staff, security, no doubt a few of them from what Trump will allegedly call "shit-hole countries" this very week. When I go to the bathroom (surprisingly empty), the woman cleaning has a knitted rainbow scarf around her head. I thank her, but she doesn't acknowledge me. No one seems terribly happy to be working the game. Maybe because Trump is here. Maybe because we're playing Alabama.

And fans of other teams hate the Crimson Tide. Sometimes that gets mixed up with the state, though having just marginally disposed of racist and alleged pedophile Roy Moore in the special Senate election, one is inclined to cut Alabamians some slack. To be fair, the whole stadium is a sea of red, and it's not just because both teams wear the same colors. Both Georgia and Alabama are red states, and I wonder how many rosy-robed fans here voted for Trump. An Alabama judge once described former Governor George Wallace, a demagogue in the same mold as Donald Trump: "[Wallace] keeps tellin' 'em, 'You the children of Israel, you gonna lead this country out of the wilderness!' Well, goddamn. We at the bottom of everything you can find to be at the bottom of, and yet we gonna save the country. We lead the country in illiteracy and syphilis, and yet we gonna lead the damn country out of the wilderness . . ." And maybe that's why some people love the Crimson Tide the way they love Trump. Because they're always on top. They are always winners. Nick Saban is gonna lead them out of the wilderness and into another National Championship. But not yet.

20–10

Halftime passes quickly while everyone catches up on their texts. People are sending pictures and Snapchats to their friends watching the game at home, or they are posting on Instagram or Facebook. I have friends in San Antonio and Italy who keep sending me game emojis. People who have no reason to be Georgia fans are completely invested in the outcome. Once we were in Seville when Spain was in the finals of the World Cup Soccer tournament; our lodging was on a big square in the heart of the city and every single bar and restaurant set up enormous television screens on the border of the square. All the patrons were sitting outside drinking and screaming at every play; everyone was unified in their desire to beat Germany, or whoever it was. It felt good to be there, to be a part of a larger organism, something that everyone agreed on and cared passionately about. It felt very human. But maybe there's another side to that, like possibly rabid nationalism.

The good part, the unifying part, seems to be what's happening here too, but not quite. The walls of the aptly named Mercedes-Benz Stadium contain a fairly rarified group, most of whom have paid full price. A man on our row walks past us on his way to the bathroom and says something to my son. After the man has gone, my son tells us what he said: "I hope you know how privileged you are to be here." This is curious and somewhat ambiguous. Does he mean my son is privileged to be watching the University of Georgia play in the National Championships? Is he privileged to see Georgia beating Alabama, to see Kirby Smart defeat Nick Saban? Is it a privilege to be in the same building as the president of the United States? Or is everyone in this arena simply privileged because they have enough disposable income to blow on four hours of football?

20–20

In the somewhat inevitable, at least to my mind, denouement of the fourth quarter, Tua rides the now rising Crimson Tide the way he might ride a surfboard in his native state. Since he's never started before and hasn't played much in other games, the Dawgs don't know what to expect from him. He's creative and unpredictable. We start to hear from the other side of the stadium, as the Alabama fans get louder and louder and the Georgia fans look more and more like deflated balloon animals. "Sweet Home Alabama" plays over the loudspeaker, a song I like, but know I'd better not sing or dance to now. The woman in front of me is no longer reaching back to give me high-fives. Someone several rows back dumps what must be a Coca-Cola onto us. I feel the sticky, syrupy mess drying in strands of my hair as the Tide gets closer to a tie. And then it is a tie game. You can almost hear the breath leaving the balloon animals as if they'd all been punctured at the same time. Alabama is going to kick a field goal in the last three seconds of the game, which seems to me to be a cowardly loser way to win. This would be a good time for the electricity to go out.

The kicker misses the field goal. The lights stay on. We're in overtime.

23–26

It's midnight. I pray for a quick ending, and hopefully a positive one for Georgia. It is quick. Georgia's Roderigo Blankenship, who should get credit for his name alone but is also a great field goal kicker, makes one, and it's 23–20. Now the ball goes to Alabama. The quarterback gets sacked, then he throws, the ball is caught, and 'Bama scores. As fast as that, all the hopes and dreams of the people on our side come to an end. Suddenly, the other side of the stadium bursts into cheers on the other side and glittery confetti explodes from the ceiling of the dome. Everyone in our section stands there dumbfounded. My husband sits down. Our daughter has her hands on her head. Our son says, "We've got to get out of here, NOW." There might be tears in his eyes. The feeling seems familiar, as if it had happened before, maybe back in early November of 2016.

Exodus

As if all the Georgia fans had the same thought at the same moment, like ants silently communicating, there's a unified and dignified movement out of their seats and into the hall. No one says anything as at least 50,000 people march towards the stairways. And just like the beginning of this disaster, we are suddenly pinned in a flesh press of bodies all moving the same way. On the stairs, one man has the temerity to squeak out, "Roll, Tide," in a tiny, uncertain voice, but he recognizes the danger of being celebratory on this side and fades into the crowd.

I am holding my husband's hand with one hand and grasping my son's sweatshirt with the other because this is the kind of crowd that would trample you in an instant, the kind of crowd where you could get shanked and your body would be carried along upright until you got outside, the kind of crowd where you could lose your children forever. My daughter is farther ahead; I can tell she's pissed and she's not going to hold anyone's hand; she's just going to get out, but we keep track of her.

The shortsightedness of the stadium planners again becomes evident as tens of thousands of sad, angry, disappointed, possibly suicidal and/or homicidal Georgia fans attempt to squeeze through two solitary exits before Alabama fans really start celebrating. Personally, I am not feeling all that bad now. It was a good game, and it was exciting; Georgia played better than Alabama. But nobody around me wants to hear it. My son starts whining about how it's a curse on Georgia teams and recounting the admittedly depressing story of the Atlanta Falcons' loss in last year's Super Bowl against the New England Patriots.

This attitude makes me think about a line from the film *Talladega Nights*, which, I should point out, is set in Alabama. Ricky Bobby, the main character played by Will Ferrell, is a race car driver at Talladega, and lives by the motto, "If you ain't first, you're last." It doesn't matter if Georgia won the Rose Bowl and the SEC Championship; it doesn't matter if they had a fantastic season and played honorably and well in their home state in the National Championships. If they're not first, they're last. This could be Trump's motto too. Trump loves winning, thinks of himself as a winner, no matter the facts. The president is no doubt now an Alabama fan even if he was a guest of Sonny Perdue because Perdue is now on the losing side. Later this week, Sonny's first cousin, Senator David Perdue, will defend Trump's profane comments on immigrants from Haiti and Africa, claiming he cannot recall the president using any such derogatory terms.

We'll Get 'em Next Year

Once outside, we head in the wrong direction and have to walk all the way around the stadium. The crowd is still eerily silent and controlled. No one screams or fights or curses. The concrete barriers around the stadium are covered with beer cans and bottles from earlier tailgaters. I think about the stadium workers and their grim, stoic faces, who will be cleaning up this mess until dawn. A tall gangly black man coming from the direction of Centennial Park walks in front of us and yells, "Fuck Alabama! Fuck Saban!" to some white fraternity guys with Georgia shirts on. They hesitantly high-five him and mildly respond, "Yeah dude, fuck 'Bama!" The frat guys walk closer together. The man keeps on walking beside the boys, mumbling to them, "Yeah, fuck that! We'll get 'em next year!" He kicks some empty beer cans and kind of trips off the curb. The fraternity boys walk faster.

CAITY WEAVER

My Magical Quest to Destroy Tom Brady and Win a Philadelphia Eagles Mini-Fridge at Super Bowl LII

FROM GQ

MANY CRISSCROSSING FACTORS combine to make football difficult to watch. The rules are completely invented from scratch at the start of every contest. It stutters along with frantic, abrupt pauses that can last anywhere from an extremely long time to 600,000 hours. The players, in their matching capris and shiny plastic orbs, are virtually indistinguishable from one another, except those players with ponytails, who are merely indistinguishable from other players with ponytails. All of which is to say nothing of the hot shame you must, if you are in any way decent, feel as you watch the odds that these vigorous young men will be able to recognize the faces of their family members 20 years hence drop in real time as they patiently bash their precious brains in for your entertainment. The game is peppered with sudden silent moments where a person, having just collided at high speed with another person, lies motionless staring up toward the sky, or translucent ethylene tetrafluoroethylene ceiling, and all the thousands of people who, seconds ago, saw that man moving faster on his feet than they probably will, instinctively lean forward with dread-tensed stomachs and wonder if he will ever walk again.

As an alternative to the bashing, the men can express political dissent, and become unemployed.

However, against all reason and morality, we do love the Philadelphia Eagles, being, as they are, from Philadelphia. And although I had never attended a football game before Super Bowl LII—had never, that I can recall, even seen an entire game on TV—I felt a desperate, primal need for the Eagles to win. If the Eagles did not win, my life would be faintly but palpably worse, at least for a period of a few hours. At the end of Super Bowl, there are 53 men on television who look like they've just arrived home to find every single one of their possessions stolen, and 53 who are laughing, crying, dancing, and praying with delirious happiness. It was very important to me that on Sunday night the latter group would be the Philadelphia Eagles, but I had no desire to see the slog leading up to that point. I could go to sleep Sunday night at 6:30 p.m., wake up Monday morning to see the score, and be just as happy—happier, probably—than if I had been made to watch the entire game unfold.

Which is why my bosses thought it would be amusing to send me all the way to Minnesota in the middle of winter to watch the game in person.

I know a haze when I see one, but I also know an opportunity for a scam. I asked that, if I go, I be allowed an opportunity to win something of value to me, such as a personal mini-fridge emblazoned with the Eagles logo for my cubicle in the office, retail value: $369.99.

And thus my Super Bowl Scavenger Hunt was born.

The terms of the hunt were thus: From a list of 25 items assembled by mysterious forces (a two-minute conversation with my coworkers), I must find or complete 13, representing one half of the list as well as the number of games the Eagles won during the 2017–2018 season. The only stipulation was that the hunt must take place entirely within the confines of the Super Bowl.

Here was my scavenger hunt list.

1. Diet Coke product
2. Bring home a handful of losing team's confetti
3. Hot dog three times
4. A personal story or previously unknown fact about Beyoncé
5. Cast a spell on the Patriots to lose (procure items on site)
6. Get an Eagles fan to perform black magic with me
7. Earn money

8. Ride on a private plane
9. Sign someone up for delivery.com using my promo code so we both save $7
10. Take a selfie with Philadelphia boy Bradley Cooper (automatic scavenger hunt win if I thank him by saying, "Thank you, Mr. McConaughey")
11. Get invited into a suite
12. Cheese steak + lobster roll (double points if consumed simultaneously)
13. ~~Find Jessica Biel~~ Make people think *GQ* employee A. J. Gibbson is more famous than Jessica Biel
14. Picture of someone dressed as Prince
15. Identify a baby under one month
16. Meet a person over 80
17. A stranger's lanyard
18. Appear on one TV show (domestic)
19. Appear on one TV show (foreign)
20. Receive medical attention
21. Meet Scientologist
22. Meet member of a player's immediate family
23. Find a Pats fan looking good
24. Greet a celebrity like I know them
25. Dead bird
26. *BONUS* Find lid

Here's what happened.

Of the 25 items on the list, slightly fewer than half seemed difficult enough to pull off that I felt they warranted a Twitter call asking for assistance.

> **Caity Weaver @caityweaver**
> **Replying to @caityweaver @chrisgayomali**
> THIS IS THE MINIFRIDGE ON THE FUCKIN' LINE. It's actually a Refrigerated Beverage Center. BUT TO GET MY LITTLE PAWS ON IT I NEED YOUR HELP WITH A COUPLE ITEMS ON THE SCAVENGER HUNT LIST. SEE NEXT TWEET.

> **Caity Weaver @caityweaver**
> If you or someone you know is at the Super Bowl and can help a poor writer accomplish the tasks on this list in order to win the minifridge of her dreams, PLEASE TWEET OR DM ME!!! GO BIRDS!!! TOM BRADY, SHOW YOUR FACE LOSER IF U AIN'T SCARED!!!!! (THIS IS REAL, I WANT THE FRIDGE) **pic.twitter.com/M5EIHyzTYt**

1. Bring home handful of losing team's confetti
2. Ride on a private plane
3. Take a selfie with Philadelphia boy Bradley Cooper
4. Get invited into a suite
5. Appear on TV (domestic)
6. Appear on TV (foreign)
7. Get an Eagles fan to perform black magic with me
8. Meet a person over 80
9. Find a Pats fan looking good (ULTRA CHALLENGE, hard to find)

For the rest, I was on my own.

Contraband Cola

I rode to the Super Bowl with three *GQ* colleagues who'd been assigned to *actually* cover the game, as well as the NFL Honors award show the night before, on social media. Two of them arrived in the lobby of our Minneapolis hotel wearing the kind of clothes you might to, say, watch a football game; the third, A. J. Gibbson (associate manager, social), entered wearing jeans, a belted suede Fendi trench coat with fur cuffs, a camel-colored Italian cashmere turtleneck, and cherry leather Chelsea boots, which had the immediate combined effect of making the rest of us look like his bumbling assistants. Upon seeing him, I petitioned my editor to modify an item on our scavenger hunt list: "Find Jessica Biel" became "Make people think *GQ* employee A. J. Gibbson is more famous than Jessica Biel."

I found the first item on my list even before making it into the stadium, in a service elevator located in the media check-in area: a rogue Coca-Cola Company product at a Pepsi-sponsored event. A man in the elevator was carrying two cases of the brand's alarmingly flavored new Diet Cokes. Although these beverages were bound for the throats and stomachs of the elites, he allowed me to take a Diet Coke Feisty Cherry, and thank God he did, because I did not see another Coke product the entire time I was in Minneapolis. (An employee in our hotel restaurant explicitly informed me, "Minnesota is a Pepsi state"—a gorgeous state motto.)

Item No. 1: Diet forager product. ACCOMPLISHED. Twelve to go.

The part of the scavenger hunt I was most looking forward to, besides soaring over Minnesota in a private jet and making tons of celebrity friends in Bradley Cooper's stadium box, was "hot dog three times." To check this item off the list, I would have to eat a hot dog three times. Not the same hot dog!

I approached the nearest concession stand, and what to my wondering eyes should appear but a single menu item called "TWO HOT DOGS." Although not hinted at in the name, "TWO HOT DOGS" consisted of two hot dogs *plus a side of fries,* for only $23, a price that included the cost associated with taking part in a living history experience in which customers learned firsthand what life was like during the Great Depression by paying $23 for two hot dogs. I decided to take a breather before my final hot dog, leaving that item temporarily unfinished.

Item No. 3: Hot dog three times. INCOMPLETE. Twelve to go.

Minnesota is the Land of 10,000 Lakes but they should call it the Land of 0,000 Lines. I'd go back again just to not wait in the lines they don't have. The vast majority of the time—at the freaking Super Bowl, with 67,612 people in attendance—there weren't lines for the food stands, or the women's restrooms, or the incredible roller coasters at the Mall of America, which I highly, highly, highly recommend. The people really are as friendly and helpful as you've been warned about. The airport is filled with spry senior citizens armed with hypotheses about what holographic images printed on paper might do to the X-ray scanners (might "set them off" is the theory; "not worth the risk").

Here's the bad thing about Minnesota: the air is so ferociously cold and dry that you are liable to crack open and bleed simply from the strain of being. And so it was, with cuticles ripping violently apart, that I completed a second task from my list: receive medical attention.

While I was receiving my Band-Aid, another woman walked in with the complaint that some part of her body "wouldn't stop bleeding." Come to Minnesota, a Pepsi state where you can't stop bleeding. The first aid station contained a robust supply of ibuprofen, Tums, and syringes.

Item No. 20: Receive medical attention. COMPLETED. Eleven to go.

Interlude: A Lidless Hellscape

Perhaps the most important task on my list was to cast a bad-luck spell cursing the Patriots with a humiliating defeat, exclusively using items collected on-site at the stadium. A kindly self-identified witch I know tried to dissuade me from performing this stunt, on the grounds that "ethically, curses are tricky," but at the end of the day I had to follow my black heart.

Prior to my arrival, I pictured myself efficiently gathering my spell ingredients like a lonely old woman from days of yore whom everyone in town suspects of being a witch, but it turns out . . . yes, she is a witch.

Here was the list of necessaries for "Bad Luck," per the source of my magic text, spellsofmagic.com:

- tape
- a pen
- paper
- one piece of mint (optional)
- one three-leaf clover
- a little bit of water
- salt
- something dear to their heart

I figured I'd beg a sprig of mint off a bartender making mojitos and swipe some salt packets from a napkin stand. Clover seemed like it might be hard to procure (1) when the city was blanketed under a fresh snowfall, and (2) inside the Vikings' enclosed stadium—but I thought I might be able to locate a microgreen garnish atop a luscious steak that I also thought I might be able to locate. A tape, pen, and paper, I was sure, would reveal themselves to me quite easily. It was the Super Bowl. Anything was possible.

Turns out most things were not possible. Not only did I not stumble upon a hidden field of clover, or steak garnished with microgreens—I couldn't find mint anywhere. One after another, bartenders shook their heads. None of the custom cocktails ("Jalapeno Pineapple Margarita," "Mai Tai," "Aviation") contained mint. No item available for purchase at the boldly named "Wild and Fresh Market" contained mint. I couldn't even find gum containing mint.

After about 30 minutes of searching (what was going on on the field, I have no idea), I came upon a promising lead: shrimp tacos. Mint and shrimp go together like dogs and logs! I ran my wild eyes over the menu description. No mint, but there *was* cilantro. It would have to do in a pinch. I asked the cashier if I could have a cup of cilantro, and offered to pay for it. She was reluctant to make me pay $11 for a commemorative Super Bowl cup just so I could have something to carry my cilantro in, but she was willing to have me pay $11 for Diet Pepsi in a commemorative Super Bowl cup and give me an employees-only paper cup of cilantro (premixed with chopped red onion) on the side. She filled my commemorative cup up to the brim with icy cold fountain soda—something I would love under normal circumstances, but this cup's purple holographic design made it extremely slippery to hold, and the cup lacked a lid.

"Could I have a lid?" I asked.

"We don't have a lid for that," she said. Odd, but not a big deal. I walked to another stand and asked for a lid.

"We don't have any lids," an employee informed me. "People leave them on the ground, so we just don't have lids anymore. Even with a bottle of water, we're supposed to keep the lid."

I had never before encountered a lidless society, and after carefully placing my commemorative cup brimming with unchecked soda on a nearby table, I sent an excited message to my editor: "No lids ANYWHERE. You CAN'T GET A LID."

"I'll give you a point if you find a lid," he wrote back.

But here's what he didn't know: I had already procured a 100 percent illegal lid for myself. [*Ed. note:* Wow.] A young man working behind the counter had discreetly slapped a plastic lid on the paper cup—designated for employee use only—containing my cilantro, to prevent it from spilling all over my bag.

"SICK," I responded to my editor. [*Ed. note:* WOW.]

Bonus Item No. 26: Find a lid. COMPLETED. Ten to go.

I am the Devil's Mistress (Part I)

Loose salt for my spell proved surprisingly hard to find, until I realized I could buy a soft pretzel and scrape off some of its enormous white crystals.

For water, I requested "the cheapest bottle of water you have" from a woman working at still another concession stand. In a manner that suggested it physically pained her to have to tell me this, she revealed that the cheapest water she could give me was $6.

For an object dear to Tom Brady, I selected a T-shirt commemorating the exciting day, with the names of all his stupid friends on the back.

I bought a commemorative Super Bowl pen (also $6) at a souvenir pop-up shop that spanned two floors of the stadium, and featured ghostly white statues of football players, benched forever in heaven.

The pop-up contained a FedEx booth where customers could pay to have their purchases shipped directly from the game. A FedEx employee allowed me to have a piece of tape for free. (THANK YOU!!!)

I tore a piece off a jumbo paper towel roll left on a table in a women's restroom and went into a stall to perform my dark deeds.

"Draw a large pentagram on the paper and write their first and last name in the center," the instructions read. "Sprinkle a little salt on the name."

"Then, drip some water on to the condiments."

"Tear up the clover and mint (if mint is present), and sprinkle on to the water."

"Place the special item on to the name. Lean down to the paper and chant the bad spell."

Good luck go, Go away. But bring all of the bad to stay. And for this spell, I must pay a price. With something dear, As well as nice. This is my will, So Mote It Be!

"Fold the paper in half hamburger style, and then hot dog style. Repeat until paper is small enough to fit in your pocket."

"Tape the paper shut and carry it around in your pocket, purse, etc."

"Remember, how long the spell will last depends not only on the strength of the caster, but on the experience of the caster as well."

Immediately after I completed this spell, the Patriots scored their first touchdown, which made me think perhaps the cilantro had been a bad idea.

Item No. 5: Cast a spell on the Patriots to lose. COMPLETED. Nine to go.

A Hologram in Real Life

Can you believe I only saw one person dressed as Prince at the Super Bowl in Minneapolis?

Item No. 14: Take a picture of someone dressed as Prince. COMPLETED. Eight to go.

I had eaten a hot dog for the Father, and the Son, so now it was time to eat one for me, Caity. To inject some color into my life, I decided to try one that was inexplicably enormous.

If you can explain the mysteries of this great and terrible hot dog, please get in touch with me. It had a very bad taste, and every time—*every time*—I bit into it, scaldingly hot hot dog water flew onto my face and glasses.

Item No. 3: Hot dog three times: COMPLETED. Seven to go.

Lucifer's Son Reveals Himself

Justin Timberlake's halftime show was one of the eeriest events I've ever witnessed. For nearly his entire performance, the tens of thousands of people seated in the stadium sat motionless. They did not dance. They did not sing. They did not talk. They simply stared politely forward, the way you might if someone were giving a mildly engaging talk just before lunch at a business conference. All sounds of screaming excitement emanated from a group of people who appeared to have been brought onto the field and clustered around Timberlake's temporary stage specifically to provide an illusion of screaming excitement. I never knew something so loud could be so quiet. When Justin Timberlake commanded the crowd to hold their phones in the air, no one complied. Before the show, folks in my section had received detailed instructions about what to do with two mini flashlights placed at everyone's seats; few abided by them. The only song to generate even a moderate crowd response was "Can't Stop the Feeling!"—a song Timberlake recorded for the soundtrack to the animated film *Trolls* about which he once said the following:

"I have always envisioned bringing the two worlds of film and music together for one epic event [and] couldn't be more excited that they will collide in DreamWorks' *Trolls*."

By far the most exciting and visually impressive moment of the performance came at the very end, after Timberlake had left the stage, when the mob of dancers who'd gathered to perform choreography with what appeared to be huge pieces of neon-colored cardboard were forced to run to the exits, to clear the field.

"That's it?" asked a woman behind me. She was correct.

I Am the Devil's Mistress (Part II)

My increasingly frantic Twitter pleas generated very little in terms of material progress, which should serve as an important reminder that the spirit of democracy and camaraderie fostered by the internet is an illusion; people do not care about you that much, and everyone will die alone, probably without ever having been the proud owner of an officially licensed Philadelphia Eagles Refrigerated Beverage Center. However, the internet was somewhat helpful in two ways:

One Twitter user brought my quest to the attention of ESPN host Katie Nolan, who offered to help by submitting a photo of herself as evidence of a Patriots fan "looking good."

> **Caity Weaver @caityweaver**
> Replying to @katienolan @emilyoestevez
> KATIE, #9 IS IMPOSSIBLE TO FIND. IT DOES NOT EXIST

> **Katie Nolan @katienolan**
> But caity,,,, **pic.twitter.com/AscaHt24cw**

What Katie did not know is that I had requested this item be added to the list as a single impossible task, to keep me humble because only God is perfect. Can a person ever truly "look good" once they have been positively identified as a Patriots fan? I contend the answer is *no*. Nonetheless, I did appreciate Katie's effort, so I awarded her photo a half point.

Later, seconds after a Patriots touchdown and subsequent crowd roar, I saw a man in a Tom Brady jersey run out of a men's room yelling, "What'd I miss?" As I watched him, he craned his neck to an elevated TV screen and unleashed a guttural

"FUCK!" his face contorting at his own misfortune. I thought that looked pretty good, so I awarded myself another half point and declared:

> **Item No. 9:** Find a Pats fan looking good. COMPLETE. Six to go.

The other manner in which social media very nearly proved helpful was when I received the following direct message from a stranger in regards to Item No. 6: get an Eagles fan to perform black magic with me.

> Hi, my cousin's husband is at the game, what would count as black magic

As it turned out, I did not need that person's cousin's husband to join hands with me in league with Satan; while I was finishing up my third hot dog, a woman in an Eagles coat approached my standing table and asked if I wouldn't mind watching her drink while she went back to the bar to get another for her husband, because they would only sell her one at a time.

"I'll do it if you perform a spell to curse Tom Brady with me when you get back," I said.

"Fine, then," she agreed in a heavy Southern drawl. (She later told me that she was from South Carolina, married to a Philly native.)

True to her word, when she returned, she chanted the following words with me over a pile of, basically, trash that I had made:

Good luck go, Go away. But bring all of the bad to stay. And for this spell, I must pay a price. With something dear, As well as nice. This is my will, So Mote It Be!

> **Item No. 6:** Get an Eagles fan to perform black magic with me. COMPLETE. Five to go.

The Dead Bird Omen

One helpful but not terribly well-publicized amenity the venue offered was free charging stations. It was at one of these that I saw a white-haired man from Philadelphia folding bills into his wallet.

"Excuse me, sir," I said. "I'm doing a scavenger hunt to win a mini-fridge with the Eagles logo on it. One of the things on my list is 'earn money.' If you wouldn't mind giving me a dollar, it would be a huge help."

"Sure," he said, and peeled off a dollar.

Item No. 7: Earn money. COMPLETE. Four to go.

"What else is on your list?" he asked.

I pulled up the list on my phone. "You haven't met Beyoncé, have you?" I asked. (Item No. 4: A personal story or previously unknown fact about Beyoncé.) He hadn't.

"I could have helped you with that one earlier," he said, pointing at Item No. 25: "Dead bird."

"You saw a dead bird?" I asked. This item was on the list because a friend had informed me that huge numbers of birds keep flying into the beautiful reflective glass of the stadium and dying.

He nodded silently.

"Where?"

"Outside my hotel."

"What hotel?"

"The LivINN," he said. "L-I-V-I-N-N. It was just lyin' there, outside the door."

"Do you know what kind of bird it was?" I asked. (Why did I ask that?)

"No," he said.

"Will you give me your email address to sign up for delivery. com?" I asked. "It's not a scam. You can unsubscribe as soon as you get the first email."

"Sure," he said. This man helped me complete two tasks in about 60 seconds, which makes him the official second MVP of the night, after Nick Foles.

Item No. 9: Sign someone up for delivery.com using my promo code so we both save $7. COMPLETE. Three to go.

The Baby of a Lifetime

Although I'd made decent progress, by the fourth quarter, I was growing despondent. The game was nearly over, the Patriots were now in the lead, and the remaining items on the list were proving impossible to find or accomplish. My evil spell had backfired, possibly due to my own use of substitute ingredients. What's worse, I had doubled its cursed impact and sacrificed the innocent soul of a woman from South Carolina who loved alcohol. I saw many men who appeared to be over 80 (Item No. 16), but they were all cordoned off in elite areas, and even if I could get to them, I was reluctant to interrupt their watching of the game to explain to these uniformed World War II veterans that I, a grown woman in a gold lamé Eagles jacket, needed their help on a scavenger hunt of my own devising. I was reduced to wandering around the main concourse asking random strangers, "Excuse me, have you or anyone you know ever met Beyoncé?" No one had. Most people seemed baffled by my question, which suggests to me that Beyoncé needs to get out and meet more people. A few folks seemed to think I was some sort of hidden-camera game show they had no interest in playing.

I was in the midst of ascending and descending stairs and escalators in random order, haphazardly traversing concourses with no direction or purpose, when I found myself next to a glass-walled studio filled with dozens of TV monitors, each blaring a different oscillating graphic ("FIIIiiirrSSSTttt DOOoooWWWnnNN!"), and decided to rest. I was soon joined there by a woman in Philadelphia gear, her arms laden with food and drink she intended to bring back to her family in the stands. She and I chatted as we watched the game on TV, unable to tear ourselves away from the screens even though we were just a few feet away from where we could watch the game live. Our mood was low when suddenly, with just over two minutes left, the Eagles appeared to score another touchdown. She threw herself into my arms. "I'm gonna cry!" she screamed into my chest. I hugged her as we both jumped up and down.

A man from behind us dismissed our joy. "They're not gonna give it to them," he said. And, indeed, when we looked back, the catch was under review. The three of us, the man, the woman, and I, pressed our faces to the glass as the action was rewound and replayed dozens of times. Catch-bobble-catch; catch-bobble-catch; catch-bobble-catch. Finally, the touchdown call was upheld. "You just won the Super Bowl," the man said. The woman and I hugged each other again, and ran off to make it to our respective seats before the final seconds of the game.

As soon as green confetti fell like beautiful acid rain, I lunged out of my seat and ran four levels through empty, echoing back tunnels to the ground, hoping that the clear "NO FIELD ACCESS" stamp on my media badge didn't matter anymore now that the Eagles had won. The first rule of Philadelphia is that there are no rules that cannot be set on fire and hurled through a storefront window in celebration. Turns out the first rule of Minneapolis is that you must respect all rules. I was stopped just a few feet from the field and forced to turn back around, which is when I saw Kevin Hart, looking dour, perhaps because he had just been forcibly removed from TV for swearing during a live broadcast, making his way down the tunnel with his entourage.

"What's up, Kev?!" I yelled. He ignored me.

Item No. 24: Greet a celebrity like I know them. COMPLETED. Two to go.

Forced back upstairs to join the disgusting ranks of the other people without field access, I bumped into another opportunity to score a last-minute scavenger hunt point: My coworker A.J. Earlier in the evening, I had jokingly given him my Eagles baseball cap to wear, and despite the greenhouse-like temperature inside the stadium, he still had it on, in addition to his suede trench and cashmere turtleneck. The result was that A.J. no longer looked simply like a well-dressed man; he looked like a well-dressed man so full of affection and respect for the Philadelphia Eagles, he was willing to ruin a fantastic outfit by wearing a dirty old baseball cap advertising his support for them.

"I'm going to pretend to interview you," I said, holding up my phone like a recorder. A few people clapped at him as they walked by. Emboldened, A.J. started pointing at people as he gave me a pretend interview. He began saying "thank you" to Eagles fans unprompted. The more he thanked them, the more they congratulated him. He shrugged and nodded when they expressed excitement. I put my phone in my pocket, ran a few yards down the concourse, and doubled back to him.

"I hate to do this," I said for the benefit of the crowd now making its way toward him. I pulled out my small notebook. "Would you mind signing?" After seeing A.J. sign an autograph for me, people began forming small lines to give him high-fives. Wary of attempting our charade for too long in one location, he and I decided to move around. He confidently began strolling around

a few various elite club levels, while I rushed along a few paces behind him, in the manner of a harried assistant. A.J. continued to
smile and nod at well-wishers and awed children. At some point,
he decided internally that he was a retired former Eagles player
and mused aloud to me, "I wish it could have been in my day, but
I'm happy they finally got it." We finally stopped wandering, not
because he got caught slipping seamlessly between club levels, but
because it was so easy as to be unexciting. At 10 p.m. on Sunday
night in U.S. Bank Stadium, it was assumed that a six-foot-six black
man in a fur-lined coat and Eagles cap was supposed to be anywhere he was.

> **Item No. 13:** Make people think *GQ* employee A. J. Gibbson is more
> famous than Jessica Biel. COMPLETE. No offense, Jessica. One to go.
> No time left.

As fans surged out of the stadium on a current of dazed emotion, I was forced to confront the barren reality of my fate, with no
officially licensed Philadelphia Eagles personal Refrigerated Beverage Center on the horizon. My drinks would forever be room
temperature, or located in a non–Philadelphia Eagles brand regu-
lar-size refrigerator far away from my cubicle. My afternoons would
be filled not with the gentle hum of drinks being continuously
cooled, but the booming silence of a distinct LACK of electricity. I
had lost, but at least the Eagles had won.

But then.

A few feet ahead of me, I saw her—a symbol of hope for the future, specifically my future, specifically my future filled with up to
20 chilled beverages at a time: a very, very young baby. (Item No.
15.) By far the youngest I had seen all night.

As if pulled by an invisible string wrapped around that baby's
finger, I glided silently away from extremely famous retired NFL
player *GQ*'s A. J. Gibbson. I peered at the baby's little face, smushed
delicately between enormous pink baby earphones. She was wearing an infant-size knit Eagles cap and crying softly to herself.

"How old is your daughter?" I asked the woman bouncing her
lightly in her arms.

"She's my granddaughter, actually," said the smiling lady, clad in
matching Eagles gear. "Two months." My heart sank. Why couldn't
this baby have been brand newer? "I think she's ready for these
headphones to come off," she added.

"Maybe she's crying because she's so happy they won," I said. The grandmother and I wished each other a good night and I walked back to collect my things. As I prepared to leave the stadium, I glanced back at the baby in time to see her being handed off to her mother. It was then that I noticed the word on the back of the beanie, spelled out in gleaming Swarovski crystals: D-A-D. My eyes flew to her mother's jersey, adorned with matching crystals: GOODE 52. Then to her grandmother's: GOODE 52. Everyone in their party was wearing the same jersey. My fingers opened Instagram so fast, my iPhone glass threatened to melt in my hands. There was the baby, on her mom's Instagram, in the arms of a beaming linebacker—Najee Goode, #52, Philadelphia Eagles.

Item No. 22: Meet member of a player's immediate family.

Like the Philadelphia Eagles, I had achieved the impossible. The mini-fridge was mine.

SUPER BOWL REVIEW: 8/10; GO EAGLES; would not go back.

JEFF MACGREGOR

Taming the Lionfish

FROM SMITHSONIAN

Friday

WE WERE SOMEWHERE around Pensacola Pass, on the edge of
the Gulf of Mexico, when the over-the-counter drugs failed to take
hold.

Just after sunrise the seas are running two or four or six feet
and at the mouth of the Gulf where the bay opens up and the tide
meets the wind from the east and the west and the north and the
south is a washing machine of razorback crests and sub-basement
troughs, waves running horizon to horizon, some as big as houses,
whitecaps peeling off the long rollers, the water every blue and
every green, the rise and fall of our little boat a series of silences,
groans, engine noises, and cymbal crashes as we pitch and roll
and the whole boatload of gear works itself loose from the fit-
tings, the tanks and the spears and the wet suits and the vests and
the fins and the buckets and the coolers and computers and the
compasses and regulators and the backups to the backups to the
backups, every dive system three times redundant now soaked and
streaming, bobbing in the bilges, and the waves coming over the
side, the top, the stern, the bow, all of us pitching and yawing and
rolling and moaning and swearing and all that gear floating at our
ankles with the bags of white cheddar popcorn and the wasabi and
the Red Vines, all of us grabbing for the gunwales or the rails or
each other, Captain Andy at the wheel calm as a vicar, Barry with
his feet planted, singing at the top of his lungs, "Welcome back,
my friends, to the show that never ends," and the planetary surge

of 500 quadrillion gallons of angry water pouring through the tiny nautilus of my inner ear on its way to my stomach. I lean over the side and throw up again. Doubled over the transom, John casually does likewise. The motion-sickness tablets do nothing.

We all laugh.

We're here to hunt lionfish.

Before we get to the marine biology, this has to be said: the lionfish is one of the most beautiful animals alive. With its bold stripes and extravagant fins, its regal bearing and magisterial stillness, every lionfish is a hand-lacquered 11th-century Japanese fan. It is a diva, a glamour-puss, a show-off. If you ran a hedge fund in Greenwich or Geneva or Tokyo, the first fish you'd buy for that 100,000-gallon aquarium in your lobby would be a lionfish. It is in every respect spectacular. And in this hemisphere it is an eco-killer, a destroyer of worlds.

Four-hundred-twenty-two words of marine biology boilerplate, a NOAA crib sheet, and a warning:

In the southeast U.S. and Caribbean coastal waters the lionfish is an invasive species. It competes for food and space with overfished native populations. Scientists fear lionfish will kill off helpful locals such as algae-eating parrotfish, allowing seaweed to overtake coral reefs already stressed by rising water temperatures and bleaching. Lionfish kill off other small cleaner-fish too, which increases the risk of infection and disease among sport fish and cash fishery populations. In U.S. waters, lionfish stocks continue to grow and increase in range. Lionfish have no known predators here and reproduce all year long; a mature female lionfish releases roughly two million eggs a year, which are then widely dispersed by ocean currents.

Two million eggs a year.

Scientific Name: *Pterois volitans* (red lionfish)

Unscientific, badass nickname: devil firefish

Identification: Lionfish have distinctive brown and white or maroon and white stripes covering the head and body. Tentacles protrude above the eyes and below the mouth. They have fanlike pectoral fins and long dorsal spines. An adult lionfish can grow as large as 18 inches.

Native Range: The South Pacific and Indian Oceans, where natural predators, including grouper, keep their population in check.

Habitat: Lionfish are found in the tropics, in warm water, and in most marine habitats. Lionfish have been found in or on hard-bottom ocean floor, mangrove, sea grass, coral, and artificial reefs at depths from one to 1,000 feet.

Non-native Range: Since the 1980s, lionfish have been reported · in growing numbers along the southeastern United States coast from Texas to North Carolina. Juvenile lionfish have been collected in waters as far north as Long Island, New York.

Lionfish are eating machines. They are active hunters that ambush their prey by using their outstretched pectoral fins to corner them. If lionfish are unable to adapt to declines in their prey, their population might decrease. In the short term, however, they will turn to cannibalism.

Warning! Lionfish spines deliver a venomous sting that can last for days and cause extreme pain. Also sweating, respiratory distress, and even paralysis. Lionfish venom glands are located in the spines on the top and the sides and the bottom of the fish. They can sting you even after the fish is dead. The venom is a neurotoxin. Once the spine punctures the skin, the venom enters the wound through grooves in the spine. If stung, seek medical attention immediately.

The guys on the dock will tell you that the sting of a lionfish is like "getting hit hard by a hammer, then injecting the bruise with hot sauce." Wear gloves.

How they got here no one really knows. Like giant shoulder pads and the music of Frank Stallone, some things about the 1980s remain inexplicable. The arrival in American waters of the lionfish is one of these mysteries. There are a couple of recurring stories, but they don't really add up to a truth. The first is that some home aquarium owner emptied a few of them into the ocean one night —the narrative equivalent of the New York City alligator-down-the-toilet story. Another story suggests a big resort hotel in the Caribbean mishandled the filtration setup on its giant destination aquarium and pumped them out into the sea. Or that a breeding pair escaped during Hurricane Andrew. Maybe they arrived here in the water ballast of big cargo ships from the Pacific.

Now they're everywhere. Like locust. That's the bad news. The lionfish has Florida in a noose, and from Mobile, Alabama, to Cape Hatteras, North Carolina, the lionfish is a blight, a plague, an epidemic. A perfect evolutionary machine for eating and ruin, every lionfish is the lace-collared cutthroat in your underwater Elizabethan costume drama.

The good news? Lionfish is delicious.

All this I learned at the Smithsonian Marine Station in Fort Pierce, Florida. They have a team of molecular scientists and marine biologists there, and benthic ecologists and visiting zoologists and doctoral candidates and postdocs and technicians and reef experts. They have a research laboratory and a public aquarium where a couple of times a day you can watch a little lionfish get fed. This is out on Seaway Drive, and on a hot spring morning the light here is like the aftermath of a blast. In fact, when you drive from here to Pensacola, all of Florida feels like a trick of the light. Overbright or too dark, at once too soft and too sharp, underwater or above it, you're never sure what you're seeing. At noon the asphalt shimmers and the sand dazzles and at midnight the stars swim in an ink-black heaven above the cypress and the slash pine. Is that a Disney castle rising in the distant murk, or just a jet of swamp gas? From Daytona to the Everglades to the Keys, from Universal Studios to the Fountain of Youth, Florida is a fever dream, an unreliable narrator. Florida is a fiction. It is an impossible place.

And that's how we all wound up in this little boat at the Lionfish World Championship. One of dozens of lionfish rodeos or derbies or hunts around the state, events like this are the first line of defense against the lionfish takeover. The premise is simple: whoever spears the most lionfish wins. Sponsored by Coast Watch Alliance and the Florida Fish and Wildlife Conservation Commission, Reef Rangers, the Gulf Coast Lionfish Coalition, and about a dozen others, over the last few years this tournament has cleaned thousands of lionfish out of the local ecosystem. In 2016 alone it brought in more than 8,000 fish—in a weekend. I'm here to watch one of five or six teams kill every lionfish it sees.

Even before dawn the marina is loud with gulls and banging halyards and happy obscenity. As the sun rises so does the wind, and wary talk of what a wild, E-ticket ride the day's going to be. Before any of us step aboard, the little boat is already filled with gear and we're still lashing coolers to the deck. There isn't a spare inch anywhere. But off we go.

Capt. Andy Ross is a fidget spinner of a man, quiet, apparently motionless, but going a thousand miles an hour. He is fit and tanned and of some glorious sun-worn indeterminate middle age. He is one of the tournament founders too, and master and commander of the *Niuhi,* a 25-foot catamaran dive boat with a small deckhouse and cabin and twin Yamaha 150s to push us out into the Gulf. Generally soft-spoken, from time to time while I'm redistributing my breakfast over the port-side gunwale, he calls out to me with a small sideways smile, "Sporty today!"

Why yes, Cap'n, yes it is.

On the other hand, Barry Shively, the mate and dive master, never stops talking. Never stops. Never stops singing or storytelling. He is a dynamo, what grandma would have called a real live wire. He dives and spearfishes mostly for fun. His day job is repairing MRI and CT scanners and other nuclear imaging equipment. He is exactly the kind of charming knucklehead savant you need on a day like today. I was able to sit upright long enough to ask him to describe the early days of the lionfish siege in this part of the Gulf.

"So, we first started seeing them showing up here probably four or five years ago. The first year we seen like one or two. And we'd alert FWC and they were like, 'Well where'd you see it? Let's get some maps going.' Then the science started and every time we came in they wanted to know . . . I mean they were meeting us at the dock asking questions. So, concern was growing and we didn't realize it was going to bloom like this. The next year, it quadrupled. And then the year after that, it was 100-fold more than the prior year. It's been an explosion and they have just taken over."

John McCain, smiling a wide smile and vomiting calmly across from me, is a sales manager from Dive Rite, a manufacturer of scuba equipment. Next to him is Carl Molitor, an underwater photographer, calm as the Buddha and somehow eating a breakfast of yogurt and fruit. Next to Carl is Allie ElHage, who has been trying very hard to light a cigarette in the wind for the last few minutes. He invented and makes and sells the Zookeeper, a length of wide, clear PVC pipe with a plastic flange at one end and a Kevlar bag at the other, into which one stuffs one's speared lionfish. He is smiling too, and when he leans back and tips his face to the sun he is a picture of absolute happiness. Alex Page, salon owner and paralegal and recreational slayer of lionfish, sits on the midships gear locker with the peaceful mien of a man on his third morning at the spa. Everyone on this little boat but me is a lionfish serial killer.

The last thing you see of Pensacola as you motor out into the Gulf are the checkerboard water towers at the Naval Air Station. That's what the town is famous for, naval aviators. Fighter jocks. And for prizefighter Roy Jones Jr. Otherwise, the travel posters are filled with beaches, seafood, board shorts, and T-shirts and flip-flops. It's the panhandle Eden.

Here's how it works, even on a day as rough as this. You and your buddies head out past the horizon, about 18 miles. You'll locate by GPS and by chart and by fish-finder an underwater structure likely to harbor a population of lionfish. Some of these structures are known to every charter captain everywhere, and some are jealously guarded secrets. There aren't many coral reefs in the northern Gulf—it's mostly a hard sand bottom down there—so these underwater features are almost entirely man-made. Picture a pyramid of I-beams six or eight feet high, or a sphere the same size. The state sinks them to promote habitat for sport fishing. Most of them anyway. There are some shipwrecks down there too, and some "habitat" sunk by enterprising locals in less enlightened times, like rusted school bus bodies and little hillocks of old appliances.

As a charter captain, Andy is a great example of a grassroots response to an environmental problem. He was taking folks out spearfishing for snapper and triggerfish and he was seeing more and more lionfish crowding them out of the habitats.

"It just seemed like a light suddenly came on. I had written in to someone at one of the local chambers of commerce, I think we've got a big problem here. We need to probably address it and I wasn't sure how to go about doing that. The Perdido Key Chamber of Commerce said, 'Well, we've got some funds available for special projects. Why don't we at least raise some awareness?' I go, 'That's a great idea. How do we go about doing it?' Let's put together a tournament. It was a little rough at first, but we managed to pull off four or five small tournaments the first year that we had some funding. That just got the whole ball rolling pretty fast."

With the water coming over the bow, you're not going to anchor, you're going to circle while your divers head down in twos and threes. The water out here is between 90 and 120 feet deep, so the divers breathe nitrox from their tanks, a cocktail of nitrogen and oxygen that allows them to make safer trips up and down and stay a little longer on the bottom. Program all that into your dive computer, and it gives back a precise dive profile: how long it takes to descend, how long you can stay, and how fast you can resurface. These are quick "bounce" dives, about 10 minutes descending, 10 minutes on the bottom, 10 minutes back. And these are all very experienced divers. But even for them, it's a bruising proposition trying to pull on gear while being flung from corner to corner, falling, colliding, tripping, swearing. Did I mention they're all carrying spears? You hunt lionfish with what amounts to a modest trident, powered by a short length of surgical tubing.

That's okay, fellas, I'll wait here.

"Are we parked?" the divers yell.

"Yep," says Andy, and the guys wobble the regulators into their mouths and roll backward into the water with a splash.

And that's how we spend the day. Two or three of us always on board and two or three of us almost continually over the side hunting lionfish. Crocs and Kevlar gloves and weapons-grade sunglasses slosh around the bilge. We circle the divers' bubbles until they're ready for pickup. A lot of the exchanges at the stern ladder go like this:

"How many did you get?"

"Twenty-five or thirty."

"How many did you leave?"

"None."

Then empty the Zookeepers into the cooler, get the lionfish on ice, and head for the next spot. Andy peers into the fish-finder; Barry tells another story; Allie lights another cigarette. It's all jawboning and affectionate insult and classic rock on the loudspeaker, "Radar Love" and PG-13 punch lines. Barry hauls the jumbo sandwiches out at midday and the Italian dressing and the peanut butter crackers and I excuse myself to go below. The boys are bringing up fish a dozen or two at a time. At one point, Alex brings up more than 100 fish himself. This is why we came. He is a giant killer.

"Be afraid, lionfish, be very afraid," says Barry.

The rest of the day is a montage of iridescent water and Tintoretto sky, wisecracks and tattoos and lionfish. The coolers slowly fill, and by late afternoon we're surfing back to the pass. The wind is up and the trip home rolls like a motocross track. "I'm tired, man," says Allie to no one in particular.

"But it's addictive, man, like Angry Birds," Barry says, and we rise and fall and ride the crests home.

Somewhere far to the east of us, over the horizon, there is an all-women's team, the first ever, and from what we can make out on the radio, they've been taking many, many fish. But it's hard to know for sure; sandbagging and gamesmanship are a big part of the competition. You never want anyone to know your real numbers until the fish are totaled on Sunday. For now, the women and their lionfish are a distant rumor.

We're back at the dock just before sunset. We might have speared more than 400 lionfish. Or we might not have. I am asked to keep mum on the matter. We are met by a couple of marine biologists. These tournaments are a terrific resource for scientists. Tonight, they're checking the females for egg sacs, researching effective ways to interrupt that prodigious lionfish reproductive cycle. They'll be at it for hours, well into darkness, and will handle every one of those fish.

As it says on Barry's Zookeeper, LEAVE NO LIONFISH BEHIND.

Saturday

It's so windy today, and the surf so much worse, that most teams do not go back out. We do not go back out.

The women's team goes back out. No one has seen them yet. They remain a whisper filled with static, a ghost across the horizon, a figment. Talk of their courage and their madness is a near constant for the day.

For the rest of us, it's a hot sun and calypso on the loudspeakers and 700-horsepower pickup trucks in the parking lot.

The point of the dry land portion of the tournament, the weekend-long lionfish festival in the small park out on the Plaza de Luna, is educational. Informational. And tasty. Once you see the banners in the little park, you begin to understand the statewide strategy for lionfish management.

"Eat 'em to beat 'em"

"Edible Invaders"

"Be the Predator"

"Remove—Eat—Report"

The exhibition tents and displays are evenly divided between things you can read and things you can eat. There are lionfish cooking demonstrations all day, given by well-known local chefs, and long lines to taste the samples. This morning it's Asian wraps done up with lionfish tenders. By noon it's a 10-minute wait to try one. One tent over, Capt. Robert Turpin of the Escambia County Marine Resources Division is delivering an informational presentation to the crowd. "Remember, folks," he says into the wind noise, "lionfish are venomous, not poisonous."

This is a central tenet of the "eat 'em to beat 'em" master plan. Consumers don't know lionfish very well. Even though a lionfish sting is sharp and painful, the meat of the fish itself is safe to eat. Unlike fugu, Japan's riskiest delicacy, lionfish is harmless. The fish has to be handled carefully when caught and when filleted, but for customers in a restaurant or at the seafood counter of their local grocery, lionfish is no more of a threat than salmon or flounder or cod. Venomous, not poisonous, is the drumbeat of the whole weekend.

Because the only way to control the lionfish invasion in this hemisphere will be to create a market large enough to turn them into a national cash fish.

But you can't do that by spearing them one at a time. Especially not at depths greater than commercial divers can safely and routinely cull them. You need to start harvesting them in large, dependable numbers. And for that, you need to figure out how to trap them. Or kill them with submersibles, drones, or remote-operated vehicles.

Walk this way to the tent of Steve Gittings, chief scientist for NOAA's National Marine Sanctuary System. If you were asked to paint the portrait of a distinguished, thoughtful, slightly-gray-at-the-temples National Oceanic and Atmospheric Administration PhD, he'd be your guy. On his display table are a number of models of a bell trap, a kind of semiautomated snare that rests on the sea bottom, then closes over, catches, and hoists up lionfish in quantity.

I asked him to thumbnail Florida's lionfish problem, just so we know.

"I think it boils down to two levels of activity that lionfish do. One is eating any small fish that they can eat, but that means those fish are not available for other fish to eat, commercial or otherwise, so that's a whole ecosystem-trophic effect. It's a collapse. Could be a collapse."

"On the other end of the spectrum," he goes on, "they're eating juveniles of the fish that would become commercially available. So,

why are people not yet saying, 'There's no more grouper. There's
no more snapper'? Well, it might be the juveniles of those species
have not reached adulthood—and won't, because they're being
eaten by lionfish. So if lionfish are eating a lot of juveniles of snapper, grouper, there's all of a sudden going to be a collapse at the
level of species entering the adult phase. That will eventually show
up as no more snapper-grouper."

That's it, that's the lionfish apocalypse. But Gittings is an opti-
mist.

"I'm still hopeful that it'll be a non-apocalypse because I hope
nature will figure it out. But, at least, as far as the evidence goes . . .
so far, apocalypse. It could be.

"But, I have to trust in nature, because for a lot of previous
invasive species, land or sea, nature eventually figures it out. With
disease, with parasites, with predators. So something's going to get
these things. Right now, they're taking over. They reproduce better than rabbits, eat like crazy, and nothing eats them.

"There are these places, though, where you just go, 'Where
are the lionfish?' So, does that mean non-apocalypse, or does that
mean they haven't gotten here yet? Does it mean they will? Does it
mean they won't? Does it mean local control is taking care of the
problem? I think it's that in large measure.

"Local control does do a lot of good. You hear people here talk
about how they are not finding lionfish near shore. That's probably because people are shooting them. The farther offshore you
get, the more fish you see.

"So, I think we have to treat it like an apocalypse, but even as
a scientist I think it's going to work itself out, and become some
kind of balance of nature."

And the deepwater traps?

"You can talk about local control in shallow water using divers.
That's doing a good job. I think we ramp it up as much as possible
to minimize anything that inhibits that from happening. But that
helps us down to that depth.

"But now we've got to tackle the deepwater problem. And do
regional control. And how do you do that? You've got to engage
lots of people, and maybe lots of different ways. I believe the fishing communities, they answer to that. I don't think that conservation people like myself can buy a bunch of ROVs and go down and
shoot them and do things. The fisherman who has a good ROV

or some other way of catching lionfish might do that, and that's a good thing, because they get to (a) kill fish and (b) sell fish and make money. And take the pressure off the other species while they're doing it.

"So that's why I got into the thinking about traps to deal with deepwater populations. My logic was, Let's design traps that fishermen would be comfortable with, which is mechanical. Fully mechanical, easily deployed, easily retrieved, you can put a bunch of them on a fishing boat. And then we've got to deal with the regulatory matters related to that."

In the next tent over, there's a beautiful mermaid in a chaise longue talking to children about ecology and our collective responsibility to the environment. There's a long line of kids—and their dads—waiting to speak to her.

Around the corner, I talk to Brian Asher, a diver and spearman, and one of the directors of SEALEG, a nonprofit trying to grow the lionfish business into sustainability.

"As a business problem, we have this incredible supply of lionfish. They're breeding rapidly. And on the other end, you have restaurants and grocery stores. You have this huge demand, and there's really no efficient way of connecting the two right now.

"The traps, though, haven't been available until the last two or three months when NOAA published the plans, and that's an inexpensive, easily deployable trap design. Taking commercial fishing operations, and having them focus on this would be . . . I mean, just huge gains can be made out of that. But it's convincing that fishing community, and then, on the flip side of that, convincing the public that, hey, this is something good to eat. And there's still a lot of resistance in the public."

Hence all the tastings. And "venomous, not poisonous."

"Right, and again, we enjoy diving, we enjoy our reefs. The first time I pulled up a lionfish, and it had a shovelhead lobster baby in its stomach, it was like, all right, game on. I want to go down, and I want to spear-fish for my allotment of snapper or grouper, or I want to pick up spiny lobster—those little bastards are eating what I am, eating my stuff! Well, someone needs to do something to fix that and it might as well be us."

One of the ways to break through with the public would be to get a big national retailer on board. Guess who's here this weekend with their own tent? Whole Foods Market.

Dave Ventura is the grocery chain's Florida regional seafood coordinator. The stores have been rolling lionfish out on a test basis for the last two years or so. The response has been overwhelmingly positive.

"Our customers here in Florida are very well educated about our ecosystem, our environment, are passionate about protecting them. They're very happy to hear that the Whole Foods in Florida has taken the lead on trying to be part of the solution to remove the lionfish from the water.

"What I can say is we've been selling lionfish for 15 months and I'm happy to report we've sold over 30,000 pounds.

"You know, everybody seems to realize that the good news is we scratched the surface. We developed a market, we know there's a market. Now it's like, hey, how do we get it on scale? How do we remove the lionfish in large volume? Once we accomplish that, then I think I can say confidently that we are making a dent, making a difference. Right now, I think we've been very successful in creating a public awareness."

And Whole Foods is developing its own product lines too, like smoked lionfish. There are a million ways to prepare it. In fact, do an image search for "whole fried lionfish." It's a centerpiece showstopper at several local restaurants, with the fins fanned golden brown in all directions. At the end of the meal, they hand out the spines as toothpicks.

So we're going to fight the rapaciousness of one species with the bottomless appetites of another. Ours. Lionfish in this hemisphere have only one enemy. Us.

But it's going to take some doing.

Because "venomous, not poisonous" sounds like something Truman Capote might have said about Gore Vidal on *The Dick Cavett Show.*

In which I speak to the mermaid

Saturday night, and there's a lionfish tasting.

This is upstairs at the Bodacious Olive, a restaurant and event space on a charming old-town stretch of brick storefronts not far from the park and the tournament tents, across from a Pilates studio.

The wind howls and low clouds worry the rooftops, but inside the Edison bulbs glow and the wineglasses sparkle and the test kitchen is as snug and clean as a catalog layout. There are 40 or so of us here, sponsors and spear hunters and dive masters, wives and husbands and scientists, captains and mates and mermaids. Celebrity Flora-Bama "chef-advocate" Jon Gibson is making lionfish tacos and lionfish sashimi and talking about sustainability and lionfish deliciousness.

There's Captain Andy, and there's Allie and Brian and John and Steve. Barry isn't here. He's across town at Pensacola State for a screening of the documentary *Reef Assassin,* produced by Mark Kwapis and edited by Maribeth Abrams. It's all about the lionfish invasion, but thanks to a scheduling wormhole these two events are happening at the same time. Some of the people *at* the movie should be here. Some of the people *in* the movie are standing right in front of me. Confused, I talk to the mermaid. Her name is Moira Dobbs. She is from Plano, Texas—where she runs a mermaid school.

I'm in italics, and a business suit.

Do you find that the kids retain the things you tell them about lionfish?

"Absolutely. And what's so great is Coast Watch Alliance not only does amazing things for the lionfish invasion issue, but they also are big into marine debris awareness and cleanup. When I do these in-character performances, if they're a birthday party, if they're an event, I bring balloons, straws, fishing line, different things that I pick up at the bottom of the ocean as a diver, and I say, 'Hey, it was so nice to meet you, when I go home look at all these things that are all over my house,' and I watch it wash over these kids. And it's creating little eco-warriors."

She looks just about exactly how you'd picture a mermaid. Pale. Pretty. Lots of auburn hair. In fact, think of Ariel easing out of her twenties, on her way to a job interview, and you'll have it. But out there under the tent, on her chaise, sun bright and the bay sparkling, wearing the tail and her magnificent fin, talking to children, the illusion is complete.

So how long have you been doing this?

"Professionally, a couple years now. I host a full-time year-round professional mermaid school, that's actually in landlocked DFW, Texas."

Do you get a lot of good turnout, in Dallas–Fort Worth?

"We do, and many walks of life, for mermaid school, and that also allows me to establish a great performance troupe that does the same kind of in-character performances that I do. Birthday parties, ocean education, library readings, stuff like that."

Are you a lionfish hunter on your own time?

"I am, I am. Yes."

So you know all these guys?

"Yes. As a mermaid and a diver."

I was going to say, do a lot of the dads hit on the mermaid, when they bring the kids over?

"We get the 'Hey, speaking mythologically, I don't know if mermaids wear tops!' We call those 'merverts.' But yes, I'm all about the banter."

So the tail . . . "That thing I was wearing today is a free-diving mono-fin embedded inside 40 pounds of platinum Dragon Skin silicone. Yeah. So you can free-dive in the ocean in that thing."

Hot, though, on land.

"Yes. It is hot. It's neutrally buoyant, and really wonderful to swim in the ocean, or pool. But it's a little rough after a few hours. I do dry out. Every two to three hours, I take a 30-minute break. You need to. Your feet are inside of that really heavy fluke. The fluke is the bottom of the tail that you see. It's kind of like being en pointe, in ballet."

So if you could tell America one last thing, as the mermaid spokesperson—

"Yes . . ."

—on behalf of the lionfish invasion awareness—

"Yes . . ."

—what would you say?

"Seek, find, and destroy, man."

Truth is, lionfish tastes pretty great. The raw flesh of the fish is opalescent, fine-grained and smooth, and nearly translucent, with a flavor to match. On the tongue, uncooked, it melts fast and tastes faintly of the sea—a memory of salt rather than salt itself. Baked, broiled, fried, poached, grilled, seared, or blackened, the meat of the fish is firm and white and buttery. It takes and holds whatever flavors you throw at it, whether you're making ceviche or fish and chips. It stands up to Cajun rub and to citrus and to wasabi and to remoulade and cilantro and garlic and ginger and cumin and aioli. It won't back down from red peppers or green chilies. It is as fearless as the person cooking it.

Everyone lines up for samples. Lip-smacking ensues.

"Don't be afraid of it," Jon Gibson says low and sweet to us all. "This is a versatile fish." He's slicing fillets so thin you could read a newspaper through them if anyone still read newspapers. "Just remember, everybody, the fish is venomous, not poisonous."

And out we all go into that windy evening.

Sunday

Most of the tents were blown down overnight, so the park looks forlorn as folks work to reset for the big day. There's Captain Andy picking up chairs and tables while Adele rolls in the deep on the PA. The early crowd is sparse, but by midmorning, even under threat of rain, the little plaza is filled again, and the music rises with the smoke from the grills and the waves pound the seawall and the crowd waiting for lionfish-stuffed jalapeno poppers is as long as the line for the crawfish boil.

You hear fragments on the wind, from the chefs and the experts and the kids and their parents . . .

"they reproduce every three or four days"

"these are fantastic"

"it's really good"

"aren't they poisonous?"

"venomous"

"go tell your restaurants you want lionfish"

"there's not much I won't eat"

Early in the afternoon, it's time for the count and the presentations to the winners. Captain Andy handles the microphone and the afternoon is an inventory of his gratitude and his enthusiasm. He and the crowd are stoked.

Biggest fish speared was a little over 17 inches.

Our boat, "Team Niuhi," finishes third, with 539 lionfish. "Full Stringer," a crew from up the road, is second, with 859 fish. Team "Hang On"—the all-women's team—wins going away, with 926 lionfish. The crowd roars and many tears are shed. Allie won't stop hugging people. For several hours.

There's a presentation of plaques and prize money and prizes, many of them quite nice, from dive gear to drones to nights out on the town, but it's pretty clearly pride everyone competes for.

Rachel Bowman is first among equals on the women's team. She is a commercial spear fisher down in the Keys and appears to be the lean, inked, freckled, and clear-eyed apex predator for the entire state of Florida.

She shoots and sells lionfish every day.

"I've got about a 40-mile range that I work, from Alligator Reef to American Shoals, and I have my spots. I have secret spots. I have public spots. The commercial fishermen in the Keys have been amazing as far as sharing their numbers with me, especially the commercial lobster guys. They know where there's big piles of rubble that other people don't know about because their traps get smacked on them. They really appreciate what I'm doing, and they help me out as much as possible. I like to think that the Whole Foods thing has made them more money because now the lionfish in their traps, they're not worth $2 a pound anymore. Now they're worth $6."

You're fighting them to a draw down there.

"Yeah, I've got commercial trap guys that tell me that last year, the lionfish numbers kind of stopped going up, and this year they've actually gone down a little bit.

"I know Dr. Stephanie Green with Oregon State University has been doing some research with the organization REEF. They found, on isolated coral heads in the Bahamas, that not only is there a decline in the lionfish population, but there's actually a resurgence of the native fish populations. What we're doing—we're never going to get rid of them—but I have to believe we're making a difference. She and I measured fish today and the whole table was covered in egg sacs. Those are egg sacs that are never going to have a chance to do any kind of damage."

What do you think of Doc Gittings's traps?

"Well, I've got a brother-in-law who's a commercial lobster trapper, and this year in three months, he pulled up 6,000 pounds of lionfish in his lobster traps. That's in sandy bottom, 200–300 feet, where divers can't go. So, maybe if he was allowed to deploy those traps when lobster season is closed, then that's another possibility."

Rachel Bowman has a diver-down flag enameled on her big toenail. She is the real reef assassin.

Grayson Shepard is the Panhandle charter captain who masterminded the women's team. Like Captain Andy, it is impossible to judge his age. He is sun-red and fit and rawboned and could be 35 or 235. He is now the Red Auerbach of lionfish, and we sat for a while to talk in the Florida Fish and Wildlife Conservation Commission motor home.

"I put together this little dream team that are just hard-core and fun as hell to hang out with. And they are dedicated and they are killers of the deep. They went with me in four-foot seas the past two days where a lot of men would not have gone. Several of my fellow charter captains canceled trips and they were freaking out. I'm like, I'm going. The girls are like 'go go go!' My buddies were on the radio like, 'Are you okay?' 'Are you all right?' I'm like, man we're fine. We're kicking ass out here."

I explained to Captain Shepard about the throwing up.

"Well they didn't throw up. The girls suited up and went down. Over and over and over again."

Captain Shepard is himself a little bit of a sentimental badass.

"This crazy little lionfish has brought together so many incredibly cool people. We all have the same screw loose in our head. That same screw makes you an interesting, easygoing kind of person. It's a little community. We all have this common obsession with lionfish. You could put all of us in a van and drive us across the country. We would get along like peas and carrots. We're best friends. When you meet us, we're all like of the same tribe. It gives us the chills."

Even with most teams canceling their Saturday fishing, the tournament still brought in nearly 4,000 lionfish. Turns out the only thing more rapacious on earth than a lionfish is you and me.

So I ask folks as they leave, "You think eating them might be able to help stop the invasion?"

And they'll say, "It's fantastic, I hope it helps."

or

"Fingers crossed!"

or

"It ain't gonna hurt. It's gonna help a little bit, I guess, but I don't know. That's a big Gulf out there. That's all they can do to try and stop it? I don't see how that's going to stop it."

*

For the last hour or two of the afternoon, everyone puts their feet up. After three days of work and worry and nausea, six-foot surf, and 100-foot bounces, there's finally time to sit around the tents and the trailers and drink spiced rum and tell some lies. This everyone does with great relief.

Music plays and the wind eases and the bay is a luminous green.

Andy says, "I think it went great. We had some tough obstacles and I was a little bit nervous that maybe we wouldn't have the best turnout and you know, under the circumstances, with the tough weather and all, I think we did a fantastic job and everybody really came together and they went out and worked real hard at getting their fish. They came in and they were all very supportive and they all had an awesome time and I think everything went very smoothly. I think it came out fantastic. I've been on the water long enough to know that you cannot predict the weather and even when you do, you're wrong."

Allie is still hugging people.

"Let's go eat," Andy says.

The Big Finish

So, quiet and tired, everyone caravans to the Sake Café, a sushi place a couple of neighborhoods over, eating what they speared, now set out on two long tables full of hand rolls and sashimi, chopsticks and wasabi and cold beer. The kitchen bustles, but the place isn't crowded. It's early yet, even for Sunday dinner in Pensacola. At the head of the longest table Andy's wearing that enigmatic smile, that sidewise Andy smile, but Barry is the one who stands to speak.

He thanks everyone for their hard work and for their excellent spear-fishing skills and for fighting this good fight. He thanks the event sponsors for their contributions and the restaurant for making dinner. He talks about what all this means to the environment and to Florida and to him. When he talks about the camaraderie of the divers and the friendship and yes, the love, he surprises himself by choking up. He gathers himself and goes on just a little longer.

"You gotta eat 'em to beat 'em," he says at the end.

And everyone applauds.

Dolly back, roll credits, that's the last scene in your Hollywood movie.

But if you're writing a magazine story, maybe you don't end it there. Not like that. Not with sushi and a speech. Too upbeat. Too certain.

Nor can your story end with that unremarkable wind steady off the bay, not with the striking of the tents and boxing of the left-over brochures, not with the loading of the vans or the vendors rolling up their banners or emptying their grills, and not with the stragglers wandering back to the parking lot under a Sunday sky as flat and gray as gunmetal.

What you want is something to remember them all, a way to think of Florida and that crazy light and that water and those men and those women and those fish.

So maybe you'll look back, no matter where you go or what you do, and see them all forever at the dock that Friday night, the whole wrung-out, laughing, groaning boatload, Andy and Allie and Barry and John and Carl and Alex and those scientists gathered around those big boxes of fish, those big coolers filled with ice and fins and Japanese fans, the sun faltering in the west, tangled in the trees, shadows long on the ground and the sky a low flame up there in the spreaders and the shrouds. One of the marine biologists leans down into the cooler and gingerly plucks up another lionfish. "I've got you now," she says to herself and for a second you don't know if she means one fish or the whole species and anyway you can barely hear her because Andy's got the stereo cranked on the boat and Van Halen is playing "Hot for Teacher." It's all a trick of the light, sure, too sentimental and too droll, but it's also true and that's the beauty of it.

It's a long fight. And maybe the lionfish win.

Maybe that's your ending.

CLAY SKIPPER

Joel Embiid Is Seven Feet Tall and Rising

FROM GQ

SO THERE HE was, in the middle of the jungle, face-to-face with a lion.

Joel Embiid was still in Cameroon then, just six years old. It didn't matter. He'd been sent away from his village, part of a tribal initiation. And now, it was kill or be killed. The young Embiid took his spear and shoved it through the lion's mouth. Then he returned to his village triumphant, the lion draped over his shoulders. And on that day, as the story goes, he became a man.

Unfortunately, it's complete bullshit.

Read enough stories about the Philadelphia 76ers' star big man —or speak to enough people who know him well—and eventually this legend will come up. It's a well-worn thread in the fabric of the myth surrounding Joel Embiid (pronounced jo-ell em-beed). That he has continued to tell it suggests both a playful charm and deft cunning at the heart of the seven-foot man. But keeping such a tale alive also seems unnecessary given the wild and improbable life that Joel Embiid is actually living right now. "I always say, 'My life is a movie,'" Embiid tells me. "Everything happened so fast."

Here's a guy who didn't play basketball until he was 15 and has, at 24, joined the first tier of NBA stars, with a positionless skill set that looks an awful lot like the future of basketball—this despite spending more time injured on the bench than in uniform in his five seasons. Then there's the fact that he barely spoke English less than a decade ago and is now the NBA's deadliest trash-talker, its most riotous follow, and maybe the internet's last good troll. He's already contending for the league's most beloved player, and might soon become its Most Valuable too. His is a *true* story crazy enough to warp the dimensions of possibility.

At age 15, as a skinny Cameroonian pushing seven feet, Embiid shows up to his first ever basketball practice. It took him months to persuade his father—fearful that the game was too dangerous —to let him play. He promptly dunks on someone. He remembers the feeling as "regular, because I'm seven feet." Basketball intrigues him. He recalls watching the 2009 NBA Finals between the Los Angeles Lakers and Orlando Magic. He'd seen people in his neighborhood putting up bricks, but here was Kobe Bryant, hitting *everything*. He wanted to shoot like that, to be more than just huge. But being huge gets him noticed nonetheless. Fellow Cameroonian and current Los Angeles Clipper Luc Mbah a Moute invites Embiid to a camp, then helps guide the young talent to his former high school in Florida. Word spreads. *Have you seen this kid? His talent is raw, but his seven-foot frame is the type you can hang hope on.* He lands a scholarship to Kansas, gets hurt, and leaves for the NBA anyway. The future can't wait. He becomes the third overall pick in the 2014 NBA Draft, tasked with saving a terrible Philadelphia 76ers franchise in a post-Iverson malaise. But then he stays hurt. For two years, he sits and people wonder whether his body is broken for good. He bides his time while rehabbing by becoming a social-media star—making himself into a Hall of Fame internet personality before he even steps on the court. When, finally, he does play, he's somehow even better than advertised. The promise was real, the hype warranted. He gets the $148 million franchise contract and becomes an All-Star.

Which brings us here, to the beginning of the 2018 NBA season. Joel Embiid looks like he might finally emerge out from underneath the shadow of the enormous expectations that have hovered over him since we first learned someone like him could exist. So maybe he can't tell this story yet, because he has no idea how this movie ends. Neither do we. Which means: we've just dropped into the world of Joel Embiid right when the wild, true story of Joel Embiid—crazy as it may already be—is just starting to get really interesting.

The smell of chicken in Joel Embiid's apartment is overwhelming—less *someone-cooked-chicken-earlier* and more *someone-is-running-a-small-Wingstop*. Unsurprisingly, there on the top of his marbled counter rest two plates of chicken wings. There are also three plates of Cajun pasta and a plate each of Brazilian cookies—"they're trash," Embiid says upon trying one—croissants, apples, and clementines hovering nearby, not to mention the beef skewers, crepes, and the rest of the leftovers I barely make out in a brief glimpse into the fridge.

"My girlfriend is coming," he tells me, which hardly feels like an explanation for this quantity of food. When I ask if he can tell me who he's dating, he says no but offers that she's "pretty big at what she does." The restless internet mob has since suggested she's *Sports Illustrated* swimsuit model Anne de Paula. (Embiid admits that dating while in the NBA is not without its challenges. "You gotta do your background check," he says. "You don't want to be that guy marrying a girl that someone else in the NBA has been with . . . I'm sure some guys end up getting married to women that have been around. And maybe on the court they also get told"—here he lowers his voice to a whisper—"Hey, I fucked your wife.")

About 15 minutes later, Embiid's bodyguard, Bubs, shows up, carrying a party-size aluminum foil tray of . . . chicken. This seems like an exercise in excess—not just that Joel Embiid has a bodyguard but that the man arrives with jerk wings. At this point, there should be enough chicken wings—though, admittedly, I didn't count—for Embiid to feed at least one person on each of the 41 floors below him.

While we talk, the 7'2" Embiid sits on the corner of his countertop—an oak tree that has paused to catch its breath. He wears a black-and-white Maison Kitsuné tee displaying the NBA logo and black Jordan sweat shorts that have the 2018 NBA All-Star logo on the right thigh, clearly a piece of swag from whatever closet comes with being honored as one of the league's best. On his wrists he has black rubber wristbands that say, ON A MISSION AND BLESSED—from a larger stash in a box nearby that also includes UNGUARDABLE, UNSTOPPABLE, and TRUST THE PROCESS. His hair—a mess of tangled twists—likely extends his height closer to 7'4". On his face the stubble is thick at the chin, patchy up near his sideburns, a sign of youth on an otherwise overdeveloped man. English is one of three languages he speaks, and when he talks the words come low and slow, blending together as if maybe they got tired traveling all the way up his torso.

He tells me that the food comes from his chef, who stops by

four or five times a week to drop off meals. It's the superstar athlete's attempt at a more carefully crafted diet, a corrective to the eating habits that became the object of scrutiny and internet laughter a few years ago, when it was reported that Embiid consumed pitchers of Shirley Temples. Embiid used to drink one (a single Shirley Temple, not a pitcher's worth) almost every day but has since cut back to merely "once in a while," he tells me while grabbing a bottled water from the fridge, as if to prove his point. (Bill Self, Embiid's coach at Kansas, tells me that Embiid was the "least mature eater" he's ever seen: "This dude would come to the house and go right to the plate of brownies and take the plate home, and that would be all that he would eat.") Of course, the diet is only one piece in a much larger puzzle, one that has proved to be the hinge on which Embiid's career swings from dormant to dominant: his body.

When it's working, he plays like an athlete the NBA has never seen before. It's not what he has—height, agility, strength—but what he lacks: the gangly clumsiness that ships standard with the awkwardly tall. People his size (other NBA stars Kevin Durant, Kristaps Porzingis, and Anthony Davis, for instance) often look as if they've achieved their height by being pulled from both ends on some sort of torturous medieval Pilates reformer. Embiid, on the other hand, looks like God hovered the computer mouse at the top-right corner of his JPEG and dragged diagonally. Odd, then, that it's been the well-proportioned Embiid—rather than the skinny guys who *look* like they're going to snap like twigs—who has spent so much of his career injured.

A bad back prematurely ended his one-year college stopover at Kansas. He was still expected to be taken with the first pick in the 2014 NBA Draft anyway, so great was the talent his body promised. Then a stress fracture in his foot in the days leading up to the draft scared teams into thinking that he was yet another big man destined to spend his career on the bench. Something built to break —no matter its promise or wingspan—will probably break.

The Philadelphia 76ers drafted him anyway with the third overall pick. Sam Hinkie, the general manager at the time, was one year into a daring plan to rebuild Philly's floundering franchise, forgoing wins in order to land high draft picks and using those picks to acquire potential franchise-altering talent like Embiid. If it worked, after two or three years, he'd have a brand-new super-team stacked with young, promising pieces. This farsighted plan was later dubbed The Process, and Embiid was its cornerstone.

The Sixers' hope, after drafting their prized—though hobbled —pick, was that Embiid would miss only a year, max. But the summer of 2015 brought more bad news: he'd need another surgery and would miss his second straight season. Hinkie's Process was either not working or taking too long—it didn't matter. He resigned under pressure and Embiid became the scapegoat. On top of the injury frustrations in his first two years, Embiid also had to cope with the tragic loss of his younger brother, killed by an out-of-control truck back home in Africa.

"All I wanted to do was go back home and, like, never come back—just disappear and stay home," says Embiid.

Instead, Embiid stayed and, with time on his hands, found a different way to neutralize those who placed the burden of the Sixers' woes squarely on his broken back. He mastered social media at a time when social media was becoming the most important outlet for the modern NBA—a place where fans and players alike could find all the league news, trash talk, and leaked J. R. Smith DMs they could ever want. (The NBA even has its Twitter handle *on* the official game ball.)

Embiid had gotten an early glimpse at the power of NBA Twitter when he became a meme the day he was selected by the Sixers. On account of his foot injury, Embiid wasn't in attendance for the draft, and so after he was picked, the ESPN broadcast cut to a satellite feed of him watching from Los Angeles. The tape delay was such that Embiid sat completely mum, expression unchanged, for nearly 15 seconds. Of course, the Sixers had been such a woeful organization that viewers were left to wonder whether Embiid's seeming lack of enthusiasm wasn't a hilarious dig at the misbegotten 76ers. Twitter lit up with jokes, all of them along the lines of: *TFW*—"that feel when" for the uninitiated offline folks reading —*you get drafted by the Philadelphia 76ers.*

In NBA Twitter, Embiid saw a natural outlet for his brand of charm, a charisma that made him popular even in his brief year at Kansas—especially with the wives of Bill Self's coaching staff. "He knew exactly which one liked to have the hug with both arms, and which one liked the left-arm hug, or which one liked the right-arm hug," Self fondly remembers. "He had that audience down perfect, where he could have people basically buying into everything he's selling. He was very, very bright that way." In the same way that Embiid could read a room, he could size up the NBA's social-media landscape—which was full of boring athletes offering boilerplate platitudes. So he behaved the way you might if, through the power of some dark magic, you woke up in the body of a 7'2" man with thirsty Twitter fingers and exactly zero fucks. He asked Kim Kardashian to slide into his DMs (before moving on to Rihanna); he retweeted his own draft meme; he nicknamed himself The Process. (Asked what happens to the Process nickname if he goes to another team, Embiid says, "I want to be in Philly for the rest of my life," which seems like something only somebody who has been in Philly for less than five years might say.)

Joel Embiid's social-media cocktails—a mix of playful antics, irony, and self-deprecation—helped defang the flood of criticism that he was still parked on the Sixers bench. Like the time he uploaded a video of him swatting the ever-loving shit out of what must be a six-year-old in front of a crowd full of people. He offset his bullying with the caption "Don't worry lil man we still got the same amount of NBA games played ha #TrustTheProcess #WeAll-FromAfrica." After two years of Embiid sitting with an injury, we didn't know what to expect from Embiid on the court—but we knew exactly what to expect from the sideline. Just as the internet was taking a turn for the worse, he was growing into its last good troll, a lovable avatar slinging viral gold.

When he finally got a chance to play, well, that wasn't so bad either. Embiid made his long-delayed NBA debut at the beginning of 2016, his third season with the Sixers—some 969 days after he'd last played organized basketball. He thought he was going to get booed. Instead, the crowd chanted, "Trust the Process!" (If you want evidence of just how beloved Embiid is, ask yourself: Who else has a *self-given* nickname that is so widely embraced?) In 22 minutes, he scored 20 points and had seven rebounds. He played 30 more games before another season-ending injury (a torn meniscus). Those 31 games, though! This was just two years after the Golden State Warriors had revolutionized basketball, pushing the game even more in the direction of high-paced, high-scoring, making the big man obsolete. And yet, already Embiid looked like the next *next* frontier, where there *were* no big and small men. Everyone would be a lab-created aberration like Embiid, a seven-footer who could dominate in the paint on offense, act as rim protector on defense, and do everything else too: pass with sharp vision, run the court on the fast break, Euro step around the big buffoons matched up against him, slash for dunks, and shoot threes, free throws, and pull-up jumpers with a silky stroke.

The 76ers signed him to a five-year, $148 million contract. That bears repeating. He'd played in exactly 31 games of the 246 for which he'd been on their roster, and yet they decided that those 31 games were transcendent enough to warrant face-of-the-franchise type of money. And it appears they were right to give it to him. Last year, Embiid averaged a double-double, became an All-Star, and finished second in Defensive Player of the Year voting. This year, he says, he'll be upset if he doesn't win DPOY *and* MVP. Michael Jordan and Hakeem Olajuwon both won it in the same year. "It would be good to follow up those guys," he says.

Perhaps more importantly, last season Embiid stayed healthy (though there was a fractured orbital bone, for which he had to wear a spooky protective mask, and he took to calling himself "The Phantom of the Process"). That's a problem for other players— not just because he's unstoppable but because it takes away their go-to trash talk too.

"A lot of guys, when they have nothing to talk [trash] about, and when they know that they're clearly not better than you, they have a tendency to talk about the past, bringing up my injury streak," he says. "I'm really not an injury-prone player. I just had that one injury that took, like, two years."

Last year he played 63 games in the regular season and eight in the playoffs. Yes, the playoffs, two words 76ers fans, until this spring, had only recently heard after the three words "did not make." But with LeBron James going west to L.A. and Joel Embiid healthy, the Philadelphia 76ers are a real threat to win the Eastern Conference. (Of Tristan Thompson's recent comments that his Cleveland Cavaliers, even without James, are still the team to beat in the East, Embiid says, "He's just out of his mind . . . He must be stupid.") He spent this offseason working on every part of his game. What did he improve? "Everything. I never thought I had any flaws, really. It's just about make sure everything I did was perfect." He's never been healthier going into a season. Through the first three games, he's leading the team in minutes (34.3 per game) while averaging 28 points, nearly 11 rebounds, and two blocks per game. It looks like he was right: The Process really *is* to be trusted.

"I'm so much better than I was last year," he says. "I just look at myself, like the only thing that can stop me is like . . ."—and here he pauses to think of something that can stop him—"nothing. That's why I'm excited."

There are 48 stories in the luxury high-rise Joel Embiid calls home. Joel Embiid does not live on the 48th floor. "I don't have that type of money," he says. "All my money goes back to Africa." (Conveniently, he just signed a new shoe deal with Under Armour, the specific details of which were not released, but it reportedly gives him gobs of money and includes charitable initiatives back in Cameroon and in Philly.)

So he settled for the 41st floor, with a view befitting Philly's new king: looking over City Hall, its glowing clock like a neighbor's extremely intrusive night-light. He heads to his bedroom, set off down a hallway. He moves as if trying to conserve energy, with a slow gait that, especially after he emerges with Ugg slippers in the place of low-top Vans, evokes the rhythmic shuffle of a pouty teenager (or an off-duty athlete). I peek around.

He's only living here temporarily—he just bought a place, but it's not ready yet—and the apartment feels that way, barely lived in. There's a room filled with boxes. The bar cart is all cart, no bar, positioned beneath some framed Benjamin Franklin stamps because: Philadelphia! The rest of the "art" includes a painting of a rooster, a photo of a bird taking flight, and what looks like a stock MacBook desktop photo that might be called "Autumn," blown up and framed. In a dark corner of his apartment sits a stack of *NBA Live 19*'s with Joel Embiid on the cover, on top of a stack of *Slam* magazines with Joel Embiid on the cover, on top of a copy of *The TB12 Method: How to Achieve a Lifetime of Sustained Peak Performance* with Tom Brady on the cover. He has not read this book—"I don't read books"—but does say he's "still got about 15, 20 years in the league," so maybe he hopes he can absorb some of Brady's longevity.

Some of this stuff is from the previous owner. Some is Embiid's. It's not clear who owns what. Except for one piece of furniture smack in the middle of his apartment: a custom-made gaming chair, complete with the 76ers logo and the words THE PROCESS printed on it. Embiid is a voracious gamer, sometimes embarking on 12-hour gaming marathons. On our way up to this place, he told the concierge to look out for a PlayStation that was being delivered. (He already has one here, but he wanted to play *FIFA 19*, which was not yet out, and the pre-release download codes they sent him were not working, so he just had a new console sent instead.)

He says the gaming chair was sent to him, which adds up, because Embiid apparently does not like to spend money. Drew Hanlen, a skills coach for a number of NBA stars including Embiid, says that in his first few years living in Philly, Joel didn't have a couch, so he'd just pull a few chairs together and play video games sitting on those.

"I'm like, 'You're a millionaire, buy a couch,'" Hanlen remembers telling Embiid. "And he's like, 'I don't need to spend money on a couch.' And then he finally got one given to him. So now he has a couch."

As Embiid tells it, there wasn't much time to play video games growing up in a middle-class neighborhood in Yaoundé, the capital of Cameroon. He was busy playing sports, or sneaking off to play sports, or running back home from sneaking off to play sports before his mom could catch him. ("When my mom found out, it was bad for me," he says.) His father—a military colonel—didn't want him to play basketball, partly because he worried it might be too physical and partly because, in his dad's head, Embiid's future had already been determined: he would go to France to play professional volleyball, a sport in which he'd shown early promise.

Of course, Embiid didn't grow up dreaming of being a volleyball player. He wanted to be . . . an astronaut, which he realizes now was a job not likely to be showcased at his middle school career fair. "[In] Cameroon, we don't know shit about space," he says. "I don't even know if there's a Cameroonian astronaut. That's what I wanted to become. I wanted to become president, and I wanted to become an astronaut. Because I was really good at math."

But then he grew into Joel Embiid and, after his dad finally relented, tabled his extraterrestrial dreams for basketball, an industry in which, unlike with space exploration, his nation did have a pioneer: Luc Mbah a Moute, currently a forward on the Los Angeles Clippers. Embiid was invited to Mbah a Moute's local camp in Cameroon, where his preternatural talents—and too-big-for-a-spacesuit size—caught the NBA player's eye. Mbah a Moute helped shepherd Embiid to his former high school, Montverde Academy in Florida, where he played a season before transferring to another Florida school, called The Rock School.

When Justin Harden, the coach at The Rock School, heard stories about Embiid at Montverde, he heard about a guy who was so new he was "like Bambi on ice." By the time he got to The Rock School a year later, his raw athleticism stood out. Harden remembers dodgeball and volleyball as particularly dangerous outlets for the young Embiid. "He'd get out there and start hitting, and everybody's scattering like roaches when the light comes on. They weren't about to get a broken face because of this guy," he remembers.

Harden recalls once walking into a basketball practice—appropriately enough, just after finishing a phone call with a college coach interested in Embiid—and seeing his big man bank a three-pointer off the backboard, a particularly clumsy way to hit a normally sexy shot. *Dude, hit the rim,* Harden thought. But then Embiid made seven more, all off the backboard, and Harden realized he was doing it on purpose. It displayed an athletic touch a man of his size really has no business having. "It's really remarkable," Harden says. "I've said it many times: I sincerely think that he probably could have done anything he wanted to put his mind to."

Embiid's mind. It's something all of those who worked closely with him highlight, an uncommon ability to pick up new skills immediately—evident even in high school—that, when paired with his physical gifts, creates an unstoppable combination.

Take, for instance, how Joel Embiid learned to shoot threes: by watching white people on YouTube. "Listen, I know it's a stereotype, but have you ever seen a normal 30-year-old white guy shoot a three-pointer? That elbow is *tucked,* man," he wrote in a piece for the *Players' Tribune.* He also famously watched, repeatedly, a tape of Hakeem Olajuwon in the hopes of perfecting the Hall of Famer's patented Dream Shake, a balletic move that is virtually unstoppable when performed by someone with the size and touch of Olajuwon. Embiid has it too apparently—just ask any of the defenders who've tried to lock him up inside, only to be Dream Shaken out of their shoes. Hanlen says most of the players he works with can learn a new move quickly, but they might take weeks to master it.

"For [Embiid], he might have me demonstrate it ten times. He might ask a few questions. He'll have me demonstrate a couple more times, and then he'll just do it full speed," he details. "And then you'll see him use it the next day, in live play, one-on-one. And you're just shaking your head like, 'How did he already have that?'"

All of this is especially remarkable when you keep in mind that Embiid's only played in 94 NBA games and, because of his past injuries, his minutes in those games were limited. He's just getting started.

"Guys like myself might have played 100, 200 games a year since I was in kindergarten," says Hanlen. "He's probably played 150 games of real organized basketball in his life."

One of those games was a road win last season against the Lakers in which Embiid scored 46 points, grabbed 15 rebounds, and added seven assists *and* seven blocks just for fun. He out-muscled everyone inside, sure, but he also hit threes and face-up jumpers, showcased a point guard–esque vision with his passing, and even displayed a delicate Euro step that's entirely too graceful for someone whose feet are the size of water skis.

Embiid says that was the game when he realized that all those people saying he could be the best player ever might be on to something. "That's when you watch the tapes [and] you start to realize that you can do this nightly," he says. "Like, no one can stop you."

In a postgame interview that night, Embiid was asked how healthy he felt; the sideline reporter wanted a percentage. "Sixty-nine percent," he said, before claiming, later, that he was from Africa and didn't know "why people were making fun of that number."

Ask Joel Embiid how tall he is and he'll lie to you. "I like to say six-eleven," he tells me before adding, more definitively, "I'm six-eleven."

He and I sit at adjacent red leather high stools. My feet rest on the bottom rung. His size 17's, still nestled into those cozy Uggs, are flat on the floor, his legs at a perfect right angle. As if I've just reminded him of a vital task on his to-do list, he picks up his phone—a small lifeboat in the ocean of his palm—and texts the 76ers' senior director of PR, Patrick Rees: "Make sure they list me

at 6'11" this year lol." (Rees will later tell me that, in the 76ers'
official listing, Embiid's height—always at 7'0" or 7'2", maybe because of his changing hairdo—is not going to change, "because
he's not 6'11".")

"People have a tendency to categorize me as a big man," Embiid
says. "I do everything that a guard would do on a basketball court,
so I want to change the game in a way that it's just positionless."

When it comes to NBA players, this is nothing new. Big guys
don't like to be characterized as, well, big guys for fear that it
makes them look like slow oafs. Though Embiid joins a long list
of NBA legends who refuse to admit their membership in the 84-
inch club—Kevin Durant, Kevin Garnett, and Bill Walton among
them—he might just have the toughest time pleading his case, as
massive as he is.

At least part of this desire to seem shorter is tied to a reluctance
to be labeled a center. There is only one spot on each All-NBA and
All-Defensive team for a center. There are three for a forward/
center (an official classification he had changed this offseason).
But it's also that Embiid cares about optics. He knows that being
seen as a slow-footed bruiser who lives in the low-post makes certain haters think he can't do what smaller guys can. And he feeds
off of that.

"I love when people talk trash. I love when people tell me that
I couldn't do this. I love when people tell me that I was gonna be
a bust," he says. "I enjoy when people tell me, you suck, you can't
dribble, you can't shoot, because it's like: gotta go to the gym."

This is the guy Joel Embiid projects to the world: confident,
unflappable, bulletproof. It's a version of the same guy who has
shot an arrow through the heart of the internet—the one who
wears his own jersey to the club, or jogs through the streets of
Philadelphia at night, or shows up at public parks and dunks on
extremely average-looking white dudes (all antics that have been
caught on camera and spread throughout Twitter, always followed
by a stream of laugh-crying emojis). It is not necessarily the same
guy you get when you're sitting across from Embiid. He can be shy,
reticent, reluctant to share. He says he's still scared to approach
a stranger and ask for directions. In conversation, he sometimes
fidgets nervously—his hands balling in his shirt, or pulling on his
shorts, feet shuffling back and forth on the floor, fingers on one

hand massaging the webbing in between his thumb and index finger on the other, dark brown eyes darting down the hallway.

"I don't have trust issues, but it's kind of hard for me to, like, trust somebody," he says. "I always analyze everybody . . . Some people talk to me and I act like I don't understand or I act like I'm not listening, but I hear everything. I observe. I see everything."

For all of us, there can often be a gulf between the person we put into the world and the person we actually are. Joel Embiid is no different. He knows how narratives take shape, which stories get retold. And while the world has taken notice of the avatar that Embiid wants us all to see, he's been watching carefully. On the other side of the carefree guy who cracks wise about killing a lion, being at 69 percent health, or YouTubing "white people shooting three-pointers" is the guy who was perceptive enough to know that we would laugh at those things, who took the time to crack the code to internet fluency, who wanted so badly to be great that he spent *hours* on YouTube watching white people shoot threes and then hours more in the gym practicing them. Always on the other side of the viral Joel Embiid is the one who's a lot more aware—and who gives at least a few more fucks—than we give him credit for. Embiid's friend Michael D. Ratner remembers seeing this side of Joel at a party a couple years back, when he was still hurt.

It was in L.A., a gathering of 30 people or so. Ratner walked away from the group and stumbled upon Embiid, sitting by himself in a dark room. Ratner sat next to him and asked what he was doing. Embiid didn't say anything, just kept scrolling through his phone. Then he pointed it at Ratner. Embiid had searched himself on Twitter and was reading tweet after tweet calling him a bum. Ratner says the one he remembers most was a tweet calling Embiid Greg Oden, the 2007 #1 overall pick who barely had a career in the NBA because of knee injuries.

Ratner recently told Embiid while the two were out for dinner that he always thinks about that moment in the dark when he sees Embiid out on the court, killing it. "You could have just given up there," he told him, "and instead you just used that as fuel." Then he noticed that Embiid had put his face in his shirt. He was crying, in the middle of the restaurant. Ratner thought Embiid was fucking with him, because, well, he's Embiid. But he wasn't.

Embiid remembers that night—and the way he was doubted

then. "People making fun of me. Telling me that I was a bust. That I was done. That I was never going to play in the NBA," he says. As he sits here with me, high above a city now eager to Trust the Process, it's the only moment when he's visibly animated. "I don't take anything for granted. I'm just grateful. I thank God every day. Now look at me. Now we're here talking about having so much potential and being a top-10 NBA player, having a whole city behind you. I never wished this."

It's true. This was never Joel Embiid's dream. He wanted to be an astronaut, remember? Instead, he stumbled into a career as one of the planet's most transcendent athletes. But he still harbors fantasies of going to space.

He knows there could be complications. He learned last year, on a visit to NASA, that he definitely can't fit in the spaceship. Plus: there's the math. Embiid says he's not so sure he's as good with numbers anymore. But he's undeterred. He figures maybe he can get into some program that'll help put him on the path to NASA. The ever-confident Embiid says it'd be "easy" to pick up rocket science once he's done with this job, dunking on people. Despite the obvious hurdles, he estimates that he could be the first seven-footer in space in a year and a half, if he really put in the time.

"I'm just too busy right now," he says.

NATHAN FENNO

A Killing Still Unresolved

FROM THE LOS ANGELES TIMES

SHERRA WRIGHT GUIDED the silver Cadillac SUV through the darkness on a mild night, seven years after search-and-rescue dogs found her ex-husband's body in a Memphis field.

The remains of Lorenzen Wright weighed 57 pounds. The coroner needed dental records to identify the man the Clippers had picked in the first round of the 1996 NBA Draft. Five gunshot wounds were visible in the withered corpse. Two in the head. Two in the torso. One in the right forearm.

The killing remained unsolved, but by last December a long-dormant police investigation had taken on new life. And a task force of federal marshals and Riverside County sheriff's deputies was tracking the Cadillac on Interstate 15 near Norco.

As Sherra drove south with her twin 17-year-old boys, Lamar and Shamar, she relived the Murrieta Mesa High basketball team's five-point win earlier that night. The twins had combined to score 32 points. Sherra told her oldest son, Lorenzen Jr., all about the game on the phone.

Then red and blue lights flashed behind them. The SUV pulled over and a voice amplified by a loudspeaker ordered Sherra to exit the car with her hands up. She started shaking.

More cruisers zoomed up. Guns were drawn, Lamar said. The twins begged their mother to keep her hands up.

They'd met about 25 years earlier, the teenage basketball prodigy from small-town Mississippi still growing into his 6-foot-11 body, and the headstrong daughter of his club coach.

Lorenzen was 16, Sherra five years older. She paid for his hot wings and iced tea on dates, as well as for better clothes, new shoes, even a custom-made suit.

"It was love and hate at the very first sight," she wrote in *Mr. Tell Me Anything*, a 2015 book featuring two characters she later said were based on her and Lorenzen. "He hated that she was all he had been warned she would be. She hated that her interest was officially sparked by a minor."

This article is based on interviews with three of the couple's six children—the first time they've spoken publicly—and others close to the family, in addition to court documents, books, public records, and media accounts.

"Ours is a Love Story, not this horror film that has been erected by the Media," Sherra wrote in a brief letter to the *Los Angeles Times*.

Nicknamed "The Howl" because he screamed after dunking the ball or blocking a shot, Lorenzen earned $55 million over 13 seasons with the Clippers, Atlanta Hawks, Memphis Grizzlies, Cleveland Cavaliers, and Sacramento Kings. Friends thought the couple put on a good show off the basketball court: the stay-at-home mother and doting father enjoying mansions, luxury automobiles, designer clothes, and a family that always appeared to be smiling.

After the Clippers drafted Lorenzen from the University of Memphis with the seventh overall pick in June 1996, Ian Rice became close friends with the young family adjusting to Los Angeles.

Then a teenage ballboy for the Clippers, Rice helped Lorenzen and Sherra move into a custom home in Playa del Rey and cared for their Rottweilers. Lorenzen lent the kid his Chevrolet Tahoe with televisions and a video-game system in the back for prom, then bought him a tuxedo and Nikes to match the cherry red SUV. When Rice graduated from high school, Lorenzen and Sherra attended the ceremony and rented him a limousine with a "CLASS OF 1999" banner.

"He was in love with her," Rice said. "She had a grip on him."

But privately there was trouble, which occasionally spilled into public view. In August 2005, police responded to a domestic disturbance call at the Wrights' Memphis home. Sherra, according to news reports at the time, had a cut on her hand and abrasions on her jaw. There were no arrests or charges.

Another time, Lorenzen and childhood friend Mike Gipson retreated to the family's RV with a couple of strippers. Sherra discovered them, Gipson said, and Lorenzen jumped out a window. Sherra forced her way into the RV, chased the strippers out, ripped off Gipson's shirt, and tore up the vehicle's interior.

In *Mr. Tell Me Anything,* a handful of violent incidents between the two main characters are folded in with allegations of infidelity and explicit descriptions of sexual encounters. Sherra told the *Memphis Commercial Appeal* in July 2015 that "99.99 percent" of the book contained true stories from her relationship with Lorenzen. She described it on social media as "my story." Lorenzen Jr. said his mother "wrote about things that really happened in her life."

The book described the wife catching her husband with another woman. The wife kicked down the bathroom door, dragged the interloper out by her hair, and repeatedly punched her. Then the wife turned to her husband and "slapped the hell out of his ass."

Lorenzen and Sherra separated in early 2009, around the same time his NBA career ended. Banks foreclosed on two of their homes, including a 17-room mansion. They had $3 million in joint debt.

A permanent parenting plan filed in Shelby County, Tennessee, Circuit Court before the divorce was finalized in February 2010 required Lorenzen to pay $26,650 a month in alimony and child support based on his previous income as a professional basketball player. It cited the couple's "extremely lavish lifestyle" and the need to continue to provide the children with benefits such as a nanny and private basketball training.

Lorenzen also had to maintain a $1 million life insurance policy, with Sherra as trustee.

A few months after their divorce, the relationship seemed to have thawed. Loren, the couple's oldest daughter, said her father wanted to remarry Sherra.

"He would tell us every day he was working to win her back," the 21-year-old said.

Investigators later found a series of sexually explicit text messages Sherra sent Lorenzen on July 17, 2010—designed, they said, in court records, to lure him to Memphis.

Lorenzen flew from his home in suburban Atlanta the next day without even packing a change of clothes.

Phil Dotson, a close friend, later told reporters that he dropped off Lorenzen and Lorenzen Jr. at Sherra's rented home on Whisperwoods Drive in the Memphis suburb of Collierville around 10 p.m. Nothing seemed amiss.

Lorenzen planned to drive back to Atlanta with a friend, Jeremy Orange, and the children on July 19, with a stop at Six Flags White Water, Orange said, but when he arrived at Sherra's home that morning she said Lorenzen wasn't there. Orange repeatedly called his friend. There was no answer.

When Gipson called Sherra, she suggested Lorenzen had run off with a lady friend. She texted Orange that Lorenzen was "probably in one of his little holes" and ended the message "LOL."

Lorenzen's mother, Deborah Marion, filed a missing-persons report July 22. When officers contacted Sherra, she told them her ex-husband had left the home around 2 a.m. on July 19 with an unknown person in an unknown vehicle.

Police sifted through a slew of theories on Lorenzen's whereabouts. Sherra suggested Las Vegas. His father, Herb Wright, thought Lorenzen was in Europe "getting his mind right." Others guessed Lorenzen had flown to Israel for a basketball tryout.

A week after her ex-husband vanished, Sherra fought tears as she spoke with reporters at her front door: "I'm not going to believe anything other than he's fine now."

The next day, she told detectives that Lorenzen had been involved in "major criminal activity," after previously telling them he didn't have any "problems, concerns or enemies." She said he left her home late on July 18 with a box of drugs and cash. Several weeks earlier, Sherra added, men in a car with Florida license plates had come to the house looking for Lorenzen.

In a separate conversation with detectives that day, Marion said her former daughter-in-law was "acting odd."

On July 28, Sherra told detectives Lorenzen had made a phone call before leaving her home around 11:30 p.m., saying he was going to "flip something for $110,000."

By then, police had linked Lorenzen to a brief 911 call made at 12:05 a.m. on July 19. The call had been lost for nine days in the confusion of overlapping jurisdictions. Police tracked it to a field surrounded by woods in Memphis—a spot Lorenzen, Sherra, and friends visited over the years to drink, talk out quarrels, relax.

Authorities discovered his body there, along with his necklace, watch, and shell casings from two guns scattered on the ground.

In the call, Lorenzen sounded overwhelmed by confusion and terror.

[Bang! Bang!]

Lorenzen: "Hey, goddamn!"

Operator: "Germantown 911. Where's your emergency?"

[Bang!]

Operator: "Hello?"

[Bang! Bang!]

Operator: "Hello?"

[Bang! Bang! Bang! Bang! Bang! Bang!]

Operator: "Hello? . . . I don't have nothing but gunshots."

Lorenzen's body and nearby evidence spent 10 days exposed to 90-degree temperatures and a half-inch of rain. The remains were essentially a skeleton.

"It was pretty much a cold case by the time investigators got it," said Toney Armstrong, a Memphis Police veteran.

Four days after the discovery of Lorenzen's body, police searched Sherra's home. Neighbors told them about an unusual bonfire in her backyard a night or two after Lorenzen disappeared. She retained a criminal-defense attorney.

Thousands attended Lorenzen's memorial service at FedEx Forum in downtown Memphis. The silver casket rested in front of the stage among a sea of photos and flowers. Coaches, pastors, relatives, politicians, and former NBA players testified to the special bond between Lorenzen and Memphis during his 34 years:

"He had unlimited potential."

"This boy, young man, was an icon to the city."

"There's gonna be rumors. There's gonna be hearsay. But God knows the truth. And they will have to stand before the Lord."

The $1 million in life insurance money arrived 14 months after Lorenzen's death.

One of the first expenses, according to court records, was $1,445 for Lorenzen's headstone engraved with a cross and basketball. After that, Sherra bought almost $70,000 of furniture and a Cadillac, Mercedes, and Lexus. She acquired a 5,300-square-foot house in foreclosure. She put $7,100 down on a swimming pool and spent $11,750 for a family trip to New York.

Sherra made cash withdrawals or wrote checks to herself for more than $344,000. She spent most of the life insurance money in the first 10 months, the records show.

"All that money she so-called blew, it wasn't spent on anybody else, it was spent on us," Lorenzen Jr., now 23, said in a recent interview. "She don't care about anything else but her kids."

A court filing in 2014 excoriated Sherra for a "lack of prudent financial judgment." Just $5.05 remained in the trust's bank account.

Meanwhile, the investigation into Lorenzen's death stalled. Memphis CrimeStoppers received only a handful of tips. The reward money remained modest, starting at $6,000 before reaching a high of $21,000.

Armstrong, the Memphis police director from 2011 to 2016, said he received phone calls suggesting police look into Sherra. A grand jury questioned her, but no charges were filed.

"The entire city wanted that homicide solved," Armstrong said.

Sherra helped start a charity for inner-city children called Born 2 Prosper; the IRS revoked the organization's nonprofit status in 2013 for not filing returns. She became a minister at Mt. Olive Number One Missionary Baptist Church in Collierville and rehearsed sermons in front of her children. She married Shelby County Sheriff's Deputy Reginald Robinson in March 2014.

"Over the past few years I have been called all sorts of things including crackhead, gold digger, stripper, murderer, whore and all other various terms," Sherra wrote on Facebook in January 2015. "I gave it ALL to God and HE worked it out and works it out!"

A reporter named Kelvin Cowans met Sherra in a Memphis-area Starbucks early in 2015. He planned to write a story for a weekly newspaper marking the fifth anniversary of Lorenzen's death. During the interview, Sherra denied having anything to do with the killing and assailed her treatment by local media and relatives who suspected her involvement.

"That bothered me—that the first time they would try to find out who I was would be when they are trying to tie me to a murder of somebody I've spent half my life with; somebody that I loved more than myself," Sherra told Cowans in an interview he recorded. "That was so hurtful."

The six-hour discussion ended only because the coffee shop closed, he told the *Times*. They started dating within a week or two. Sherra divorced Robinson a few months later and eventually moved with Cowans to a white brick home in Sugar Land, Texas, with five of her six children. Lorenzen Jr. had left for college.

Sherra cheered her children at high school basketball and

volleyball games. The couple watched *Game of Thrones* and *Grey's Anatomy*. And Cowans said Sherra kept spending: a gray Jaguar, a BMW, $15,000 for Christmas. Even after the insurance money ran out, she had property and other assets left over from the marriage to Lorenzen.

Not everything was normal. Cowans recalled that Sherra sometimes paced the street in her bathrobe while shouting into her phone. He couldn't figure out what precipitated such intense conversations and tried to block them out.

A few nights each week, Sherra retreated to the couple's walk-in closet to pray, usually with a pillow and blanket. Most of the closet belonged to her: mink coats, Rolex watches, about 300 pairs of shoes, more than 200 purses, and an abundance of designer clothing. Cowans sometimes heard crying and incomprehensible speech coming from the closet.

On one occasion, Cowans said, Sherra walked into their bedroom in the middle of the day, played Lorenzen's 911 call and asked if he thought an indistinct voice on the recording sounded like a man or woman.

"She'd have this scared look on her face," said Cowans, who later split with Sherra and wrote about their relationship in the book *The Whispering Woods of Sherra Wright*.

Repeated court fights with Herb Wright, the executor of Lorenzen's estate, kindled Sherra's anger. In one clash, she alleged that Lorenzen didn't make alimony and child support payments before his death and petitioned Shelby County Circuit Court in February 2016 to take the money from the estate.

"Lorenzen's family questioning her about anything would always set her off . . . It was real bad. It was just ugly," Cowans said. "Looking back, now I believe Sherra felt like Lorenzen wronged her so it really didn't matter how she treated him or his family."

Sherra bolted awake one night breathing heavily. She usually didn't talk to Cowans about the constant nightmares.

This time, though, she said Lorenzen had called her down a street in their old neighborhood.

"You know I love you," Lorenzen said. "Get over here."

He reached out, she said, and crumbled into dust.

Sherra and Cowans broke up in February 2017. She and the children moved to Riverside County, where her brother, Marcus Robinson, worked as a pastor.

Tim Robertson, an old friend, became her third husband. They settled in Murrieta. Loren learned about the marriage when Sherra mentioned it during a casual phone conversation.

Sherra ferried the younger children to practices and games, hosted their friends, retweeted basketball highlights from the twins, and finished writing the sequel to *Mr. Tell Me Anything.*

When she floated the idea of pursuing a job providing in-home medical care, the children recoiled. She had been a stay-at-home mother their entire lives. They didn't want that to change.

"I know how much she has sacrificed over her whole life just trying to protect us and make sure we're okay," Lorenzen Jr. said.

Unknown to the family, the hunt for Lorenzen's killers had taken on new life. The Shelby County Multi-Agency Gang Unit received an unspecified tip in spring 2016 that led it to reexamine the case. Officers dubbed the effort Operation Rebound because it was a second chance to bring closure to Lorenzen's family. They investigated the murder as if it had just occurred, even retracing his final steps in the field.

Each tip and piece of evidence pointed to a murky lake next to a landfill in Walnut, Mississippi. It had been searched without success earlier in the investigation after a tip from one of Sherra's cousins, Jimmie Martin. Investigators tried again.

On June 27, 2017, an FBI dive team found a semiautomatic nine-millimeter Smith & Wesson pistol in the lake. Ballistics testing matched the shell casings near Lorenzen's body.

About four months later, investigators secured a court order to monitor Sherra's phone calls. They announced the pistol had been found, then intercepted a call by Sherra that seemed to imply an informant led authorities to the weapon.

"Someone done sent somebody somewhere to get something," she said in the call.

Cowans texted. He thought Sherra would be relieved the pistol had been found. Instead, she sounded worried, even agitated. He didn't know what to make of the response.

Four days after the intercepted call, investigators said, Sherra flew to Memphis and met with Billy Ray Turner—a convicted felon who served as a deacon at the Collierville church she once attended. A relative of Sherra told investigators the ex-wife and Turner had been in a romantic relationship at the time of Lorenzen's murder. Loren disagreed.

"He was not my mom's secret lover," she said.

Turner had also been named in Lorenzen's death in 2010 by two tipsters to Memphis CrimeStoppers. It is not clear why those tips didn't advance the case.

(Speaking generally at a news conference about the case last December, Memphis police director Michael Rallings said tips don't always give authorities sufficient evidence to make an arrest.)

In another intercepted phone call, investigators overheard Sherra tell an unknown person that when police searched the home on Whisperwoods Drive in August 2010, they missed three guns.

Police arrested Turner in Collierville on December 5. A week and a half passed before the task force pulled over Sherra's Cadillac SUV on the 15 Freeway in Norco.

The twins started crying, Lamar recalled. They had no idea what was happening. Officers removed the children from the Cadillac one at a time. They seated Lamar in the back of a cruiser. An officer told the boy they were arresting his mother for killing his father.

The prosecution's case centers on Martin, an aspiring Memphis rapper who used the stage name Triksta.

In addition to providing the tip about the pistol in the lake, Martin alleged that Sherra paid him and Turner in a failed attempt to kill Lorenzen to collect the life-insurance money. According to the complaint, the men tried to kill Lorenzen at the suburban Atlanta townhouse in early 2010. They entered through a window Sherra left unlocked, but Lorenzen wasn't there.

After Lorenzen's death in July 2010, Martin told authorities, Sherra and Turner had "confessed to him that they had murdered Lorenzen Wright."

Martin is serving a 20-year prison sentence for second-degree murder in the shooting death of his girlfriend. He didn't respond to an interview request through his attorney.

Sherra and Turner have pleaded not guilty to first-degree murder charges. Five years passed between Martin's tip about the gun and their arrests.

Most of the case file is sealed, the people involved remain tight-lipped, and prosecutors haven't offered an explanation for the delay.

An orange jailhouse shirt had replaced Sherra's designer clothes in late January when she arrived in Memphis after a cross-country trip in a prison transport bus.

During a hearing May 30, Shelby County Judge Lee Coffee read a series of reports about Sherra's behavior in jail. The previous day, the judge said, she directed "abusive, profane language" toward guards. Coffee described the words as "so foul, so offensive, so incendiary that I will not even publish these statements in this courtroom." Six minutes after the outburst, she allegedly stripped naked and attempted to stuff items into a toilet to flood the cell. The judge said she told guards she was "going swimming, y'all."

One of Sherra's former attorneys, Blake Ballin, suggested at the time the incident raised concern about her mental health. The judge increased Sherra's bail to $20 million.

"It's all like a terrible dream, all of it," Sherra, now 47, wrote in the letter to the *Times* delivered by Loren. "From his murder to my arrest, unreal. But, I have grown as a woman of God that is putting my hope in the Lord. I believe, with the help of the nation, I will make bond . . . I can't wait until the day that I sit down for a 'real' documentary or movie with the TRUTH in it."

The letter ended with a plea for supporters to write her in jail, raise bail money, and buy the sequel to *Mr. Tell Me Anything*.

"Stay tuned for my upcoming book during the Christmas holiday," Sherra wrote. "Be blessed."

On August 22, Coffee ordered Sherra to undergo a mental evaluation. No trial date has been set.

Her new attorney, Juni Ganguli, said his client "misses her children terribly" and maintains her innocence.

The six children—who range in age from 11 to 23—are adamant their mother was not involved in their father's death.

"Not my mom, not Sherra," Loren said.

The children created a GoFundMe in late June to help bail out their mother. The "Bring Mommy Wright Home" campaign, seeking $500,000, accused prosecutors of "having no case other than lies and fabrications."

More than two months later, it hadn't raised a dollar.

BOB HOHLER AND PATRICIA WEN

Gladiator: Aaron Hernandez and Football, Inc., Part One: The Secrets Behind the Smile

FROM THE BOSTON GLOBE

SPORTS AGENT Brian Murphy and one of his top young clients, Aaron Hernandez, had a lot to celebrate in the late summer of 2012. Murphy had just helped the star tight end secure a $41 million deal with the New England Patriots, and Hernandez had told a crowd of reporters that being a Patriot had purged him of his reckless ways.

But, as Murphy flew into Boston, to meet with Hernandez at his condo, he had another matter on his mind. A little thing, perhaps, but also a measure of how much his client had really changed.

A local Toyota car dealer had loaned Hernandez a silver SUV with the expectation of some free Patriots tickets and promotional appearances. But Hernandez, then 22, hadn't done his part.

This was no way to build a reputation, Murphy told him. To earn respect you have to honor the deals you make.

"No, no," responded Hernandez.

He reached into his closet and pulled out a rifle.

"I get my respect through weapons."

Murphy told a grand jury later that he chose to interpret that encounter, never reported on before, as a joke.

He now knows it was another warning sign missed. There had been so many and would be many more, missed or minimized by Hernandez's friends, family, coaches, and associates as his star soared, then plummeted toward murder, prison, and suicide.

Infamy outran fame—in the end, it wasn't close. What was so obvious about him—his athletic gifts, his outsized persona, his growing taste for violence—proved to be so much less important than what he'd kept hidden.

And he hid a lot. A Spotlight Team investigation found a man who lived a life of secrets—about his childhood, his football career, his sexuality, his drug habits, and his fascination with violence. On closer examination, much about him was not as it seemed or has been commonly reported.

Much of his unraveling occurred in plain sight, but those who profited from his on-field heroics rarely troubled to look or care. In life, one of the National Football League's star gladiators was not who he seemed to be; the elite athlete behind the dimples and the goofy grin was degenerating into a reckless thug. In death, Hernandez provides a damning example of the indifference big-time football often shows to the price some of its players pay.

For Hernandez, as for so many, the proof is now best seen on a microscope slide—his brain was ravaged by CTE, the devastating disease caused by hits to the head, of a severity never seen in someone so young.

This portrait of Hernandez was filled out by scores of interviews across the country and volumes of previously undisclosed information, including thousands of court and government records, and text messages, emails, and images that Hernandez sent and received.

Also by his own words and voice. *Globe* reporters obtained recordings of nearly 300 phone calls Hernandez made from jail over a six-month period while he awaited trial. His conversations with family, friends, and former teammates open a window on his life the public has never seen.

Those calls reveal many things, some of them appalling, some bizarre, some pathetic. He tried to understand what had become of his life but couldn't. But he was clear that his football celebrity, and all that went with it, had meant very little in the end.

"You have to find inner peace to be happy. Nothing you do is gonna make you happy. Nothing you get is gonna make you happy," Hernandez said on one jail call. "Just like me, like by having money . . . having everything in the world, I still was miserable. Know what I mean?"

Like Father, Like Son

The misery of Aaron Hernandez was, for almost all of his short life, obscured by the myths and secrets of Aaron Hernandez. It was a pattern that went back to his earliest days, to the foundation stories of his childhood, to three key relationships in his life that were nothing like what they seemed.

First comes his father, Dennis, nicknamed The King. In Bristol, Connecticut, people trying to fathom Aaron's epic fall said that he never got over the loss of this larger-than-life patriarch. The school janitor who dreamed of athletic greatness for his sons died abruptly after a routine hernia surgery at age 49.

Aaron had adored his dad and lost his way when he was gone, the story goes. Maybe that's why this good boy went bad.

It was a myth and behind it lay misery, the Spotlight Team review found.

Aaron and his older brother were often beaten and brutalized by their dad. Aaron didn't cry at his father's funeral, and people took note. He kept it all inside.

Maybe that's what he couldn't get over.

His only sibling, Jonathan Hernandez, now 32, told the *Globe* that he and Aaron lived in constant fear of their father's beatings, which were so severe and routine that Jonathan once threatened to call authorities rather than keep it a private family matter.

"I picked up the phone once to call, to seek help," the brother said in his first interview on the subject. "And his response was, 'Call them.' And he handed me the phone, and he said, 'I'm going to beat you even harder, you and your brother, and they're going to have to pull me off of you when they knock down the door.'"

The beatings inside their Greystone Avenue home were often about the tiniest of transgressions, and sometimes related to the father's drinking. But there was a special fury when The King felt his two sons were not trying hard enough in school or sports, said Jonathan, whose upcoming memoir, *The Truth About Aaron,* is due out later this month. Sometimes the boys couldn't see any cause for the beatings at all—a kind of impulsive lashing out that Aaron would also manifest in the years to come.

Outside the family home, the image of Dennis Hernandez was quite otherwise. In the traditional working-class city of Bristol, some 18 miles west of Hartford, he was generally regarded as a local success story. He was the scrappy kid who grew up in a family with Puerto Rican roots. People knew he had had his share of run-ins with the law, but they saw him pull himself together as a teenager and become a Bristol Central High football star and a football scholarship recipient at the University of Connecticut in Storrs.

Dennis married Terri Valentine, also a graduate of Bristol Central, and they settled into jobs with the public schools—she was a secretary and he worked as a custodian. They seemed to have much to be admired, even envied, in this sports-crazy town that became home to the headquarters of ESPN. Above all, they had two good-looking, athletic sons who broke records under the bright lights of Muzzy Field.

First to shine was Jonathan, then known as DJ, who would follow his father's footsteps and get a football scholarship to UConn.

He'd done so well, but at a price.

In his interview with the *Globe*, Jonathan wept several times recalling painful parts of his childhood that no one had discussed for decades. He recalled a Fisher-Price game table at their home in which one of two long sticks was frequently missing: his father used it in his assaults.

Only later in life—and with some counseling help—has he been able to better cope with his past.

"You realize . . . that's not how other families do it. You're just like wow, you don't have to hide at home if you get a C? Like really?"

He said he and his brother were raised believing that seeking psychological help for problems was a sign of weakness.

Some outside the family did get a hint of the harshness inside the Hernandez home.

Jeff Morgan, a former assistant football coach at Bristol Central, remembers Dennis as an old-fashioned disciplinarian, but one time he wondered if Dennis took it too far with Aaron.

"I know one time (Aaron) went to a senior dance as a freshman. I guess he was drinking before he went to the dance, and they threw him out of the dance at the school. Then, the next time we saw him, he looked like I guess his father did discipline him some."

When asked how he knew that, Morgan responded, "He had a black eye. I'm assuming that's where that came from."

Dennis Hernandez also once brought his rough ways to the football sidelines, where he was often on hand to cheer his boys on.

When Aaron was just eight, he had a youth tackle football coach named Tim SanSoucie, whose son was Aaron's age and would later become a high school quarterback throwing touchdowns to Aaron. Aaron's father made it known he didn't think much of SanSoucie's coaching decisions. After a heated exchange of words, Aaron's father got physical.

"He promptly turned around and clocked me one across the face, broke my glasses off my face," said SanSoucie in an interview in his son's home in Las Vegas.

Police responded, but the matter was later resolved through small claims court when Aaron's father was ordered to pay for the broken eyeglasses. That money was never paid.

These episodes never fundamentally changed the good-father image that people around Bristol had of Dennis—though there were murmured words of something ominous back in his college days. In retrospect, it looked like a harbinger of the trouble that would tempt and envelop Aaron.

Two days after UConn lost the final game of its 1977 football season, a police officer from Plainville, Connecticut, was killed in a bungled home burglary, and detectives ended up questioning Dennis.

He was a person of interest for a reason. The *Globe* uncovered a police affidavit that says Dennis Hernandez, while not involved in the cop killing, tried to help the burglars evade police. One of the burglars was a football teammate at UConn and Bristol Central.

Dennis, then a junior, was never charged in the case, but he was finished at UConn, where records show he was also on the brink of academic failure.

The turbulence of his personality—and past—was felt most by those who lived with him.

Much later, Aaron, in tapes of jailhouse phone calls obtained by the *Globe*, reflected on his father's dark influence on the family. In one conversation, he described growing up in a household where there was "arguing 24/7" and where there was a lot to argue about.

Terri and Dennis went through many tough times as a couple. Records show that after they married in 1986, they got divorced in 1991 when Aaron was a toddler, and then remarried again in 1996 when Aaron was six. Also in 1999, when Aaron was nine, the couple filed for bankruptcy, with credit card and other debts.

There were other troubles. When Aaron was three, his father was arrested and charged with trying to buy cocaine from an undercover officer. His mother was also once arrested for being part of an underground sports gambling bookie operation, out of the family home, when Aaron was 11.

Aaron, in the jailhouse calls, recalled scenes of his father being tossed out by his mother—and then always allowed back.

"My mom went through a real lot with my father," he said in another call. "But she just believes in—she loves someone, she just always sticks by them."

Brutality was not the entire picture. Jonathan said his memories of childhood can be confusing, as the terrifying ones are mixed in with very warm, tender, and loving memories of his father. He recalled the family watching TV together on the couch, eating homemade brownies as a family, and playing sports in the yard. He recalled his father inventing makeshift games with paper bags and yarn for the boys to play.

He said his father helped the two of them at sports practice and games—and that he dearly wanted them to excel in life.

Still, abuse was one of his major motivational tools, though the beatings tapered and eventually stopped as the boys got older, Jonathan said.

Teenage Exploration

Aaron would mature into a football player of a skill and local renown his father never knew. But here too, the gap between the local fable and the reality opens wide under scrutiny.

Hernandez looked like the image of one sort of young athlete on the field but off it, secretly, was another.

The lush green turf of Muzzy Field was where Hernandez could escape the stress of family strife. It was also a place where he could show off his genetic good fortune: uncanny athletic ability that included lightning-quick speed, nimble hands, and exceptional eye-hand coordination.

In his elementary years, Hernandez was a skinny kid, but by high school he quickly became a man among boys, almost reaching his full height of six feet, two inches and filling out a sturdy muscular build. He wasn't a motivated worker in his earlier years, but by high school he was practicing harder than anyone else. He seemed determined to be a star.

He also had his trademark dimpled smile, dark handsome looks, and an easygoing side, which drew many friends and admirers. Among them was Shayanna Jenkins, a female classmate whom he dated for a time in high school and who would years later become his fiancée.

By his junior year, he had become an exceptional pass receiver, particularly with Tim SanSoucie's son, Dennis, as the quarterback. They were one of the most prolific passing tandems in the state —nine touchdown completions in the first four games. In Hernandez's junior year, he caught 67 passes for a total of 1,807 yards, a Connecticut high school record.

The two teenagers also shared a life outside football. Dennis SanSoucie told the *Globe* he and Hernandez smoked a lot of marijuana—before school, before practices, and after games. It would become the beginning of Hernandez's lifelong relationship with getting high, even before big games.

Dennis SanSoucie recalled the first day of junior year walking with Hernandez near the high school.

"We were baked," said SanSoucie, who later joined the Marines.

For the first time publicly, SanSoucie also talked about a now-and-then sexual relationship he had with Aaron, which began in middle school and continued through high school.

"Me and him were very much into trying to hide what we were doing. We didn't want people to know," Dennis SanSoucie said in an interview.

SanSoucie said he and Hernandez worked hard to keep their relationship a secret. In their traditional community of Bristol, where Dennis was bound for the military and Aaron for big-time football, it was not something they wanted people to know about.

For Aaron, it would not have played well at home, especially with his dad.

Dennis Hernandez had long had concerns that Aaron, as a boy, had a feminine way about him—the way he stood or used his hands, his brother said. He also remembered one of Aaron's early ambitions that sent their father over the edge.

"I remember he wanted to be a cheerleader. My cousins were cheerleaders and amazing," Jonathan said. "And I remember coming home and like my dad put an end to that really quick. And it was not okay. My dad made it clear that . . . he had his definition of a man."

The home environment, in general, was deeply homophobic.

"'Faggot' was used all the time in our house," Jonathan said. "All the time. Standing. Talking. Acting. Looking. It was the furthest thing my father wanted you to even look like in our household. This was not acceptable to him."

Hearing this sort of harsh talk must have been hard for a teenager exploring his sexuality, though Aaron kept his thoughts to himself. He was also privately nursing another sort of sexual hurt.

Jonathan said that Aaron disclosed later in his adult life that he had been sexually molested as a young boy. Jonathan declined to say more to the *Globe* about this revelation. One of Aaron's lawyers in his criminal case, George Leontire, also said Aaron had spoken to him of sexual abuse as a child. Neither the brother nor the lawyer was willing to identify the perpetrator.

Aaron's sexual complexity was one of his closest secrets, one he hinted at only rarely. His high school quarterback friend was similarly circumspect, and for many years.

SanSoucie said he has finally come out in his late twenties to family and friends, after Hernandez's suicide, despite the difficulty in doing so. He believes that Aaron would be proud of him—for that and his publicly acknowledging their past relationship.

"I really truly feel in my heart I got the thumbs-up from him," he said.

"He Didn't Get Back Up"

Before his father died during Aaron's junior year, Aaron had informally accepted a football scholarship to UConn, which would have cemented the special UConn Huskies tradition in the Hernandez household. But Aaron's outsized talents—and work ethic—captured the attention of college recruiters across the country. Soon, he was getting calls from such places as the University of Michigan, Notre Dame, Boston College, and the University of Florida.

Aaron got a taste of the national media scene too, as reporters peppered him about where he would take his top talent. At the time, he also began talking about his father in glowing terms, reinforcing the glossy image that many in Bristol saw of the supportive sports dad.

"I wish my dad was here now that more schools are coming. Notre Dame just came on recently and it really makes you think. It just makes me think more," Hernandez said in a *Hartford Courant* article. "My dad would have been able to help me out even more. But I'm pretty sure he would have wanted me to go UConn. My family wants me to go to UConn and my heart's at UConn."

But that commitment would waver as he began to be courted by the University of Florida and its legendary college coach Urban Meyer, known for his win-at-all-costs philosophy.

Outside the recruitment whirlwind, Aaron entered his senior year as a teenager searching for his identity—and a good time. He kept up decent grades, but also maintained a vibrant social life, which started to include a sizable amount of drinking, along with smoking pot. On the field, he continued to dazzle crowds with his knack for outmaneuvering defenders.

But in one game against Maloney High School of Meriden, he gave the crowd a scare when he was knocked down by a blindside hit to the head and lay motionless before a hushed crowd.

"I saw him get hit, and I saw him go down. And he didn't get back up," said Lorrie Belmonte, a registered nurse in Bristol who was in the stands. "And Aaron would always get back up. And then the coaches went out on the field and . . . he must have been totally out of it because they called . . . the ambulance [that] was standing by. And so the EMTs immediately came up on the field and got him and took him."

This was 2006, and scientists were just beginning to establish a link between blows to the head in football and the disease now known as chronic traumatic encephalopathy, or CTE. Soon, researchers would also begin to understand the damage of subconcussive injuries, which may not have immediate symptoms, but still cause profound damage. That research would affect not only professional players, but millions of children who play contact sports.

The pace of CTE research was accelerating, but there was so much that wasn't known, and the NFL and youth football leagues were largely downplaying the health hazards for players of all ages.

Aaron's concussion sidelined him for one game. Then he came back and finished out the season. He was named Connecticut's Player of the Year.

"You're Gonna Die Without Even Knowing Your Son"

As Aaron was juggling college decisions, he was also painfully moving between two homes. He had become alienated and full of anger at his mother after his father's death. It was a rift that would last for years, another betrayal for Aaron to try to make sense of, another well of misery.

Among Aaron's relatives based in Bristol, he was closest to a cousin, Tanya Singleton, who was about 14 years older. She was like an older loving sister he never had—and someone he could totally trust.

After Aaron's father died, he learned what seemed unimaginable: his mother was in a serious romantic relationship with Tanya's husband, Jeff Cummings. It came as a shock to Aaron and Tanya —and over the years the two grew even closer through shared anguish. Tanya would divorce her husband and see him move in with Aaron's mother.

Aaron was crushed and enraged, and his loyalty shifted even more to Tanya. He began spending long stretches at Tanya's house on Lake Avenue, which was across from an athletic field where Aaron used to play youth football. It became like a second childhood home.

It was a warm, nurturing house that seemed to have an open door to anyone. It was also a house that drew in all kinds of stragglers and drifters, including many with long rap sheets.

It was a place where prosecutors say Aaron got needed solace but also acquired the swagger—and the street-wise mentality—of the wrong crowd.

In later years behind bars, Aaron would have phone calls with his mother in which it was clear he was trying to repair their ruptured relationship. The conversations could be tender, but also blunt—and often profane.

In one, Aaron suggested that she never helped fully treat his attention deficit hyperactivity disorder as a boy.

"Matter of fact, you're the reason I never could pay attention in school and shit. You were supposed to get me my medication," he said in a call in the fall of 2014.

"Yeah, I knocked you over the head with a frickin' hammer. That was your medication," she replied.

Later in that same conversation, his mother seemed to equate the effects of an ADHD medication with a dangerously addictive drug.

"That's what Adderall is: B-L-O-W," she spelled out over the phone.

The two went back and forth repeating those letters because Aaron couldn't figure out what she was trying to spell, until his mother became frustrated and blurted out: "Cocaine, dipshit! That's what Adderall's like."

Aaron's mother, Terri Hernandez, declined the *Globe*'s request for an interview.

In another of their jailhouse calls, Aaron lamented that he long felt he could never be fully open with her.

"There's so many things I would love to talk to you [about], so you can know me as a person," he told her. "But I never could tell you. And you're gonna die without even knowing your son."

The strains of this relationship were apparent to many of Aaron's closest friends and family, but not to the college recruiters and coaches assessing his rare ability as a football athlete. In wooing Aaron, they felt they needed his mom on their side—she was, after all, the only parent of this rising national star who tragically lost his father in high school.

It was their story, and publicly they would play their roles in it well.

Meyer, one of the nation's top college coaches, traveled to Bristol. He visited Aaron's childhood home and met with his mother.

There was another visit. Hernandez's high school principal said he also met with Meyer. The Florida coach asked for something that took the principal by surprise.

Meyer wanted Hernandez at the University of Florida—and soon.

NICK HEIL

Is Kilian Jornet for Real?

FROM OUTSIDE

AROUND 2 A.M. on May 28, 2017, Kilian Jornet crabbed across Mount Everest's North Face, alone, delirious, at nearly 27,000 feet, and far off route. He was descending from the 29,029-foot summit, his second trip to the top without supplemental oxygen in seven days. But now he was lost and couldn't recall how he'd gotten there; his memory from the past hour was blank. It was snowing, the slope growing icier and more precarious with every move. "I thought maybe I was having a nightmare," Jornet told me recently, "and that I would wake up in Base Camp. I dropped a rock to see how steep it was, and I realized it was not a dream and that I needed to wait until daylight so I could see before making any more decisions."

At first light, he discovered that he had strayed more than half a mile from the North Ridge, the route that would take him to the North Col and down to the relative safety of advanced base camp (ABC), at around 21,000 feet. That left him perched dangerously near the top of Everest's soaring 7,000-foot north wall. Eventually he was able to navigate using GPS waypoints on his watch, traversing slowly back to the route. He had no radio or satellite phone, and no way to alert his lone teammate, the filmmaker Sébastien Montaz-Rosset, or the handful of friends he'd made since being on the mountain. Far below, at ABC, they peered anxiously through a spotting scope in search of Jornet, now hours overdue.

Everest was the culmination of the Summits of My Life project, which Jornet began in 2012 in an attempt to establish speed records on a collection of iconic peaks, including Mont Blanc, the Matterhorn, Elbrus, Denali, and Aconcagua. By then, at age 24, racing had lost its luster. He continued to compete—he liked meeting people, enjoyed the milieu—but he'd already won every-thing there was to win, often multiple times, including marquee pain parties like Colorado's Hardrock 100, the 106-mile Ultra Trail du Mont Blanc (UTMB), and Alaska's brief but brutal Mount Marathon. Summits was a chance to pursue more imaginative, in-dependent projects, moving how he liked, fast and free, on his own schedule. It had a tragic start. While attempting the first ob-jective, the Mont Blanc traverse, his partner, world-champion ski-mountaineering racer Stéphane Brosse, was skinning beside Jor-net above the Argentière Glacier when a large cornice broke off between them, pitching Brosse 2,000 feet to his death. They had been separated by only a few feet. For months, Jornet could not understand why it had not been him.

Despite the tragedy, Jornet went on to flash up and down the other peaks, setting records, traveling light, deploying his bohe-mian brand of mountain endurance, and often doing in hours what took other experienced climbers days. With support from his main sponsor, Salomon, and help from his friend Montaz-Rosset, Jornet produced impressive documentation of each mission: pho-tos, blog posts, data, and several films. By the time he arrived at Everest in 2017, his third trip there in as many years, he was one of the most recognized athletes in adventure sports, with a robust social media following, including nearly 250,000 on Twitter and more than half a million on Instagram. Some fans even referred to their Salomon running shoes as Air Jornets.

Many people, myself included, had tuned in to his feeds during the Everest expedition, only to find them frustratingly quiet. When the news emerged, on May 28, that Jornet had climbed Everest not once but twice in a single week, and that he was claiming a new speed record, it seemed extraordinary to the point of confusion. Two ascents, back-to-back? Without oxygen? By himself?

I was intimately familiar with Everest's north side. In 2007, I'd climbed to the North Col, at 23,000 feet, while working on a book about the mountain. I knew the perils of Jornet's route via the Northeast Ridge and had written about the disturbingly high num-ber of people who'd died there. I'd never heard of anything re-motely like Jornet's achievement—four trips above 8,000 meters in less than a month—which quickly made headlines around the world. There was some predictable grumbling. "The public only understands velocity, they don't understand climbing," said Himalayan gadfly Reinhold Messner, dismissing the feat as merely racing, not mountaineering. But the occasion was largely celebrated as a historic milestone.

"I can't imagine trying to recover and climb again five days later, physically and emotionally," says alpinist and guide Adrian Ballinger, whose own oxygenless ascent of Everest coincided with Jornet's. "I climb at altitude and recover pretty well, but this is a whole different level."

That summer, Jornet went on to notch a string of performances that were, even for him, astonishing. Two weeks after Everest, he set a blazing pace in a road half marathon in Norway that ascended more than 5,500 feet, cranking out miles in under six and a half minutes on an 8 percent grade and winning in 1:30. By August, he had won Hardrock, the Marathon du Mont Blanc, Switzerland's ultracompetitive Sierre-Zinal, and the Glen Coe Skyline trail race. In early September, he placed second at UTMB, 15 minutes behind his Salomon teammate François D'Haene, a veritable photo finish after 106 miles. Jornet won, or nearly won, everything he entered.

The Everest feats, meanwhile, started coming under scrutiny. Where was the proof, critics demanded—the summit photos, the GPS track, the witnesses? Why did arguably his greatest accomplishment, in a career strewn with meticulously documented accomplishments, remain fuzzy? Forums like LetsRun hosted heated threads dissecting the issue in granular detail. In early 2018, the Spanish climbing magazine *Desnivel* ran a cover story calling Jornet out, stating, "He did not show definitive evidence of what he had done." When I reached out to Himalayan Database, the Kathmandu-based organization that has been verifying Himalayan mountaineering since 1991, it had not confirmed either of the climbs. It was impossible not to wonder, in a post–Lance Armstrong fake-news world, if something was amiss.

Most people know Jornet as a runner, but that is only half the story, maybe less.

"I don't like to put tags on things," says the 30-year-old. "I like to move on mountains in different ways. In summer it's logical to go on foot. In winter, in snow, I go on skis."

It's January, and I've come to Romsdal, on the western coast of

Norway, to go on skis with Jornet. He and his fiancée, the Swedish ultra-runner Emelie Forsberg, moved here in 2015 to escape the maddening sports crowd of France's Chamonix Valley, where they previously resided and are huge celebrities. To friends he is Kiki, to fans he is the Extraterrestrial, but in Norway, he gets to simply be Kilian. Their home, a renovated farmhouse, located on three scenic acres surrounded by mountains, that they call Moon Valley Farm, is quiet and private, the way they want it. They don't go out much. You can count the restaurants in nearby Andalsnes, the town of 2,300 where I'm staying, on one hand. The closest bar is 30 miles away. "Sometimes after climbing, my friends take a beer," Jornet says in fluent but heavily accented English, "but I am like, why?"

In person it's easy to see how Jornet is so fast. At five-foot-six and 128 pounds, he's like a jockey with keg-size quads built from years pistoning up steep slopes. His upper body is slight, streamlined. He does "a little stretching," he tells me, but largely eschews lifting weights or other types of cross-training. I ask him, half jokingly, what he can bench-press.

"Zero! Nothing!" he says. "I have no absolute strength."

He's joking, sort of, but point taken: Jornet has spent most of his life developing the physiology he needs for mountain terrain. Anything else was a waste of time.

I'd first learned of Jornet through my own inexplicable midlife addiction to ski-mountaineering racing—aka skimo—an Alps-born sport that entails hauling ass up and down wintry mountains on featherweight touring gear while dressed in a skintight onesie. Jornet is a world champion; I'm a flailing amateur who cuts a lumpy profile in Lycra. Jornet rarely slows down long enough to accommodate journalists, but last October he underwent surgery on both shoulders to address chronic dislocations, and was straightjacketed in matching arm slings for weeks. He'd just started training again when I showed up, and the prospect of chasing the very best around the Norwegian mountains made me as giddy as a teenager.

One morning I join Jornet and two of his local friends on a mission he tells me will last "a couple of hours." Deep into hour three, there is no end in sight. There is no Jornet in sight either. He has vanished, far ahead, leaving only a skin track that, in the squally weather, is disappearing fast. Eventually, worried that I could get lost forever in the whiteout, I bail. I don't hear from Jornet for another four hours. "Still up," he texts, "but will be back in town in an hour."

Forsberg laughs when she hears the story. She calls this Kilian Time.

"Friends will visit and ask about a route, and Kilian will say it takes three hours, but for them it's like 15," she says. "You learn with him that you have to make your own calculations. If we're going to the mountains and he estimates seven hours, I pack food for ten."

Sometimes, Kilian Time turns sketchy, like in 2013, when he and Forsberg ended up on the Frendo Spur outside Chamonix, a technical route of rock, ice, and snow, in running shoes, and required a rescue from the gendarmerie. I ask Forsberg if she worries about her partner.

"Of course," she says. "I'm not afraid because of his capacities; things that look like risks to others are within his experience and knowledge. But I'm afraid of nature. He's out there a lot, and I know things can happen in the mountains."

For all of Jornet's impressive performances, my record-scratch moment was his appearance in a 2013 documentary about steep skiing called *T'es Pas Bien Là?* (*Downside Up*). The film, by Montaz-Rosset, centers on Vivian Bruchez, one of France's most skilled extreme skiers. But there is Jornet, right next to him, scritching out turns on 55-degree blue ice, downclimbing Class 5 rock and snow, slipping across knife ridges so narrow and airy that his skis stick out in both directions. I've watched the film dozens of times, and it never fails to leave pools of sweat under my palms.

"His versatility as an athlete is unparalleled," says Mike Foote, who has twice finished second to Jornet at the Hardrock 100. "I don't think there's anyone who brings his level of imagination and creativity to the sport. I think that's how he keeps things fresh, how he doesn't burn out."

Jornet's origin story is mythological. He grew up in Refugi Cap del Rec, a backcountry hut in the Spanish Pyrenees, where his parents, Eduoard and Nuria, worked as caretakers and mountain guides. No TV, no Xbox, no internet, just his year-younger sister, Naila, for company and the wild peaks outside the door. At three, he competed in his first cross-country ski race, the 12-kilometer

Marxa Pirineu. At 10, he completed a 42-day through-hike of the Pyrenees with Nuria and Naila. His parents had split by then, and Eduoard had moved into a neighboring hut, but soon, Jornet says, it seemed normal, he and his sister rotating each week between the two parents.

At 13, Jornet applied to the Center for Mountain Skiing of Catalonia (CTEMC)—a kind of Spanish version of Vermont's Burke Mountain Academy, but for skimo racing. In other countries, skimo is a fringe sport, but in Spain, it is more popular than either cross-country or alpine skiing. Jornet was two years too young for the program, but he didn't quite fit into a typical high school. Nuria worried about him. "There was a moment when he was a teenager that I saw his attitude had a destructive point," she told me. "That's the reason why I look for help at the school."

She believed CTEMC would provide an outlet for his irrepressible energy. The school agreed. "I remember perfectly when he was explaining to us his projects of great mountain crossings," recalls Jordi Canals, Jornet's coach at CTEMC. "When he talked, he had a special shine and determination. We decided to admit him because we thought it was better that he was in our group than just alone in the mountains."

Athletic training at CTEMC was carefully prescribed and supervised, but Jornet was hard to restrain. He would routinely ride his bike to school, work out all afternoon, and then ride home—25 miles each way. When the snow melted, he began running mostly as a way to stay in shape for skimo. Once, to see how his body would respond, he stopped eating altogether, continuing with his workouts while subsisting only on water. He lasted five days before he passed out, midrun.

Early on, Jornet's unique qualities amazed and perplexed his coaches, most notably his "extraordinary recovery from strenuous trainings," as Canals described it. "He has this resistance to osteoarticular and muscular lesions"—the bone contusions and muscle strains commonly triggered by demanding exercise. "A lot of athletes with smaller training loads have lots of trouble."

When I spoke to Canals on the phone, I asked him what was the most amazing thing he'd seen Jornet do. He thought for a moment, then told me about the vertical kilometer event at the 2014 Skyrunning World Championships in Chamonix. Kilian had just returned from setting a fastest known time on Denali (11 hours and 48 minutes), where he had spent a month "eating poor meals, sleeping in a tent in snowy and cold conditions, doing long alpine routes." In other words, *not* training for an event that is essentially a 30-minute all-out uphill sprint. "When he won, I said to him, 'You didn't deserve to win this race.' And he said, 'Yes, I'm very surprised too. But I felt very well.'" Canals recalled. "That is Kilian."

The downside of excellence is that it invites skepticism, something Jornet encountered early on. In 2008, at age 21, he showed up at his first UTMB having never raced in anything longer than a marathon. He pulled away at mile 40, en route to vanquishing a field of older and more experienced vets. The French organizers were not happy. Ten miles from the finish, at the last checkpoint, they detained him for more than an hour. They accused him of cheating—of using a pacer (he wasn't) and not carrying the mandatory gear (he was). Despite the delay, he crossed the finish line first, by more than an hour, but was not declared the winner until the next day.

"I was just going to get in my car and go home," Jornet recalls. "I was like, Fuck you, fuck the race and everything."

He was still a student then, studying exercise physiology in Font-Romeu, France, living in shared housing, stretching what little money he had to keep him in pasta and olive oil. He'd learned enough at CTEMC, he believed, to be able to coach himself. He lived to race but didn't race to live. There was little money in his sports: purses were skimpy, and there was no Olympic skimo or trail running. Even after his UTMB win, when Salomon signed him to a full-time contract, it only meant bigger bags of pasta and, at events, an occasional hotel room instead of the back of his car.

He couldn't know at the time that ultra-running was poised to take off, particularly in the United States, where Christopher McDougall's 2009 book *Born to Run,* about the Mexican Tarahumara and the Copper Canyon Ultramarathon, sparked a trail-running boom. Between 2007 and 2016, the number of races in the United States exceeding 26.2 miles more than tripled, according to *UltraRunning* magazine, from 480 to 1,473, and a new cast of stars emerged: Scott Jurek, Krissy Moehl, Anton Krupicka, Jenn Shelton, and others. Jornet would soon eclipse them all.

His rise to fame not only inspired many runners and skiers

but invited study and emulation. Some have speculated that the early commitment to skimo built the machine that powered his mountain-running dominance. Splitting his year between the two disciplines helped stave off the overtraining and burnout that has plagued so many talented runners—a strategy that's now employed by top competitors like Krupicka, Foote, and Rob Krar.

Even among elites, Jornet appears special. In 2012, his VO_2 max was recorded at 92, one of the highest values ever seen. He has a near-miraculous ability to recover quickly from workouts and races. Until his recent shoulder trouble, he seemed impervious to injury. Echocardiograms revealed that his heart has adapted to the stress of training with very little malformation, such as thickened ventricular walls, that often affects other elite athletes' performances. And he has cultivated a monklike devotion to training, technique, and equipment that he deploys through 1,200 hours of yearly practice.

"If genes dictating performance are like a row of light switches, all of his are flipped on," says Eric Carter, 31, a member of the U.S. ski-mountaineering team. "I've trained with him, working as hard as I can, soaked in sweat, and the guy is still in his down parka, chatting away."

Jornet is a private person, but he is a very public athlete, and his workouts are readily accessible on Strava and Movescount (Suunto's proprietary site). The volume is startling. Three days before the Marathon du Mont Blanc, he ran up and down the Mont Blanc massif—14,000 vertical feet—in seven hours. His "taper week" prior to the Hardrock 100 in July included a 35-mile ascent of Mount Eolus and a 26-mile run up Mount Elbert, both Colorado fourteeners.

I started to question if these feats were even possible without some kind of pharmaceutical or other assistance. It saddened me to feel suspicious, but who could forget the now-infamous 2001 Nike ad in which Lance Armstrong says, "What am I on? I'm on my bike, busting my ass, six hours a day. What are you on?" Yet credible doping allegations followed Armstrong throughout his career. There was his relationship with Michele Ferrari, the disgraced Italian doctor, and accusations from former teammates and friends. With Jornet, there have been occasional whispers of foul play but nothing concrete, just garden-variety trolling and speculation that could reasonably be chalked up to professional jealousy.

Doping would be risky to try to hide. As a member of both the World Anti-Doping Agency's regulatory program and Athletes for Transparency, Jornet must provide records of his whereabouts and doctor prescriptions, and he could be tested as often as once per month by an administrator who shows up at his door unannounced. And while Jornet now makes a six-figure salary through sponsorships, skimo and ultra-running don't offer anything close to the financial rewards that tempt athletes in cycling and marathon running, sports plagued by doping scandals.

"There's no incentive," says John Gaston, the top U.S. skimo racer, who spent the year training and racing on the European World Cup circuit. "There's hardly any money in our sport. And now you see people catching up to him. The competition is tight. If you get to know him, I think he loves the mountains too much to compromise the world in that way."

In recent years, Jornet has transcended traditional endurance sports, establishing himself in an elite club of adventurers that is reinventing high-mountain objectives. In Norway, Jornet showed me a spreadsheet he'd made, prosaically titled "Cronology [*sic*] of Significant Events Related to Going Fast in the Mountains." It contained hundreds of entries, covering everything from trail running to steep skiing, tracking all the way back to the year 1040 with a running contest that Scottish king Malcolm Canmore hosted to find a speedy courier. The document was exquisite in its geekiness. Jornet wasn't merely a participant, he was a scholar.

Three years ago, he began teaming up for occasional climbs with the late Ueli Steck, aka the Swiss Machine. It was a natural partnership. Steck was the preternaturally talented sport climber who could flash up technical routes faster than almost anyone. Jornet was the aerobic monster who could grind fast and forever on little food or water. In 2015, they joined forces to billy-goat up the north face of the Eiger via the classic 1938 route. A typical round-trip of the route requires three days. It was Jornet's first time, but the pair summited in four hours and were back in town in less than 10.

In April 2017, Jornet was on Cho Oyu, in Tibet, when Steck died on Nuptse, Everest's 25,791-foot neighbor. Steck had been acclimatizing, alone and high on the mountain, when he fell to his death. Beyond losing a friend, Jornet had lost a special peer he could consult with. "We talked a lot about what it means to move in the mountains," Jornet told me. "Ueli was coming from a supertechnical background—like pure difficulty—and I was coming from endurance. We were both trying to learn from each other."

Like Jornet, Steck had encountered controversy around certain climbs, including what may have been his biggest achievement: a 28-hour solo ascent of Annapurna's lethal south face. Steck produced no summit photos (he claimed that his camera had been knocked out of his hand by an avalanche) or GPS data (he didn't record any). Nevertheless, based largely on the credibility of Steck's previous accomplishments, he was awarded the Piolet d'Or, climbing's highest honor, for the Annapurna ascent.

The case leveled against Jornet's back-to-back Everest climbs is similar: a lack of documentation verifying a historic accomplishment. The dispute is being pushed primarily by a single individual, a climber named Dan Howitt based in Portland, Oregon. After the climb, Howitt produced and circulated a 19-page document that reviewed, in painstaking detail, Jornet's ascent of Cho Oyu, in early May, and both of his Everest climbs later that same month.

Howitt's case against Jornet focuses on two main points: no persuasive summit images and questionable GPS data. Given the significance of the claims, he convinced a British website called Mount Everest the British Story, to publish the document in full in the summer of 2017. The report sparked widespread debate. It also prompted threats directed at the website's staff via online comments and Facebook. "Some people enjoyed the read, but most disagreed with what Dan had written," Collin Wallace, the website's founder, wrote me in an email. A few critics warned that they would "give the website a bad name" and that Wallace should "get legal advice about publishing the article." Concerned about losing the audience it had taken him a decade to build, Wallace promptly removed the piece.

Howitt persisted, however, lobbying media outlets, including *Outside,* and claiming that he could prove Jornet had come up short, at least on the first Everest ascent. When he compared Jornet's summit track on a topographic map with Adrian Ballinger's, Jornet's route appears to terminate in a different location, presumably below the summit. (Jornet's watch had inexplicably recorded part of the descent for the second climb, but nothing more.)

Howitt's report raises legitimate questions, but it mainly delivers uncertainty—by no means proof that Jornet is a fraud. That's a common phenomenon in our digital age. Wade into the online record-keeping of nearly any endurance sport and you'll encounter a few obsessives who've made a hobby out of endlessly questioning and parsing the latest FKT. Howitt has assumed this role in the mountaineering realm for nearly two decades. A climber who has claimed speed records on Mounts Rainier, Hood, Adams, Shasta, and others, he had waged a years-long crusade against the late Chad Kellogg, a well-respected mountaineer from Washington who claimed FKTs on Rainier and elsewhere.

Jornet remained largely quiet as his accuser continued his media campaign. He eventually responded to the allegations in December, but the defense was thin: his GPS had malfunctioned, and photos and video were embargoed until a documentary film, *The Path to Everest,* was released in the spring. That same month, he appeared on the Talk Ultra podcast, hosted by Ian Corless, and offered up additional details, but it hardly put an end to the controversy. The cover story in Spanish climbing magazine *Desnivel,* which relied on Howitt's report, was published the following month.

One evening in Romsdal, I join Jornet, Forsberg, and their friend Ida Nilsson, the elite Swedish runner and skimo racer, for dinner. Forsberg grows much of their food on the property. For dinner she's prepared a rich lentil stew and fresh bread made from locally produced spelt flour.

After the meal, I ask Jornet to walk me through the Everest climb. I expect the question to mark the immediate end of the dinner party's convivial vibe. Instead, Jornet seems happy to go over it in detail. We settle on the couch next to a wood-burning stove, in front of his laptop, where he shares his collection of photos and videos.

Jornet tells me that they spent less than a month total in Tibet, the first 10 days on 26,864-foot Cho Oyu, before moving on to Everest Base Camp, at the foot of the Rongbuk Glacier. It was a small team—just Jornet, Montaz-Rosset, Forsberg, and their Nepali cook, Sitaram.

Back in Norway, prior to the trip, Jornet and Forsberg had pre-acclimatized for one month, cranking out high-intensity intervals on a stationary bike while sucking reduced oxygen through a face mask. It seemed to work: Jornet arrived in the Himalayas feeling better than he had on his previous two trips. Forsberg eventually turned back before the top on Cho Oyu, but Jornet reached the broad plateau on May 14. Howitt and others have said it couldn't be claimed as a summit, and Jornet agreed: he acknowledges that he merely reached the plateau. But that was enough. Cho Oyu was only a preamble for the two weeks ahead.

Forsberg returned to Norway for a race, while Jornet, Montaz-Rosset, and Sitaram set up on Everest's north-side moraine. It was a comically tiny headquarters: a mess tent and three small personal shelters, nothing like the sprawling expeditions that bloom around Base Camp each spring. On May 18, after a one-night layover at advanced base camp, at 21,300 feet, Jornet made a trial run—literally—on some sections. He was ascending nearly 1,000 feet an hour, an impossible pace, all the way to 27,500 feet. "I did some stupid sprint on the North Ridge," he laughs, "because I could." The summit glistened temptingly less than 2,000 vertical feet above and Jornet felt great, but he stuck to his plan: descend to Base Camp, recover, and make an actual attempt in a couple of days.

As he narrates, Jornet cues up a series of images and video clips he took with a GoPro along the route. On May 20, he departed Base Camp at 10 p.m. to make his first try for the summit. By the time he reached the North Col, at 23,000 feet, he felt terrible and began wrestling with stomach problems. He was moving, as he says into the camera at one point, "So. Fucking. Slow."

It was almost sunset by the time he turned onto the Northeast Ridge, the nearly horizontal mile-long approach to the summit that includes three prominent steps. He was alone now, plodding forward. There is a dimly lit final photo on the ridge and then video of his face in the darkness, illuminated by the GoPro's small bulb. In the clip he's sitting, breathing hard. Over his shoulder, briefly catching the light from his camera, I glimpse prayer flags, the only evidence that it's the summit. "It was hard to film," Jornet says. "It's the last thing I was thinking about."

Next he took me through his second climb, including getting lost on the North Face. The weather was worse—windy and cold —but he felt better and moved more quickly, again summiting in the dark. He shows me another clip, but just of his face, no flags this time. He's wearing a face mask and seems profoundly tired. I'd watched a lot of footage of Jornet in the preceding months, from various races and climbs, and I realized that this was the only time I'd ever seen him looking exhausted.

He never claimed a speed record, he tells me. Early reports of an FKT were based on hasty press releases sent by his media team. (The FKT honor remains with Christian Stangl, who made the ascent in 2006 in 16 hours and 42 minutes, about 18 minutes faster than Jornet.) What he's certain of is that he summited both times. When I ask what he made of all the questioning, he only offers casual indifference—it's the media making hay.

Jornet sits back in his chair. Outside the window, the January supermoon is rising above the fjord, bathing the landscape in a monochrome of blue and white. "You don't think about much up there," he says. "You only really think about moving. I remember I could see lights from the south, people just starting their climb from the South Col. But that's about it."

My last morning in Norway, I load into Jornet's Mercedes Marco Polo camper van for a short trip to a jeep road along a nearby fjord. Jornet wears ski boots while he drives. We park and he's ready to skin in minutes, while I fumble with my gear.

"So, I think I go ahead and do some trainings now," he says. It's almost a question. Would I mind?

"Great!" I say. "I'll see you up there."

I know my way. It's the same zone we skied on the first day of my visit, a soft snow cone of a summit 3,000 vertical feet above. The sky is overcast but unthreatening, and I'm relieved to ski at my snail pace. Jornet has done his best to be accommodating, and I've tried my best to keep up. After four days, I'm beat.

I watch Jornet glide away on the snow-covered road, graceful, weightless. After an hour of steady effort, my base layer soggy with sweat, I reach the top. There are 360-degree views of the valley, the undulating fjords, the craggy peaks of the Troll Wall to the north, stabbing the sky. I look behind to find Jornet blasting up the slope toward me. As we remove our skins, I ignore the fact that this is his second lap. For the moment, I'm his equal, another friend in the mountains, gliding off the summit and down onto an apron

of spongy snow. It's blissful being back on the right side of grav-
ity, swooping and whooping through clusters of scrub oak and fir.
I encounter him again, briefly, back at the road, skins on, poles
pumping, chugging back uphill for his third run.

If Jornet was anything other than what he would have us believe, I found no evidence of it. Perhaps there was another, simpler
explanation for his back-to-back Everest summits. Steve House, the
alpinist and author, believes Jornet is an example of what happens
when you log an average of almost 1,000 hours a year for 17 years
—the compound interest of nearly two decades of progressive
training. "All this volume allows him to do such a wide range of
things," House told me, "and to do them well." They are collabo-
rating on a book for uphill athletes.

I spoke with Jornet again a few weeks after my trip to Norway.
He'd been busy. He sent me a thorough rebuttal he composed to
address the Everest claims, including numerous details about the
GPS data, photo and video analysis, and a timeline of events. He
was circulating his response to the media and the Himalayan Database, which still hadn't confirmed his climbs.

I read through the report. As with Howitt's, there was no single
piece of information that closed the case. But as a whole, it was
the most convincing argument he'd made yet, laying out the in-
tricacies of GPS tracking that help explain why his and Ballinger's
summit routes don't align. Still, Jornet seemed resigned to the fact
that clarity might be impossible. "I think there will always be fans,
and there will be those who doubt," he said. "I don't want to spend
time on the haters, but I understand about proof."

Jornet had also stormed back to racing, climbing, and skiing.
In February, he placed first in the vertical and fourth in the individual race at the Puy Saint Vincent Ski Mountaineering World
Cup in France, his first competition since surgery. A week later,
not far from his home, he logged a first descent on a 55-degree
pencil couloir on the Troll Wall that set the extreme-skiing world
convulsing with adulation. And he'd started planning Summits of
My Life 2, a preliminary list, at least, that included "projects bigger
than Everest."

In March, Jornet competed in the Pierra Menta, a four-day race
often touted as the Tour de France of skimo. On the fourth and
final stage, he and his teammate, Jakob Herrmann, were leading

and poised for the overall win when Jornet crashed on a downhill section and fractured his fibula. The injury would keep him in a cast for six weeks, but the prognosis was favorable. When I last heard from him, a few weeks after the accident, he sounded upbeat and optimistic, and he intended to be racing again by July. He was, it seemed, superhuman, but also human, after all.

KATHRYN MILES

Is This Man a Victim?

FROM DOWN EAST

MONINDA MARUBE'S FAME came to him unexpectedly. Which isn't to say the competitive runner wasn't seeking stardom. On the contrary, he came to the United States from his native Kenya dreaming of high-profile victories and lucrative sponsorships from companies like Nike. Instead, Marube has acquired a celebrity he never anticipated—as the face of human-trafficking survivors in Maine and nationwide.

In that capacity, he has stood on the steps of the U.S. Capitol alongside Maine senator Susan Collins, who praised him as "a person of remarkable courage and commitment." He's been the subject of newspaper, magazine, and radio stories and multiple documentary projects. He's spoken at conferences and workshops and shared billing with Maine governor Paul LePage at the state's Summit on Human Trafficking. On a CNN segment covering Marube's 2015 attempt at an awareness-raising cross-country run, the network's morning anchor declared, "You can't believe in this day and age that that's happening—slavery and human trafficking. But, you know, he is living proof that it is."

I heard about Marube from a filmmaker who'd interviewed him for a documentary. I listened, enthralled, as the documentarian retold Marube's story: How the runner had traveled to Coon Rapids, Minnesota, expecting to train with an expert manager, only to be exploited in unimaginable ways. How, even with his passport confiscated by his trafficker, he'd managed to escape under cloak of darkness, thanks to a dramatic rendezvous. How Border Patrol officers were so taken by his story that they let him go, despite his being out of status. How he found his way to Maine, thanks to big-hearted patrons, where he reinvented himself as an advocate and activist.

When I contacted Marube last summer and asked whether I could interview him for a magazine profile, he was arguably at the height of his fame. Weeks before, he had reported to his local newspaper that he'd successfully outrun two black bears that had given chase while he was on a dawn training run in his adopted hometown of Auburn. The story of Marube's escapes—from the bears and from his trafficker—had gone viral, appearing in outlets around the globe, with coverage of one or both from the BBC, NPR, *Good Morning America, Time, Sports Illustrated,* and others.

Marube invited me to meet him on campus at the University of Maine at Farmington, where he was starting his sophomore year. He seemed eager to share his story.

Marube and I met one afternoon in September in the lobby of the university library. He was wearing a tracksuit and hooded sweat-shirt, and with his reedy build, he could easily have passed for a decade younger than his 39 years. He was as mild and charming as friends and supporters had described him to me: soft-spoken, almost formal in his politeness, with a beatific smile. We chitchat-ted about late summer weather and the school year. Marube, who is undocumented, is studying community health at the western Maine liberal arts college, which he says he attends on a partial tuition waiver negotiated by Dan Campbell, his primary benefac-tor and the university's track coach, with whom Marube lives in the summer and who pays the remainder of the runner's tuition. (The university will not confirm details of enrollment or financial aid status.)

Marube suggested we move to a picnic table on the quad, so we chose a sunny spot and settled in for a multi-hour interview, dur-ing which he unraveled his long, complicated story.

In March of 2010, after a few years competing internationally in Europe, Asia, and Australia, Marube traveled for the first time to the United States to run in Arkansas's Little Rock Marathon. He had a temporary visitor visa and an open-ended return ticket with what he thinks was a six-month window. Upon arrival, he dis-covered that the race offered no prize money. He won anyway, but with nothing to show for his victory, Marube resolved to stay in the

United States longer than he'd planned, accepting an invitation from a friend and fellow Kenyan to board with the man's family outside Dallas.

When the house began feeling crowded, the friend suggested Marube travel to Minnesota to train with another Kenyan expat, named William Kosgei, founder of a successful running club that managed and facilitated the travel of East African runners. Kosgei agreed, and Marube boarded a bus for the comfortable Minneapolis suburb of Coon Rapids.

He stayed in Kosgei's house for nine months, during which time, he says, the manager confiscated his passport and visa, pocketed all but a fraction of his appearance fees and winnings, and prevented him from communicating with the outside world via phone or internet. For lack of money, Marube says, he was forced to run in dozens of races, but he didn't retain enough of his own race income even to consistently afford food, which Kosgei did not provide. Marube says he was forced to share a single room with many other runners. When we first spoke, he told me he couldn't remember their number or sleeping arrangements; later, he said it was five to seven runners, with some on mattresses on the floor.

While under Kosgei's management, Marube says, he overstayed both his return ticket and the duration allowed by his immigration form. His visa may also have expired—he can't remember for sure —but he was definitely in the country illegally. He feared arrest if he tried to leave or approached authorities about his treatment. Anyway, he says, Kosgei so closely monitored his athletes' comings and goings, there were few opportunities for escape.

One day, Kosgei allowed several runners to accompany him to a grocery store. There, in a brief unsupervised moment, Marube befriended a Kenyan truck driver who was also shopping, and he memorized the man's phone number. Later (possibly the next day, possibly several days later—Marube has said both), he tricked Kosgei into returning his passport and immigration documents (he has given conflicting explanations as to how). Then he used a neighbor's phone to call the truck driver and explain his plight, and the sympathetic driver offered to meet him at a nearby truck stop and drive him to Texas.

On the appointed night, Marube told me, he snuck away from the house, together with a runner who I'll call Faith (she has requested anonymity), who also sought to escape Kosgei's abuses.

Away from the house, the two runners split up. Marube rendez-voused with the trucker, who delivered him out of Minnesota.

In Texas, he lived for months with Kenyan acquaintances; he was broke and slept on a bedbug-ridden mattress. In late 2011, he wrote to organizers of the Santa Barbara Marathon, which he'd won the year before, racing under Kosgei. The race's organizers offered to fly him out (elite runners are often paid fees and ex-penses to register, to raise a race's profile), but with his immigra-tion status expired, Marube requested a bus ticket instead. Then, en route to Santa Barbara, at a checkpoint on the Texas–New Mex-ico border, Marube's Greyhound was boarded by officers from the U.S. Customs and Border Patrol. They detained him after check-ing his expired documents, but Marube says they were so inspired by his story, they let him go free, admonishing him to get his pa-perwork in order and then driving him over an hour to return him to his bus.

"They told me this," Marube said in a 2016 documentary about his trafficking. "'You are a special case. We have never let anyone free.'"

The next day, Marube won the Santa Barbara Marathon and set the course record. At the post-race party, he approached one of the race's organizers to ask if he could receive his winnings in cash; the organizer was Dan Campbell, who'd come to Santa Bar-bara to assist the race's founder, a native Mainer he'd coached years before. Campbell was moved when Marube told him of his desperate circumstances back in Texas, and he invited the runner to move to Maine, to live with him, his wife, and his daughter. So in early 2012, Marube came to Auburn and moved in with the Campbells.

During that first interview, Marube and I talked at our picnic table until the sun began to set. Here and there, throughout our conversation, Marube paused to greet fellow undergraduates walk-ing by.

"They call me 'grandfather,'" he told me and beamed. More than one journalist has described his grin as "infectious." Many students, he said, come to him as a mentor and a confidant—a shoulder to cry on when a relationship ends, an inspiration when coursework seems stressful. When he came in second in the Maine Marathon in 2016 (he won in 2014), he was greeted at the finish line by a throng of UMF students, some of whom he works with as a volunteer coach for the school's cross-country team. They waved signs with slogans like UMF BEAVERS LOVE MONINDA, and some wore T-shirts promoting his anti-trafficking, anti-obesity campaign, The Moninda Movement.

Before we finished, I asked Marube for some details that would help me flesh out the story and contact other sources. Where was the truck stop where he'd met his rescuer, and what did it look like? Marube said he was no longer sure. What was the truck driver's name, and could I contact him? Marube told me he'd long since forgotten. What were the names of other runners who were with him in captivity in Coon Rapids? Marube said he couldn't remember any, except that of the woman he escaped with, which he came up with later, in a follow-up call.

On a number of points, in fact, Marube was vague on details — some of those above he filled in or clarified in follow-up interviews. At first, he told me he was holding back certain information to someday publish in an autobiography. But when I pressed him on a few points, he admitted that his memory simply failed him in many cases. This is not uncommon among trafficking survivors, as I later heard from Annalisa Enrile, a clinical associate professor at the University of Southern California who specializes in the experiences of trafficking victims. "There's a lot of trauma and PTSD there," Enrile says. "In a lot of ways, you exist in someone [else's] psychology even after you're removed from the situation. So you have a shifting narrative—your natural defenses keep you in denial."

Marube and I agreed to talk again a few weeks later. We shook hands, and he gave me one last infectious smile.

Human trafficking is among the planet's most pervasive crimes. It is also one of the least understood. It is not the same as human smuggling, which the United Nations and U.S. Department of Homeland Security define as the illegal transportation of people. It is also not the same as unfair or exploitive labor practices—paying less than minimum wage, say, or ignoring safety requirements, breaching child labor laws, or permitting workplace harassment.

Human trafficking is the forceful or fraudulent recruitment of someone for his or her labor. It is coercive servitude—a form of modern-day slavery that generates billions of dollars each year for those who perpetrate it. It is often delineated into two separate forms: sex trafficking and labor trafficking. Of these, the former has received the most attention in this country, which can make the latter all the more difficult to identify.

Because human trafficking is also one of the planet's most underreported crimes, it's hard to put firm numbers to its extent. Globally, experts say, human trafficking likely counts at least 27 million victims at any given time. In the United States, the majority are trafficked in the sex industry, but not all—fully a third of trafficking victims are exploited for other forms of labor, things like felling trees, washing dishes, or braiding hair.

"There's this image of trafficking victims as women chained in basements or held in shipping containers, but that's not what we see," explains Daniella Cameron, director of Anti-Trafficking Services at Preble Street in Portland. "Really, the only demographic trafficking victims share is that they often come from vulnerable populations."

In states like Minnesota and Maine, dominated by industries with transitory labor forces like tourism and agriculture, seasonal turnover can make it easier for trafficking victims to go unnoticed. In 2011, the year after Marube says he was trafficked, Minnesota's Department of Public Safety identified more than 50 trafficking victims in that state, working in everything from landscaping to retail to child care. Advocates suggest the actual number of victims is exponentially higher.

No agency or organization in Maine keeps official statistics on labor trafficking. What data about trafficking does exist comes by way of a recent study commissioned by the Maine Coalition Against Sexual Assault. It estimates that, in a state with a population of just 1.3 million, more than 200 people are victims of sex trafficking annually. Only about 14 percent of those ever report the crimes committed against them.

"For many trafficking victims, there's a great risk in reaching out," Cameron explains. "Some worry there will be retaliation against them or their families, or they don't have legal status."

Many of those trafficked don't even realize they are victims of a crime. That was true in one headline-making scandal last year, which uncovered high school students from countries including Paraguay and Nigeria brought to New Jersey under false pretenses to play basketball. The foreign students arrived without the necessary immigration approval, were bounced between people posing as their guardians, and were denied basic needs like winter clothing and allowances for food. Similar stories of trafficking for athletic purposes have emerged from Arkansas, Arizona, Georgia, and elsewhere, where international basketball students have been found living in abusive conditions, not enrolled in schools, or without proper clothing and personal supplies.

Thanks to language barriers, cultural differences, and the transitory nature of competition, the arena of international pro sports can be especially difficult to police. Last year, in a joint investigation, three European news agencies reported on the routine exploitation of professional Ethiopian runners in oil-rich nations seeking athletic prestige. The head of the International Association of Athletics Federations, track and field's governing body, described the abuse as trafficking and called for an investigation. (An IAAF spokesperson referred me to the organization's independent ethics unit for details of that investigation; the unit didn't respond to multiple contact attempts.)

Bridgette Carr, who directs the Human Trafficking Clinic at the University of Michigan Law School, has worked on cases resulting from foreign-student basketball scandals. She isn't aware of any trafficking cases involving runners, but she believes they might be out there.

"Whether it's sports or any other industry, trafficking is horrible," Carr says. "But at the end of the day, it's also just powerful people taking gross advantage of unpowerful people—and that's a lot more common than we'd like to admit."

William Kosgei denies that he is a human trafficker. Marube's story, Kosgei says, is false, and he finds it "very wrong and morally sickening."

Last October, I flew from Maine to Minnesota to visit Coon Rapids, some 10 miles north of Minneapolis proper, hoping I could see firsthand some of what Marube couldn't remember and get the details I'd need for a story. I hadn't planned on contacting Kosgei, in part because I wasn't sure whether he was dangerous. It was only a 24-hour trip, during which I hoped to get a look at the house where Kosgei lived with his runners—and maybe, if I was lucky, find one outside the house who'd talk to me. I wanted to see the suburban blocks where his neighbors were evidently unaware of a trafficking operation in their midst, as well as the streets where

Marube would have taken his training runs. I wanted to find the truck stop where he'd made his dramatic rendezvous. And, if I'm being honest, I did hope to observe William Kosgei.

So after exploring Coon Rapids and searching in vain for anything in town that might be described as a truck stop, I drove to the address I'd found online for Kosgei and his Duma Runners Club. In a tree-shaded neighborhood full of cul-de-sacs, I spent less than an hour parked outside the duplex townhouse before a car pulled into the driveway and Kosgei stepped out. I recognized him from photos on the web: fit, in his forties, his head shaved or bald. He went inside and came out again a few minutes later, wearing a tracksuit. Then he got back in the car and drove off.

I followed, and I soon found myself pulling into the parking lot of Coon Rapids High School, where I knew from some web sleuthing that Kosgei is an assistant cross-country coach. I watched from the lot as he greeted and then ran through some warm-ups with a group of gangly teenagers. A few minutes later, a pair of adults in workout clothes, who I pegged for Kenyan runners, showed up in their own cars—evidently unmonitored and unescorted—and started training with the high school kids. For over an hour, I watched the practice unfold. Sprints. Stretching. Kosgei seeming to joke around with his runners. The whole scene just seemed so normal.

When it was over, after I'd watched Kosgei drive off and the man and woman who I presumed to be his runners leave separately, I texted Kosgei at a number I'd cribbed from the web. I wrote that I was a journalist and asked whether I could meet with him and his club the next morning, before my return flight.

Kosgei wrote back immediately. He apologized: he had to work early the next day (as a tech at a lens manufacturer, I would learn) in order to leave early for cross-country practice in the afternoon. However, he wrote, his wife and the runners who stayed with them would be happy to host me at the house. With some hesitation, I accepted the invite.

The next morning was cool and rainy, and I spent the better part of it in the kitchen in the Kosgeis' townhouse, sitting around a large table with seven elite Kenyan runners from the Duma Runners Club. Nicole Kosgei, a polite native Minnesotan and real estate agent, welcomed me in before apologizing that she had to take her kids to a dentist appointment. She invited me to stay as long as I'd like, then left me alone with the runners.

The kitchen was steamy and smelled a bit like a locker room. The runners shared with me a traditional Kenyan tea, hot and sweet and poured from a blue plastic pitcher. Among them were several extremely accomplished athletes, including a world champion marathoner. I was still cautious about the circumstances and told them only that I wanted to know about their experiences training as international runners with Duma. A few had run with the club for several years, and they told me they tend to spend six months in the United States during the race season, then six months back in Kenya—two of them are police officers there. They showed me the two rooms they stayed in, which reminded me of places I'd lived in college. Everyone agreed the house was too small for everyone to be comfortable and that seven runners was probably too many at one time. They also said they were making the most of their cramped quarters. I asked whether they held their own passports—they said they did—and whether Kosgei was a fair manager. They told me he was.

I watched some of the runners scroll through Facebook and exchange texts with their families back home—most had their own cell phones—and others make plans with friends to go into Minneapolis that afternoon. If their movement or communication was restricted, I saw no indication of it. Before I left, a couple of them asked if we could take selfies on the couch. By the time I was back in my car, they'd texted me the images.

Back in Maine, I called Kosgei and came clean about my reasons for visiting. We spoke at length. He denied Marube's accusations, gave me permission to use his name in this story, and insisted he has nothing to hide.

Kosgei also put me in touch with Faith, the runner with whom Marube told me he escaped Kosgei's house. She currently lives in Washington State with her husband, another Kenyan runner. Over the phone, Faith denied several of Marube's claims. Kosgei never held her passport, she said, and she didn't flee his house with Marube but stayed in a different house altogether and left Duma both amicably and some time later on. Her training and treatment in Coon Rapids, she said, were favorable.

I also spoke by phone with Richard Kandie, who now lives in Wisconsin and trained with Duma Running Club for years, starting in 2008. Kandie and his wife, runner Rael Murey, were also among the runners at Kosgei's house with Marube in 2010. He too says Kosgei treated them fairly, that he remembers no restrictions on phone or internet usage, was in no way prevented from coming or going, always held his own passport, and has no memory of Marube mentioning his immigration documents being withheld. And although he admits he wasn't privy to Kosgei's arrangements with other runners, Kandie says the manager took 15 percent of his race income, the industry standard (Marube says Kosgei took a 20 percent cut), plus a reasonable amount for expenses.

When I called Marube some weeks later, I told him about my trip to Coon Rapids, and what Kosgei and his two fellow runners had said. "Okay," he said, without hesitation. "I think what you are trying to dig into has a lot of tribal stuff going on." At Kosgei's, Marube explained, he had been the only member of his Kenyan ethnic group. He's a Kisii; Faith belongs to the Kikuyu, and both Kandie and Kosgei to the Kalenjin. In Kenya and abroad, there is enmity among these groups. Tribal prejudice, Marube said, likely explained Faith's and Kandie's denials.

Later, in a fact-checking session with his immigration lawyer present, Marube elaborated, saying that Kosgei had, in fact, singled him out because of tribal prejudice. He wasn't actually sure, he conceded then, whether other runners had their immigration documents taken or what their financial arrangements had looked like. And other, favored runners, he said, did indeed have internet access on Kosgei's computer; it was he, specifically, who was barred from using it.

The explanation that Marube was uniquely persecuted contradicts what he first told me, as well as what he's told audiences as recently as April, at a UMF conference on human trafficking that he helped organize. It also contradicts two formal accounts Marube has given to law enforcement and immigration agencies.

In 2012, Dan Campbell introduced Marube to Auburn police chief Phillip Crowell, cofounder of a faith-based, anti-trafficking organization called the Not Here Justice in Action Network and a seven-year member of the Maine Attorney General's Human Trafficking Work Group. Sometime after their acquaintance, Marube learned about a visa available to victims of certain crimes. It wasn't until he visited an immigration lawyer, he later wrote in an affidavit, that he told his Auburn hosts about his mistreatment by Kosgei. Thereafter, in 2014, Crowell arranged for Marube to sit down with two special agents from the Homeland Security investigations unit of U.S. Immigration and Customs Enforcement, in order to formally disclose his circumstances in Coon Rapids.

The agents determined that Marube's account was insufficient to prompt a federal investigation. But in the record of his testimony, and in a subsequent signed statement accompanying a visa application, Marube was explicit that all—or, at least, other—runners with whom he shared Kosgei's house had experienced the same exploitation and mistreatment.

Those 2014 and 2015 documents also make no mention of the truck driver—neither the meeting in the grocery store nor the truck-stop rendezvous, both central to the escape narrative that Marube has often shared in the years since. Instead, Marube stated in both documents that his friend in Texas, with whom he'd first stayed, simply arranged a ride for him out of Minnesota. When asked about this in a fact-checking session, Marube acknowledged that he'd left out some details: he did meet a Kenyan trucker in a chance encounter at a Minnesota grocery store and then subsequently escape with him, Marube explained, but in between, he contacted his friend in Texas, who it turned out unexpectedly knew that very driver. So both accounts were true.

Marube's two recorded statements also suggest that he and Kosgei were unacquainted before Marube went to Coon Rapids, and that his Texas friend had arranged his Duma training. That's what Marube told me and again later verified in a fact-checking session. But Kosgei provided me emails dated March 2010, purportedly between him and Marube, in which Marube appears to contact Kosgei just a week after arriving in the United States, reminding him of having met in Kenya and discussed visas and a potential training arrangement. What's more, the emails allegedly from Marube seem to imply that he was unsafe in Texas, being monitored by his host and prevented from communicating. "When you are threatened [*sic*]," reads one, "you can fear to even leave especially if you have nowhere to go."

Other stories of Marube's, not related to his trafficking, simply proved difficult to verify. There are the black bears, of course. And there's the story Marube told me of having received a special guest pass from a supportive government minister, allowing him to stay and train at a Kenyan military barracks. A military attaché at the Kenyan embassy in D.C. rebuffed this claim. "No such individual has been granted unfettered access to and accommodation in any of our military bases or installations," he wrote. "As a matter of fact, there is no such practice for runners in Kenya to gain free access to our military facilities, unless they are actually employees of Kenya Defence Forces."

A spokesperson for the U.S. Customs and Border Patrol, meanwhile, said he'd found no record of Marube's Greyhound bus detention. That doesn't mean it didn't happen, he said, but international travelers with expired legal-visitor status cannot reapply without returning to their homeland, so the agents' supposed admonition that Marube get his "paperwork in order" would have been nonsensical. Anyone found out of status "would be processed accordingly," the spokesperson said, and a failure to do so would likely be grounds for discipline or dismissal.

Though they challenge the neat narrative around which he has built an advocacy platform, none of the inconsistencies in Marube's story, denials from other sources, or unverifiable claims necessarily mean that Marube wasn't in some ways mistreated or even trafficked while in Coon Rapids.

In all, I and *Down East* editors contacted eight former Duma runners who have stayed with William Kosgei. Only the two with whom Kosgei put me in touch had no complaints about their treatment there. All said that their movements and communications were unrestricted. All said they held their own passports and immigration documents, although two said that Kosgei had asked or offered to hold theirs. The same two said that Kosgei had sponsored their visas, complained that he sometimes threatened to have runners sent back to Kenya, and claimed he later somehow caused their visas to be revoked while they were out of the United States. Four had complaints about their financial arrangements; they thought Kosgei had charged them more commission than he did other runners, up to 18 percent, and/or that they were charged more for expenses than was fair, or more than they'd been promised. Some said he could be stingy, others lewd. Kosgei, for his part, says that managers become targets for complaints from runners who underperform. Even those runners who felt somehow wronged stopped short of saying they were victims of human trafficking.

In 2015, a documentary called *The Long Distance* made a small splash in running circles. Directed by German filmmaker Daniel Andreas Sager, the English-language film follows two Kenyan runners during a season of competition in Europe with a veteran German manager. A condensed version of the film is available on the YouTube channel of German public television. In one scene, a runner receives her payout, her disappointment evident as the manager deducts for travel, room and board, his fee, and more, leaving little bottom line. In another scene, he chastises his runners for a poor performance, and in yet another, the runners debate the financial calculus of attempting an extra marathon they'd rather not run versus returning home nearly broke.

"Modern slavery," reads one characteristic YouTube comment. The word "slavery" pops up repeatedly in other users' comments: "They're treated like slaves." "Definitely exploitation." "Shocked, dismayed, and disgusted." "I hope someone in the UN or similar org sees this film . . . this is almost considered slavery, these athletes are being held hostage."

And yet, the film's director points out, what some viewers see as bondage, the manager and the runners considered banal enough that they allowed a film crew to document it. The manager and his wife were pleased with the film, according to Sager. "I can understand both opinions," he says.

Sometimes an instance of labor trafficking is obvious. Other times, what constitutes any of the three main pillars of trafficking—force, fraud, and coercion—is in the eye of the beholder. Alicia Peters is associate professor of anthropology at the University of New England and the author of *Responding to Human Trafficking*. She says it can take a lot of nuance and experience to identify when a crime has taken place.

"Trafficking and exploitation occur along a continuum, so there are certainly gray areas," she wrote to me in an email. "But case law and screening tools have added clarity over time."

Those tools include verification systems and in-depth questionnaires administered by staff trained to identify trafficking and distinguish it from "mere" exploitation. But a lot of communities lack those resources. In Maine, for instance, just two of the state's 16 counties have federally funded trafficking service providers, which means the only way for most labor-trafficking survivors to be identified is by Good Samaritans or referrals from government agencies or community organizations. Awareness of the problem may be on the rise, though: this April, state legislators overturned a veto to pass a law that, for the first time, defines criminal forced labor in Maine and prohibits the withholding of passports, threat of deportation, or unfair compensation for work.

Whether Marube's situation would meet the thresholds established by such statutes and screening tools is unclear—he has not participated in any formal victim assessment—but U.S. Citizenship and Immigration Services will weigh his case. In 2015, Marube filed his application for what's known as a U visa, a class of admission granting permanent residency to victims of certain crimes willing to assist law enforcement with the investigation and/or prosecution of those crimes. The application requires a law enforcement official's certification, indicating the applicant "is or has been a victim of" a qualifying crime and has cooperated (or might cooperate). Marube's included his own notarized statement, as well as a certification signed by Auburn police chief Crowell.

I asked Crowell about that document, which includes a line leveling Marube's most disturbing allegation, one the runner doesn't speak of in documentaries or interviews: "He is aware of some female runners who have been forced into prostitution by the running club owner." In a fact-checking session, Marube and Dan Campbell explained this charge is based on a single instance of hearsay, of another (male) runner telling Campbell of Kosgei having propositioned a female runner to sleep with his friends for room and board. "Is there evidence of this sex stuff? No," Marube said. So I didn't understand why Crowell would include it, and why he'd certify Marube's victimhood "based upon an investigation of the facts" and "under penalty of perjury" when neither the Auburn PD nor any other agency had pursued an investigation. Crowell wrote back in a statement:

"Moninda was advised that based on what he was able to share with us, we would not be pursuing the case. This does not take away the fact that a person reported he was a victim of a crime and he was willing to cooperate . . . It is the responsibility of the governing body to determine if the testimony provided by the victim meets the threshold of issuing the U visa."

Marube's application is still in the agency queue. The U visa is granted to just 10,000 applicants per year, and for the past three years, the quota was met before a judgment was made on his materials. While awaiting adjudication, applicants are legally permitted to remain in the country.

In my last interview with Marube, I asked him how he felt about the prospect of Kosgei being formally charged and perhaps going to prison. Trafficking comes with a maximum sentence of 20 years, although it can be extended to a life sentence if there are aggravating factors like prostitution. Marube hesitated. "I'm not a judge, and I don't want to judge," he said. "If the law says that's the way to go, then who am I to say no? If the law says I'm the one in the wrong, then who am I to say, also?"

After a while, Marube told me maybe it would be better if I didn't write the story at all.

"Someone's going to get hurt," Marube said. He might be right, I told him. There's Marube himself, of course. And there are those who've supported him, both formally and informally. There's William Kosgei, who has been accused of crimes he may or may not have committed. And then there are an unknown number of trafficking victims and survivors who may not come forward if they fear they won't be believed. For their sakes, if for no others, I have wondered at times if I should have taken Marube's advice and not written this story at all.

It's those victims that Bridgette Carr fears for. The director of the trafficking center at the University of Michigan Law School worries that publicly dissecting stories like Marube's can make it harder to prosecute perpetrators of trafficking—and harder for people actively involved in criminal investigations to get visas.

"I know from my own cases that victims of human trafficking— even those with significant, credible, and independent evidence of their trafficking—often face an uphill battle to be seen as victims and to find safety and support," she told me. "Our sex-trafficking clients are still more likely to be convicted of prostitution than be identified as victims."

Too many Americans, Carr says, have a hard time believing that human trafficking occurs here. We're like the host of the CNN segment on Marube—incredulous that slavery could be a part of our modern experience of the world. But there can be more insidious factors, she says, like the fact that trafficking victims often don't look the way we want them to. They are runaways or homeless. In some cases, they are drug addicts or prostitutes. They're not as winning or as eloquent or inspirational as, say, Marube.

"When they don't present that way, it can be easy to lose sympathy," Carr says. "We all want to subscribe to the myth of the perfect victim."

ABE STREEP

What the Arlee Warriors Were Playing For

FROM THE NEW YORK TIMES MAGAZINE

STARTING AT NOON on February 23, the town of Arlee, Montana, evacuated. Most of its 600-odd residents drove 70 miles south through Missoula and then into the Bitterroot Valley, a river corridor full of subdivisions, trailers, exclusive private communities, and ammunition stores. The crowd filtered into the gymnasium at Hamilton High School, wearing red shirts and pins bearing the faces of the Arlee Warriors basketball team, who that evening would be playing the Manhattan Christian Eagles.

Manhattan Christian is a faith-based private school near Bozeman. Arlee is a public school on the Flathead Indian Reservation; about half the town is Salish, descendants of the people forced out of the Bitterroot in the 19th century. Manhattan Christian's boys were tall and muscled; most of Arlee's players were well under six feet and on the thinner side. Manhattan Christian arrived in a sleek black bus with aerodynamic curvature and tinted windows; Arlee came in a yellow Blue Bird. The February 23 game would be a rematch of the previous year's Class C state championship, which the Warriors won. On one wall of the gym, Manhattan Christian had hung a banner reading #UNFINISHED. Arlee had their own banner, but they did not need it. They had Phillip Malatare.

Phil is 18 and six feet tall. He claimed to be 167 pounds, but that seemed generous. His normally angular face was especially gaunt that afternoon, a result of a nasty cold. But he had a reputation in the state: for his routine triple-doubles, his no-look passes thrown around his back at a dead sprint, his unguardable pull-up jump shot, the speed and body control that made it all possible.

His parents, John and Becky, arrived at 9 a.m. to watch the day's earlier games and to stake out seats. The Malatares never sat together at games. "It just works better," Becky said. "I like to kind of breathe." John wore a red T-shirt adorned with a Salish phrase that translates as "I'm proud of my warriors."

Ten minutes remained before warm-ups. Normally, at this point, the boys would be making fart jokes or talking about video games. Now, though, the Warriors left the locker room and gathered in a hallway. A cameraman lined the players up. They were silent. The light on the camera blinked, and Phil spoke.

"We, the Arlee Warriors," he said, "are dedicating this divisional tournament to all the families that have lost a loved one due to— um—" He tripped up, and the cameraman asked for another take.

"We, the Arlee Warriors," he said, "are dedicating this divisional tournament to all the families that have lost a loved one due to the pro—due to the pressures—"

Phil tried again: "We, the Arlee Warriors, are dedicating this divisional tournament to all the families that have fallen victim to the loss of a loved one due to the pressures of life."

"We want you all to know," said Greg Whitesell, one of Phil's co-captains, "that you will be in our hearts and in our prayers as we step onto the floor to represent our school, community, and our reservation."

Lane Johnson, the power forward, spoke: "As a team, we rely on each other to get through the challenges on the court or in life." Then Isaac Fisher, the six-foot-nine center, said, "To all the youth on the Flathead reservation, we want you to know that we stand together with you."

Darshan Bolen, the sixth man and Phil's cousin and foster brother, said, "Remember, you are the future." Phil wrote that line. Then Will Mesteth, a co-captain and the team's only other senior, closed it: "Please help us share this message and join our team as we battle against suicide."

Only about half the Warriors could legally drive, and many struggled academically. But as state champions, they were kings on the Flathead reservation. They came into the season hoping to defend their trophy; Phil and Will also wanted a chance to play in college. But by the evening of the Manhattan Christian game, the season had transformed into something else entirely.

The videographer turned off his camera, and the Warriors retreated into the locker room. The boys could hear the gym rippling with noise. Then the drumming started.

Highway 93 connects Missoula, a booming college town, with Polson, on the south shore of Flathead Lake. Driving north out of Missoula, you pass a few gas stations, then wind through tight timber. A large casino emerges on the left, and then, just north of an overpass for migrating wildlife, the land yawns open to reveal a spectacular landscape. A timbered ridge rises to the east, out of which flows the Jocko River, fat with snowmelt in the spring. The highway curves through ranchland, then briefly splits to accommodate Arlee's five-block downtown. Tourists who stop at the charming huckleberry-themed restaurant or the coffee shop and art gallery don't always realize they're guests of a sovereign nation: the Confederated Salish and Kootenai Tribes. One mile later, Arlee is gone.

The town is named for a Salish subchief. In 1871, Arlee, a Nez Percé by birth, acquiesced to the U.S. government's demands that the Bitterroot Salish relocate. This put him at odds with the head Salish chief, Charlo, who stayed in the Bitterroot Valley until 1891, when he marched north under military escort. Embittered, he had called Arlee "that renegade Nez Percé." On the reservation, the Salish were forced together with the Pend d'Oreille, their historical allies, and the Kootenai, a northern tribe with a different language. Government officials assigned them Anglicized names, and in 1909 Congress passed legislation opening the reservation to settlers. Many tribal members sold their allotted land, and Chief Charlo died in 1910; Native youth were forced into a Catholic boarding school, where nuns told the children that the devil was in them. The town of Charlo, 30 miles from Arlee, is now almost entirely white. Arlee is not. The town's most popular gathering places are Wilson's, a grocery store; a community center full of basketball courts; and the gleaming gymnasium that looms over the one-story public high school.

Because of its size, Arlee competes in Class C, the division representing Montana's smallest schools, most of them in mining and ranching towns or communities in Indian Country. The state's seven reservations—home to members of the Salish, Pend

d'Oreille, Kootenai, Blackfeet, Gros Ventre, Sioux, Crow, Northern Cheyenne, Assiniboine, and Chippewa-Cree tribes—share
a deep passion for basketball. In 1904, just 13 years after James
Naismith invented the game, a team of Native girls at a boarding
school near Great Falls competed in a tournament at the World's
Fair in St. Louis and were proclaimed world champions. In 1936,
a team from the Fort Peck Reservation won a state high school
championship; its stars, three brothers, went on to anchor a group
that beat the Harlem Globetrotters.

"Indian ball," as it became known, was characterized by full-
court-press defense and high-scoring, improvisational fast breaks.
The game is predicated on speed and cooperation. "It's not very
individualized," says Don Wetzel Jr., a Blackfeet Nation descendant
who manages the Montana Indian Athletic Hall of Fame. "You're
not taught to be like that. To make your people happy is one of the
greatest things you can ever do." High school stars from the past
remain celebrated today: names like Jonathan Takes Enemy, Sha-
ron LaForge, Elvis Old Bull, Malia Kipp, and Mike Chavez remind
people of on-court triumphs and, in many cases, off-court trials.

Montana's best-known reservation teams have come from the
plains east of the Rocky Mountains: from Lodge Grass, on Crow
Nation, and from Browning and Heart Butte, on Blackfeet Nation.
But for the past decade, the basketball program in Arlee, which
is in the foothills of the Mission Range, has touched the hem of
this elite. In 2005, a group of parents, including John and Becky
Malatare, started a youth basketball clinic. Between 2009 and 2013,
Arlee's boys went 88-34; the girls went 105-39 between 2011 and
2016. During that time, both teams secured divisional titles but
fell short at the state level. Zanen Pitts, a 32-year-old rancher and
Pend d'Oreille first descendant, took over as the boys' coach in
2013. He installed a system that combined the freewheeling speed
of Indian ball with defensive strategies borrowed from college programs. "There is a structure to our chaos," Pitts says.

In 2014, Phil Malatare entered high school. He had dedicated
most of his young life to two pursuits: horn hunting—searching
for the freshly shed antlers of bull elk—and playing basketball at
the community center. His arrival turned the Warriors' defense
into something terrifying. During his freshman year, the team lost
in the state semifinals; during his sophomore year, they reached
the championship; last year, they went 25-1, and Phil played nearly

every minute of the championship run. Just before the end of the game, someone in the crowd called him a redskin. Then, in the final seconds, he jumped for a rebound that clinched the victory. In his bedroom, he hung news clippings of his victories and defeats, for motivation, along with the cleaned skull of a buffalo he killed.

After last year, Phil was the only Class C player named to the ALL-USA Montana Boys Basketball team. This fall, when the *Great Falls Tribune* previewed the state's best high school players, it listed Phil first. Watching Phil on the court, Wetzel got to thinking about Old Bull and Takes Enemy, each of whom he played against. "He's more like Elvis," he says. "Elvis was deceptively quick. Phillip is flat-out quick." Don Holst, a former head coach for the University of Montana and a principal of Arlee's elementary school, saw it differently. Old Bull was a shooter; Phil, he says, has "this innate ability to see things." Pitts earnestly compared him to the NBA star Russell Westbrook. "I like Russell's pull-up jumper a *little* better," he once said. Whenever Phil arrived at basketball camps, kids flocked to him. At one game, his father heard a boy scream: "Phillip Malatare touched me!"

John Malatare, a Salish and Cree wildland firefighter, wanted Phil to cash in his ticket to leave the reservation while it was still good. "A lot of these colleges in Montana," John says, "will give a Native kid one chance." On reservations, basketball stars become symbols of hope, but many have struggled to replicate their high school success in college. Wetzel played at Montana State University at Billings, but he left the team after having a child in his sophomore year. He went on to a career in public education. Not everyone has been so fortunate. In 1991, *Sports Illustrated*'s Gary Smith wrote about the Crow stars Takes Enemy and Old Bull, who both struggled with alcohol. Others have gone to college, only to leave after feeling homesick.

Pitts says that in five years as head coach, he has had three college coaches ask if prospects are Native, openly worrying that they might not last in school. Women from Montana's reservations have carried a similar weight. In 1992, Malia Kipp, from Blackfeet Nation, entered the University of Montana, starring with the Lady Grizzlies for all four years. "I felt if I didn't succeed," she once said, "others wouldn't get the opportunity."

According to Pitts and Wetzel, the skepticism Native recruits face is owed to cultural misunderstanding, and the inadequate support systems in place as a result. "Those coaches need to do a better job of sustaining 'em," Pitts says. "They need to understand what they're coaching." That meant recognizing the gravitational pull of home for players from reservations, but also the genuinely distinct sports culture incubated there. Kids who grow up playing Indian ball on the reservation, whether or not they are themselves Native—the Arlee Warriors are Salish, Navajo, Sioux, Pend d'Oreille, and Blackfeet, but also white, black, and Filipino—can find the college game as alienating as campus life. For Wetzel, the businesslike nature and slower pace of college ball was challenging. "It's conformity," he says. Wetzel thinks schools should recruit multiple reservation players at once, the way the Lady Grizzlies did a decade ago, following Kipp's success. "I rarely see two Natives on the court at the same time at a college level," Wetzel says. "It does bring some magic."

Pitts, for his part, just wanted his players to get the opportunities they deserved. That meant a lot was riding on Phil. A good student with a supportive family, he was covered by local newspapers with headlines like "Unstoppable." Pitts thought he had been touched by God. Sometimes he found himself pleading with him to thrive in college. "You're doing this for every kid in the world," he says, "that's ever looked up to a basketball player coming off the rez."

On November 15, the evening before the season's first practice, 13 boys sat anxiously in a small classroom in Arlee's gym. It was 5 p.m. and already dark outside, signaling the beginning of western Montana's long winter. Coach Pitts stood at the front of the room in baggy jeans, a baseball cap covering his sandy hair, dried manure on his boots.

"We're here for a purpose," Pitts said. "That purpose is to win a state championship. I'm going to chew on you, I'm going to break you down, I'm going to build you back up." He said he was going to change their lives. "This is so much bigger than you." He outlined the rules. Guys who disrespected teachers would not play. Guys whose parents complained about court time would not play. Latecomers would not play. Exceptions would be made only in extreme circumstances: "If you want to go hunting, you've got some huge buck figured out, call me."

Pitts cued up a highlight reel from last year's championship season and left the room. Will Mesteth often watched the tape at night; it made him feel all warm inside. But it just made Phil sad, because his two best friends had graduated, and he wanted another championship. He also wanted, desperately, to make it as a Division 1 college player.

When the tape finished, Phil walked to the front of the room in a camouflage hoodie and a backward hat. "Everybody's going to be intimidated," he said. "And we got to make them intimidated. And that is going to be how it's going to be."

The first game of the season was on December 8, against a larger school from the Rocky Boy's Reservation. A couple of thousand fans filled the gym at a tribal college 40 miles north of Arlee. Will's hair was shining in a double braid courtesy of his mother. Phil was wired even though he had spent the morning deer hunting.

"We're not nervous," Pitts said.

"I'm nervous," Phil said. His teammates appeared relieved.

On the mirror behind Pitts was a flier for a suicide-prevention hotline; all but three of the tags on the bottom had been ripped off. He opened a box, revealing sleek, hooded warm-up shirts. The boys' nerves melted away in a chorus of hollering. Pitts choreographed the team's entrance, instructing the boys to fan out onto the floor once Will's grandfather, father, and uncles hit the drum and started the honor song. "I want everyone to know," he said: "The champs are here." The boys fell silent, and Pitts prayed:

> Our Father in Heaven
> We bow our heads humbly before you
> For the great opportunity that we have to play this game.
> To separate ourselves from the world.
> We ask, Father,
> That thou will bless us with strength and wisdom
> And give us the ability to be safe.
> Bless our opponents
> That they also can come out and perform at their highest potential.
> That they can be safe as well.
> And most of all,
> Let the refs keep up.

Before the previous season's championship game against Manhattan Christian, David Whitesell, Arlee's superintendent, spent long hours considering what might follow a loss. In the event, Whitesell was planning to increase counseling both for the community and the team. It was a lot, he said, "to place on the shoulders of a bunch of adolescent boys."

The cause of his concern was a proliferation of suicides that had swept the Flathead reservation in recent months. It started in the fall of 2016, with a few teenagers. Then in the winter, just before the 2017 divisionals, the Malatares awoke to discover that a close friend had taken her own life—a woman Phil considered to be "like an auntie," and an aunt of Will's by blood.

Pitts and John Malatare told the boys that when people came to see the Warriors play, they briefly escaped their worries. But the suicides continued; they had become what public-health professionals call a cluster. In April, a former Warrior who quit the team shot himself after attending the funeral of a friend who committed suicide. The former teammate survived, but Pitts was haunted. "The adversary is so strong," he said. "It's just there."

Between November 2016 and November 2017, there were 20 deaths by suicide on the reservation, according to Anna Whiting Sorrell, an official with the tribal health department. Phil said he had known "a few" people who had died by suicide. Asked to clarify, he said, "Twenty or thirty."

In 2016, the Centers for Disease Control released a study examining suicide rates among Americans by race and ethnicity. In 2014, the last year for which the researchers compiled data, non-Hispanic Native women between the ages of 15 and 24 committed suicide at a rate of 15.6 deaths per 100,000, or three times the rate of non-Hispanic white women and five times the rate of non-Hispanic black women of the same age. Young Native men had a rate of 38.2 deaths per 100,000 people. Among young people, the suicides often come in clusters, as happened in 2013 and 2014, on Arizona's Gila River Indian Reservation; in 2015, on South Dakota's Pine Ridge Indian Reservation; and last year, on the Flathead reservation. Some there, like Pitts, blamed technology, social media, and bullying. Others looked to the boarding schools that removed a generation of children and created a cycle of abuse. Whiting Sorrell had come to think of suicide—along with alcoholism and drug abuse—as a symptom of intergenerational trauma, the inherited grief among indigenous communities resulting from colonization. Whitesell said that the community's kids needed to learn to "survive their past and their present."

Part of that, he thought, was getting kids to talk openly about mental health. Upon taking the superintendent job in 2015, Whitesell sent the school staff to prevention training and had them take what's called an adverse childhood experiences (ACEs) quiz, a 10-question test to assess trauma. According to ACEs data the CDC collected in 2010 from more than 53,000 people in 10 states and the District of Columbia, 40.7 percent of participants reported no adverse childhood experiences, while 14.3 percent reported four or more, scores that were linked to increased health and behavioral risks. "I scored a seven," Whitesell says. Many kids in Arlee, he says, would most likely register right around there. That trauma can manifest in many ways. Suicide, Whitesell says, was "an option. It can't be an option."

In the fall, Whitesell's son Greg, the Warriors' co-captain, got a concussion playing football, his fifth, and had to stay home from school for three weeks. He struggled to eat and felt depressed. That confused him, because he was a star and a state champion. He almost felt as if he had no right to be sad, and that just made it worse. Greg didn't hunt like Phil and Will; off the court, he loved video games and hanging out with his friends. Now Greg started to isolate himself and to sleep a lot. "I was tired of being depressed," he says. "You just get tired of everything."

One night he sent a despairing text to a couple of friends. He was considering climbing out his window to start running when he saw headlights in the driveway. It was two teammates, Lane Schall, a gregarious ranch kid, and Darshan Bolen, Phil's cousin and foster brother. Greg told them he didn't want to live anymore.

Dar sat with him while Lane went to get Greg's mother, Raelena. She spoke with her son for about 45 minutes, then took Greg to a hospital in Missoula, where Whitesell met them. (He and Raelena are divorced.) Greg spent that night in a bare room with scratches on the wall. "I felt like I didn't belong there," he says.

The hospital staff determined he wasn't an immediate risk and sent him home. For weeks Raelena woke up every couple of hours to check on her son, and Greg regularly saw a counselor. Then basketball season started. He kept his experience private until he learned that a younger teammate was battling depression, at which point he told the kid he had been through similar struggles. Lane and Dar never talked publicly about that night. But, Greg said later, "if they didn't show up, I don't think I'd be here now."

*

In December, in a game against a team from Seeley-Swan, Phil racked up 48 points, 16 rebounds, and nine assists in 24 minutes of play. Afterward, Adam Hiatt, the head coach from Montana Tech, a college in Butte that competes in the National Association of Intercollegiate Athletics conference, texted Phil, hoping that he would enroll.

But Phil had other ideas. Sometimes he envisioned going to a powerhouse program like Oregon, but the idea of leaving Arlee caused an almost physical discomfort. He had been approached by a Division 1 school in Washington, and a small California school had offered him a full scholarship, but he brushed them off. The path to reconciling his athletic ambitions with his desire to stay close to home ran through Missoula: the college town just 24 miles south of Arlee, home of the Division 1 University of Montana Grizzlies. But the Grizz had offered Phil only an invitation to walk on, meaning he'd have to try out and pay his own way.

Tech, on the other hand, was offering a full scholarship. Phil was the team's No. 1 recruit. Becky liked the idea. But Phil said he needed more time, and sure enough, soon a coach from the Grizz reached out again. "They're dangling that carrot," Becky said.

By January 9, the Warriors were 8-0 and had outscored their opponents by an average of more than 40 points per game. That evening they played Mission, a larger high school in St. Ignatius and a rival, just up Highway 93 from Arlee. In the stands, Becky sat next to Hiatt. "He's the best player in the state," the coach said of Phil. John Malatare sat a couple of rows away, calling out traps.

Sitting with Hiatt, Becky digressed, as is her habit, talking about her son's dietary preferences—"Phil doesn't eat salad; he eats chicken"—and how he and John would leave in the middle of the night to hunt buffalo.

"That's crazy," Hiatt said.

But mostly Becky discussed Will Mesteth and how much Phil loved playing with him. "They grew up together," she said. A few minutes later, Will carved his way to the basket. "Will, No. 3," Becky said suggestively. "There he goes." And then, a few minutes later: "No. 3, his grandma is a Malatare. So they're related." But Will's shot was off. In the stands, his dad, Big Will, yelled, "Get him the ball!"

Will's parents had him when they were in high school, and he was largely raised by his *tupye*, his great-grandmother. Will got into powwows as a boy, singing and dancing; his grandfather gave him the claw of a black bear for protection, and he kept a collection of more than 20 pairs of Air Jordans. Will's mother, Chasity Haynes, is Salish and Navajo, and now works in the Salish and Kootenai Tribes' enrollment department. Big Will—no one calls him Will Sr.—was a Sioux and Salish football star who went to play at the University of Montana but got kicked out before he played a game. Now he was a cop on the tribe's drug task force. Big Will desperately wanted his son to complete college. But Will's college prospects depended on the intensity of his defense and the accuracy of his three-pointer.

Will struggled early in high school, compiling a string of F's and skipping class, sometimes to care for his *tupye*. But a teacher named Jennifer Jilot helped him, and he raised his grades enough to be academically eligible by his junior year. Then he made the all-state team for Class C. He didn't say much, but when he spoke, teammates and opponents alike listened closely. When it came to basketball, Will said, "pretty much everyone in the state knows who me and Phillip are." But in Jilot's classroom, Will curled up on her couch and hugged a pillow like a child. Jilot was deeply proud of his academic progress. She thought she might cry when he graduated.

Arlee beat Mission by 18 points, but in Pitts's and the other coaches' estimation, it was a lackluster night; the Warriors played selfishly. At the next practice, an assistant named Francis Brown-Lonebear accused the boys of playing "Missoula ball." That was about as exciting as watching Flathead Lake freeze. "I want to be *gone*," Brown-Lonebear said. "If you don't understand that, you don't understand about Indian ball."

John Malatare sat in his friend T. J. Haynes's truck, hurtling through the darkness. T.J. wore a wool cap with elk teeth affixed to the brim. A tribal cop who worked with Big Will, he grew up with John. Now each was a foster parent; it was T.J.'s wife who committed suicide the previous February, before the state tournament. He was raising nine kids.

John and T.J. had heard that buffalo were moving out of Yellowstone National Park, so they had loaded up T.J.'s trailer with snowmobiles and rolled south at 2 a.m. In the 1870s, the Salish moved a few calves into the Flathead reservation, building up a herd that was later used to revive the flagging Yellowstone population. Now the Salish are one of six tribes with treaty rights allowing them to hunt Yellowstone's bison when they move out of the park.

On the ride down, the men rubbed their hands and whistled in anticipation. Sometimes the hunters just stood in line waiting for the bison to cross onto Forest Service land, and sometimes animal rights protesters tailed them. Even so, John would rather hunt buffalo than anything else. "The first time I shot one of these, it was a whole different feeling," he said. "It was just the respect." He and T.J. talked about their disdain for trophy hunters who sell the hides. "Phillip, he sleeps on his," John said. "Got to keep the fan on just 'cause he stays so warm!"

He considered his son's college prospects. He wanted Phil to get back to the Montana Tech coach. He knew Phil wanted to play for the Grizz, but he didn't know what to do. Should he go knock down the coach's door and ask what it would take? He thought of a friend who had played college ball. The coach had given him a hard time. "I said, 'They're testing you out,'" John recalled. "'They're seeing how tough your willpower really is.'" But his friend quit. John said, "Proven point right there." Native kids got one shot.

A track star in high school, John always wished he had pursued athletics more seriously; Terry Pitts, Zanen's father, a retired coach and former tribal councilman, thought he could have been an Olympian. John met Becky, who was a descendant of European settlers and played basketball against his sisters, at age 22. Becky went on to work for a Missoula hospital, handling accounts, while John was hired by the Forest Service, digging breaks around wildfires. When he started out, "We heard a lot of, 'What are you Indians doing here?'" he recalled. "I had to work extra hard to prove that I could do the job." John became a supervisor, earning a good living, and when Phil was in sixth grade, four of his cousins, including Dar, came to live with the Malatares and their three children. After that the Malatares kept getting calls from the tribe, asking them to foster more kids. They came and came, sometimes for days at a time, sometimes more. Mounds of laundry piled up in the kitchen.

When Phil was six, he told his parents he was going to be a

professional athlete. By the time he was a freshman, he said he wanted to be the best basketball player Montana had ever seen. John realized he hadn't considered his own life once his son's career ended. "What are we going to do if he doesn't continue and play through college?" he asked. "I don't know. I don't know if I've thought that far."

Dawn revealed a blue, snowed-in landscape. T.J. and John parked at a pull-off, stepped out of the truck, and fired up their snowmobiles. A wolf ran past. The men hopped on the sleds and tore off into the lodgepole. They wound up a long curving track to an overlook from which they could see wide plains and craggy peaks, but no buffalo. They descended into low timber and split up. T.J. wound his way a bit farther, then stopped. A herd of bison moved slowly through the trees, followed by hunters on foot and, behind them, a group of animal rights campaigners documenting the kills. Shots rang out, and the herd split up, some moving toward private property, some back toward the park boundary.

An hour or so later, John and T.J. met back at the truck. John hadn't caught the herd. "Everyone without sleds killed 'em," John said.

"Them protesters must have pushed 'em all onto that private property," T.J. said.

Over dinner that night at a sports bar, they joined a group of Salish hunters, who talked basketball and hunting and foster-parenting. At one point, one of the men tried to imagine life with endless buffalo. "Used to be a perfect world," he said.

"Sure ain't now," T.J. said.

On the way home the next day, John considered the state championship in Butte, six weeks away. With seven games remaining in the regular season, the Warriors were undefeated. John had already booked his hotel room. "Stars are going to have to start falling out of the skies," he said, "for us not to be there."

By early February, Phil was averaging 23 points, 10 rebounds, seven assists, and six steals a game. He needed to decide about Montana Tech, but he didn't have a clear feeling. Then one day he was driving out to one of his horn-hunting spots, hoping to clear his head, when he received a text from a coach at the University of Montana. Phil called the coach right away, and the coach asked if he wanted a spot on the team. Phil pumped his fist and politely said that yes, he'd like that very much. In a follow-up call with Phil's parents, the Grizz offered Phil a "preferred" walk-on spot, meaning he was guaranteed a place on the team but would have to pay his own way. Phil told the coach he was in. (Rachi Wortham, an assistant coach at the University of Montana, said, "We can confirm recruitment," but he declined to comment further.)

After the call, John sat down in his leather recliner and exhaled. Becky was still partial to Tech—the school had great academics, and the free ride wouldn't hurt, given that the Malatares still had two more kids to put through high school and college. But Phil had made up his mind. He called Adam Hiatt to relay his decision, but he asked his parents not to share the news widely. He didn't want to disrupt the Warriors' playoff run.

The season came down to three weekends in late February and early March: the district championship, the divisional championship, and state. By this point, Will had rediscovered his shot, and the Warriors played with devastating joy. In the last regular-season game, Phil and Will combined to score 72 points.

Pitts called a coach from a Montana college, gushing that Will had a 35-foot shooting range, defense that can't be taught, strong grades. The coach wanted to know about Will's family. Pitts said that Will's father was a cop and that if the coach gave him a chance, his mother would "have him there tomorrow." Assuming his most authoritative sales voice, Pitts declared that Will would make it: "I'd stick my job on the line for him." The coach said he'd think about it. Pitts hung up and shook his head.

On Tuesday, February 20, just before divisionals, word spread of a suicide: a teenage basketball player from Two Eagle River, a competing team on the Flathead reservation. Pitts was worried. "The next week or two, another kid might do it," he said.

The divisional tournament was held in Hamilton, in the Bitterroot Valley, the ancestral homeland of the Salish. On the bus ride down before the first game, Pitts asked the players if they wanted to make a statement about the suicide. The boys thought it was a good idea and settled on a video as the way to do it. They decided that Phil would speak first and Will last, but when the camera rolled, Phil got nervous. One player didn't: Greg. His voice was calm and resolute. "I was focused on helping these people," he later said. "It felt awesome."

*

In the locker room, after the camera turned off, Phil and Will coughed violently. After catching his cold, Phil had gone out to check some cows on a cousin's ranch in subzero temperatures earlier in the week. Will, meanwhile, had some as-yet-undiagnosed illness that had caused him to lose 25 pounds since the beginning of the season. In recent weeks, blood had showed up in his urine. He sought medical attention only after his mother, his coach, and Pitts's wife, Kendra, an emergency medical technician, insisted. "If you tell me I can't play," Will recalled telling a doctor, "I'm going to play."

Will and Phil had carried two pillowcases into the locker room. In them were a pair of war bonnets adorned with golden-eagle feathers, which Will's grandfather, who worked at the Salish language school, had made by hand. When the boys put on the bonnets, their teammates stared. Then Will's grandfather hit the drum and started the honor song, and the cousins sprinted onto the floor.

The Arlee crowd stood, everyone scrambling for their smartphones to capture the moment. Phil's grandparents, Bear and Irma, weren't sure about the bonnets; if a feather fell out, they might have had to do a ceremony on the court. But it was different for John. He hadn't always felt that his son had fully embraced Salish culture. Now, seeing Phil in the war bonnet, shaking the opposing coach's hand, he thought his heart might burst through his rib cage.

A couple of minutes into the game, Phil sprinted into the locker room, where he threw up. Then he checked back in, and the team ran an isolation play pitting Phil against Manhattan Christian's best player, Caleb Bellach, a six-foot-five junior and the coach's son. Phil dribbled between his legs three times as he approached Bellach, then feinted a hard crossover to the left but brought the ball back to the right and was gone. Another defender came to meet Phil, but he spun and jumped to his left, rising toward the rim with two hands, then pulled the ball down and scooped it to the right. His body moved one way but the ball went the other. The defender followed his body, and Phil softly laid the ball in.

At halftime, Arlee was up 39–30, and Phil threw up again. So did Will. In the third quarter, Manhattan closed the gap. Then, in the span of a minute, Will hit a three-pointer, made a layup, stole the ball, and threw an around-the-back pass to Greg for two points, at which point the crowd detonated. Arlee won, 69–60. The announcer, a white man, marveled at the noise. "You think this many people lived in Arlee?" he chuckled, out of range of the microphone. "Nobody's guarding the stores tonight."

The next day, the Warriors released their suicide-prevention video on Facebook. As the team warmed up before the divisional finals, Anna Whiting Sorrell, who helped oversee the tribe's response to the 2017 suicide cluster, was sitting in the stands. She considered the video in the context of the teenagers who, after the Parkland shooting, advocated gun control. "Maybe," she said, "it's kids saying: enough." She continued: "Maybe these kids can. I want them to just be happy and enjoy their lives. They chose to engage. They've all been there. They say, enough."

The team hoped a few thousand people might view their video. But within 24 hours, it had been watched nearly 86,000 times. On Monday, the team, inspired by the reception, skipped practice to make another, this one an elaborate production with alley-oops and war bonnets. As they were finishing, a coach from Two Eagle River arrived in a black suit. He had come from the wake for the boy—his player—who committed suicide the week before divisionals. "I just wanted to say thank you, guys," he said in halting breaths. His chest heaved, and he told the Warriors to bring home the trophy.

A long silence followed. Then someone asked: "Can we hug him?"

Phil embraced the man, and everyone else followed.

"I'm not scared one bit!" Phil screamed. It was halftime of the state semifinal game, and the Warriors were losing by six to Scobey, a fast team from near the Canadian border. In the locker room, Phil coughed rapidly. "I like it when we're down!" he yelled. "When we come back and beat their ass, that's going to be better!" Then he threw up and took the court.

In the third quarter, Pitts unveiled a brutal press. The team's defense was designed to tire the opponent out until, all at once and in a great rush, the boys unleashed. With less than three minutes remaining in the quarter and Arlee losing by four, Pitts hopped up and down on the sideline and screamed. In a moment, the boys were everywhere. The next 60 seconds passed in a blur of steals and turnovers. Greg and Will each hit a long three-pointer, the second giving Arlee its first lead. Then, as Scobey brought the ball up, Greg and Phil smacked the floor. Phil took off in a straight line for the ball handler, who looked terrified; he ripped the ball away and flew off for a layup. He sprinted back down the court, beckoning to the crowd. The cheers sounded like the inside of a breaking wave.

In just over two minutes, Arlee had scored 14 unanswered points. After the game, Pitts teared up, thanking the boys. Then the Warriors watched Manhattan Christian win, setting up one last rematch. A couple of hours earlier, in a hallway of the Butte Civic Center, the father of one of Manhattan Christian's players said he just wanted everyone to have fun. "It's not life," he said.

The following morning, Becky and John Malatare staked out their seats for the final by 11 a.m., nine hours before tip-off. By game time, Senator Steve Daines, whose son previously attended Manhattan Christian, was in the crowd. Shortly before tip-off, Chasity did Will's hair by center court. Phil got an IV of fluids, his third of the week. Then he joined his teammates in a practice gym, where Pitts told the boys to enjoy the moment and prayed to God and the Creator. Then Phil spoke.

"It was a pretty short year, wasn't it?" he said to his teammates in a dry, cracking voice. He turned to Lane Johnson, who would be guarding Bellach: "Hound that guy!" Then he turned to Isaac. "Dunk it. Rip that rim off! Will, Greg, freaking rip that net off!" He told them, "Don't get down if we go down by two points. We've been down. All right, boys? Come out, battle for me. Battle for Will. Battle for each other. Let's make that crowd happy."

Now the long, slow cadence of Phil's voice changed. It got small and rushed, and he started to cry. Normally the team ended these huddles by chanting "brothers" and "family." Now, though, Phil said, "'Love you' on three." He counted—one, two, three—and his team chanted: "Love you." Then Big Will and Will's grandfather and uncles hit the drum, and Phil and Will sprinted onto the floor in war bonnets, Greg trailing them in a Navajo headband. On the east side of the Civic Center, the town of Arlee rose as one.

Bear and Irma Malatare sat in the second deck. Nearby, David Whitesell held up a smartphone, filming the game. Down below, Becky, sitting near Adam Hiatt, looked on calmly. Chasity sat courtside with her five other kids. She knew Will was risking his health, but rest was not an option: "It would kill him." Nearby, Will's *tupye* sat in a wheelchair, wearing a pin showing her great-grandson's face. John Malatare's jaw rotated in small movements, a beaded Warriors medallion around his neck.

Manhattan Christian won the opening tip-off, and Bellach hit a three-pointer. Then Phil threw a no-look pass off Isaac's hands, Will missed a three, and the game turned ugly. Phil missed his first five shots; Will made only one of four. At the end of the first quarter, Bellach blocked Phil's shot, and the game was tied at 10.

In the second quarter, Will missed two more three-pointers, and Manhattan's boys began to nod their heads. With a few seconds remaining in the first half, Phil dropped the ball to Will about 10 feet behind the three-point line. Will eyeballed the waning clock and fired a wild shot toward the rafters. The ball ripped through the net, the buzzer sounded, and Will pumped his fists and screamed. He made two more three-pointers in the third quarter, and the score was 40–36 Arlee going into the fourth. Then Phil took over.

He rebounded a missed three-pointer and bullied in for a layup. While nearly lying on the floor, he tossed the ball to Isaac for a basket. When Manhattan closed to within two, Phil drove, scored, and was fouled. With a four-point Arlee lead and less than one minute left, Phil whipped the ball to Isaac for another layup. But in the season's final moments, it was Will who stood at the free-throw line, preparing for two shots to seal the state championship. In the stands, Jennifer Jilot whispered to Will: "Just breathe." Twice the ball rolled through the net, and Jilot wept.

On Sunday, the Warriors returned to Arlee led by a fire truck and tribal police escort. Afterward, the team gathered on the bus to listen to an elder. She said that the kids would crash, and that a time would come when they would feel alone. She asked them to forgive themselves. "It's temporary," she said. "It's like the breeze. It will be gone."

The next day most of the boys called in sick to school. The second prevention video was on its way to reaching one million views. Pitts started receiving congratulations from public officials: a call from the governor's office and letters from all three members of Montana's congressional delegation. Senator Jon Tester released a video saluting the Warriors' efforts alongside Senator Cory Booker of New Jersey. The team was arranging to speak with the Tribal Council and younger students at neighboring schools. Pitts called it "the Warrior movement."

Becky Malatare received a gracious message from Manhattan Christian's coach, Jeff Bellach, thanking her for the opportunity to compete against Phil. On Wednesday, Will went to the hospital, where he discovered he had been playing with walking pneumonia and an enormous kidney stone. He elected to delay its removal until after three all-star tournaments. College recruiters had reached out to him following the championship, and he needed one more push to get into school.

That night, Big Will went on a difficult call. He arrested one of the players from the previous year's championship, a freshman at the University of Montana. The police said the boy had been present at a shooting, and he would later be charged for accountability to attempted deliberate homicide. Big Will apologized to the boy's parents before driving him to Missoula.

One afternoon that week, Phil got his spotting scope and drove his red Chevy toward one of his horn-hunting spots, a ridge from which gullies descended to a river. He pulled over and fastened his scope to the open passenger window. The snow was still deep up top. He scoped until he found a herd of about 100 elk. "Can't hide forever!" he said. "I'll walk all this even if it don't melt. If I know they're dropping, I'll go in there." But the herd was mostly dark: cows. He was looking for the big, tawny bulls.

As he scanned the hills, Phil thought about this summer. He figured it would be his last as a kid. He planned to be starting for the Grizz by the time he was a sophomore. He wondered about the temptations of college. "After a big win, am I going to want to go be dumb?" he asked, as if it were a question he couldn't possibly answer.

He thought about his father and T.J., who could walk these hills for a full day without eating. Phil couldn't do that. He discoursed on the supremacy of brown antlers—which are fresh with blood —to white ones. "White's old, brown's new," he said. "Put it this way: You rather have a Lamborghini or a Subaru?"

A Subaru, I said.

"But if you lived in California?"

Phil didn't want to live in California. "Every one's like 'Oh, you need to get out of here,'" he said. "Which I believe. But if you love where you live, why not live there? No use movin'."

Once I asked him about the pressure of making it with the Grizz. He said that he was "all in," but that if it didn't work out, that would be okay. "It's my life," he said. What did that mean, anyway, to make it? Was it a jersey entombed in glass? Phil couldn't take that with him when he died. He was going to play ball as long as he could, but when it ended, he wanted to be a game warden, like T.J.'s father, Tom Haynes, so he could work in the mountains.

As chance would have it, Tom drove by just then. Maybe he was out busting someone for illegal firewood cutting. Phil went back to scoping; he had found three bulls bedded down in the snow. He was hoping one would drop its antlers right there. "That's my dream," he said—to see one shed through the lens of his scope. It had never happened. "Come on, guy," he said to the elk. "Lose your horns." His right eye affixed to the scope, the boy in constant motion was absolutely still. Only his left eyelid fluttered. "I wish I could sit here all day," he said. He stared into the wilderness, wondering what would happen.

On Sunday, March 11, Arlee hosted a *syulm,* a dance celebrating warriors returning from a victorious battle, for the team. About 350 people showed up to the community center's basketball court. The gym smelled of turkey, fry bread, spaghetti and meatballs. Irma and Bear Malatare arrived early. Irma was thinking of buying a 15-passenger van so she could take the whole family to Phil's college games. She went inside while Bear stood out front in an Arlee Warriors state-championship jacket, long arms dangling at his sides.

Bear had been reading a history of the Cree. He normally didn't dwell on the past. He never told Phil about his time at the boarding school, when teachers beat him for speaking his language. "We can't constantly sit and cry about what they done to us," he once said. But the book made him think about his grandparents' migration from Canada, and his own father, for whom Phil was named, and his time with the nuns; the constant efforts at assimilation and extermination.

"We're not supposed to be here," he said, his face turning momentarily dark, his immense hands clenching. Then his hands released, and a great smile worked its way across his face. "We're still here," he said.

He walked inside, where mothers danced around the laughing boys, shoving them playfully down to the court. The world is never so hopeful as when the old honor the young.

TIM LAYDEN

Fists of Fury

FROM SPORTS ILLUSTRATED

START WITH THE image, a still life of protest. It captures a vital moment in history, yet its meaning evolves, as time measures what has—and has not—been learned. It tells the story of a battle fought, in a war neither won nor lost, but ongoing. Of a place and a time, not so different from here and now. Of sports and division, it was fifty years ago this month. "Fifty years! Can you believe that?" says Tommie Smith, a man of 24 in the image, a much older man of 74 today. Fifty years.

In the scene, Smith stands on the top of the Olympic podium, the number 1 painted beneath his feet, which are purposefully sheathed only in black socks, with a single black Puma sneaker also perched on the platform. He is a black man wearing a black scarf beneath his red, white, and blue USA sweats, and a black glove on his right hand, which is thrust skyward, his arm so straight, it looks as if he is trying to reach into the gray overcast and bring rain. This was on the evening of October 16, 1968, in Mexico City. A Wednesday.

Many Americans saw this scene on square black-and-white televisions while eating dinner. Smith had won the gold medal in the 200 meters. It hangs from his neck as "The Star-Spangled Banner" plays. His head is bowed, his face intense. Behind him, facing the medalists' flags, is bronze medalist John Carlos of the United States, then 23. The two men were training partners of a kind in California, but not close friends. Carlos is also shoeless in black socks, a sneaker on the platform. Beads hang from his neck, behind his medal. He has a black glove on his left hand, which is raised. His arm is slightly bent, his pose more casual than Smith's, but no less forceful and eloquent.

There is a third man in the image, silver medalist Peter Norman, a 26-year-old Australian. He is wearing the green uniform of his country and, like Smith and Carlos, a white button pinned to his chest. Norman is looking up at the flags, smiling. Fifty years.

That is the singular moment, one of the most iconic—and important and controversial—in sports history. This is a story about that moment, but just as much about the moments that followed, laid end-to-end, repeated, until they span months and years and decades, and encompass lives and legacies. Smith and Carlos were young black men protesting racial inequality, using the platform of the ceremonial playing of their national anthem at a sports event. Where they raised their fists, a half century later Colin Kaepernick would take a knee. "We're trying to recapture terrain that we thought was once conquered," says Harry Edwards, the septuagenarian sports sociologist who as a 25-year-old instructor in 1968 organized the movement that led to Smith's and Carlos's protest.

The moment defines Smith and Carlos, as Kaepernick's defines him, and always will. It extracted a cost—opportunity lost, money never earned, families tested and broken. They were heroes to some, pariahs to others, lauded and threatened and belittled. Smith, as sweet a mover as ever set foot on a track (Lord, to have seen him race Usain Bolt), never ran another race after the Olympic final, not uncommon in his era but poignant against the backdrop of his last performance. Carlos ran for only one more year.

Both men only found footing in society many years after Mexico City and, ever so gradually, gained acceptance as leaders. In 2005, a 22-foot statue depicting the scene on the medal stand was dedicated at San Jose State, where both had been students and competed. Three years later ESPN awarded Smith and Carlos the Arthur Ashe Courage Award, and in September 2016 they were recognized at the White House by President Obama with members of the '16 U.S. Olympic team. Yet now they grapple with the state of race relations in their country, which some days makes them wonder what they accomplished 50 years ago. "Many struggles are not final victories," Edwards says.

And each wonders alone. Both men have family and friends and the hard-earned respect of millions, but they do not have each other. Smith is a sharecropper's son, raised picking cotton in California's San Joaquin Valley, serious and dutiful. Carlos was born and raised in Harlem, with the soul of a hustler. They have never been close. "Oil and water," says Smith's wife, Delois. The protest and all that followed did not bring them closer.

Smith and Carlos see each other on occasion—at various reunions of the 1968 Olympic team, or for paid speaking gigs. They are a set of two, keen to experiences that no other human—except perhaps Kaepernick, who has met with both men—can understand. Yet they are not a pair. They are one, and one.

It is no simple matter to gain access to Smith or Carlos to talk to them about their story. They know how its meaning has evolved, and how it is acutely relevant. But their reticence is understandable. Both are weary. Carlos is as game as ever to take on the system (you'll see); Smith, as ever, is more cautious (you'll see).

I started asking in late February, with emails and calls that went unanswered. I asked mutual friends to help. Nothing. Smith and Carlos speak in public regularly and sometimes together, but rarely these days sit for media interviews.

In late May, I received a reply from Delois, who handles most of Tommie's affairs. (She is his third wife; they have been together for 21 years.) The email: "Call me tomorrow," and a phone number. When I called, Delois talked about the many times her husband had signed the cover of the May 22, 1967, issue of *Sports Illustrated,* which featured the 22-year-old Smith uncoiling from starting blocks in gold sweats, next to the headline: "Blazing Quarter-Miler." (He did not enter the 400 in Mexico City.) She also asked, "Is this a paid interview?" I told her that it was not. "I am going to grant you this interview with Dr. Smith," Delois then said, cheerfully.

Tommie Smith has lived in a modest, two-story brick house in Stone Mountain, Georgia, since 2005, when he retired after 27 years as a teacher and coach at Santa Monica (California) College. We talked in his basement, which is a staggering monument to not just the evening of October 16, 1968, but also to his remarkable (and remarkably short) track career, to his life, to a vital era in track and field, to the Olympics, and to activism. The room is alive with memories. An Olympic flag, swiped by Smith from the Mexico City Olympic Stadium before the protest, decorated with the signatures of U.S. teammates Jim Hines, Al Oerter, Jim Ryun, and others. A framed *Newsweek* cover from '68 with the headline, "The Angry Black Athlete." A picture of his childhood home in rural Lemoore, California. Another of his junior high basketball team, with Smith towering over his teammates as a 6'2" eighth-grader. Dozens of black-and-white action photos of Smith setting some of his 11 world records between '66 and '68. And several shots of the medal stand protest, some signed by Carlos and Norman.

Smith settles into a lounge chair and leans forward, engaged. "I don't talk to everybody," he says, "because I don't want to fight what's going on now in the country. I only want to talk about my belief in what I was doing." When, in the course of a two-hour interview, the subject turns to today's racial climate, Smith speaks slowly and carefully. He knows who he is and understands the power of his name. "I have to make all my words count," he says. "Have things changed in fifty years? Not as much as I hoped they would. At times it's as bad or worse than it was in the '60s because there are more things to become agitated about. And the people to fight those negatives are fewer because black folks don't have that leadership, black or white, like Dr. King or the Kennedys."

Minutes later he resets, seeking an uplifting turn: "It's moving in a positive direction."

When I ask him if he approves of President Trump (and his policies), Smith says, "His tenacity, but not where it's going. Nobody thought he would be here, so you have to admire . . ." Smith stops and points his finger at me. "Now don't you say Tommie Smith likes Trump. Any leader needs to be strong, but not to the point where he becomes a tyrant. Like Putin. Putin is a tyrant."

Carlos lives 20 minutes south of Smith. Fifty years after sharing the podium, they could shop at the same Kroger and both fly out of Hartsfield. That has not brought them closer. "People said we would be joined at the hip," says Smith. "That has not been the case. We're totally different people. I'm quiet and reclusive; he says what's on his mind. I'm an introvert; he's an extrovert. I count to 10 before I throw a rock and then maybe I throw a Wiffle ball instead. He throws the rock."

Between February and late June, I called Carlos half a dozen times and sent an equal number of text messages. Colleagues who know Carlos told me that he was finished doing interviews. Forever. After leaving Smith's house, I made one last call, and Carlos answered. Then he threw some rocks.

"Tim!" he shouted into his phone. "What the hell do I have to do to get you to stop calling me? I've been talking about this s— for fifty years, and ain't nothing changed since Mexico City in 1968. Nothing! I've spoken and spoken and spoken, and it ain't gonna make no difference. It ain't enough. I could die and come back in another life, and things would be the same. You have to agree with that."

I suggest that a story might amplify his message. "You write your article in *Sports Illustrated*," says Carlos. "You think that evil is defeated because people read that s—? That ain't gonna happen, my brother."

At 73, John Wesley Carlos is a proud and passionate man, unfiltered. A few weeks later I talked with the oldest of his three children, Kimme, who is 52. "My father is a private person," she said. "But if you do talk with him, he will speak from the heart. It's all on the table." I spoke with John for 17 minutes. His initial response— *it ain't gonna make no difference*—sounds at first like resignation, but it's actually anger. Where Smith is careful and largely muted on social media, Carlos posts and shares furiously on two Facebook pages. Where Smith assiduously avoids the bullring of public discourse, Carlos seeks it, on his terms, advocating change. Last May he posted a 347-word criticism of the NFL's anthem policy and the president's support of that policy.

I asked Carlos why he still fights. "Look at what you have in the White House," says Carlos. "That's the outer layer of America. That's the president, supplying his base. He called young black men sons of bitches for kneeling. Sons of bitches! He said they weren't respecting the military. What did he ever do in the military? What did any of his children do in the military? And then you've got police officers out there shooting young black men, and nobody is prosecuted. Nobody is sent to jail. It's the same b— today that it was fifty years ago."

Carlos was not impolite in this exchange. He was full of life and fury. Only on the subject of Smith did he mellow ever so slightly, shifting from prose to poetry. "You look at Dr. King and Malcolm X," says Carlos. "Each of those men had different methodologies for dealing with the complexities of society. But both came to the fight with courage. When the dust settles, okay, Tommie Smith and I walk together for eternity, but we never got the chance to be together."

With that, Carlos ended our conversation, but for this: He added suddenly, "Hey, Tim. I'm done. That's all I got. Okay? That's it. Okay?"

Okay.

The Mexico City protest was not spontaneous. It was part of an 18-month movement organized by Edwards. He had been an athlete at San Jose State, and that is where he first began organizing student protests. A boycott of the 1968 Olympics by black U.S. athletes had been discussed privately, and the idea went public after Smith won two medals at the World University Games in Tokyo in September '67, when Smith affirmed the possibility to a Japanese reporter. In late November the vague boycott talks coalesced into the formation, under Edwards, of the Olympic Project for Human Rights (OPHR), which made four demands: the expulsion of apartheid South Africa and Rhodesia from the Olympics; the removal of IOC president Avery Brundage of the United States, who had vigorously supported the awarding of the 1936 Games to Hitler's Germany; the hiring of more black coaches at college sports programs; and the restoration of Muhammad Ali's heavyweight championship title (which had been stripped in April '67 after he refused induction into the Army).

In late 1967, Smith and his San Jose State teammate Lee Evans, a 400-meter runner, committed to the boycott. According to an *SI* story that December, Smith said to Evans as they walked out of Smith's apartment, "All I hope is that this [boycott] does some good, that it doesn't create any chaos."

But America was already ablaze in chaos. In the summer of 1967, there were race riots in Detroit and Newark. In January '68, the Tet offensive fueled antiwar sentiment and spurred demonstrations. On April 4, Dr. Martin Luther King was assassinated in Memphis. Two months later, presidential candidate Robert F. Kennedy was killed in Los Angeles. But despite growing frustration among African Americans, the Mexico City boycott lost steam for many reasons, not least because many athletes didn't want to sacrifice years of training for a cause. They wanted medals.

Boycott talk became protest talk, but no roles were assigned. Athletes would make their own choices. Ten days before the opening ceremony, at a student protest in Mexico City's Tlatelolco plaza, government troops killed scores of protesters. (The exact number has never been determined.) There was fear in the air when the Games began on Saturday, October 12. Facing death threats at home and if he went to Mexico, Edwards did not attend. He would watch the Games from Montreal, where he was attending a writers' conference.

Events willed Smith and Carlos forward. Before the start of the track and field competition, USOC officials arranged for Jesse Owens, a national hero for his performance at the Berlin Games, to speak to the black athletes. He discouraged them from demonstrating. "Jesse told those guys, 'If you do, you'll never get a job,'" says Edwards. "[U.S. 400-meter runner] Vince Matthews stood up and said, 'I already don't have a job.' In 1968 a black athlete didn't get a job. Maybe you got a job at the parks and recreation department in the town where you grew up."

But the first black American to win a gold medal embraced Owens's words. On the night of October 14, Hines became the first 100-meter runner to crack the 10-second barrier with fully automatic timing, setting a world record of 9.95. His protest was that he declined to shake Brundage's hand, a significant act that went largely unreported. He stood at attention for the anthem. "Jesse Owens was our leader, and we were under his instructions to do what was right and acceptable," says Hines, now 72 and living in his native Oakland. "I also followed my own instructions with respect to Brundage."

Two nights later was the 200 meters. Pressure was building within the OPHR. Hines had not been a part of the OPHR meetings. On the afternoon of the 16th, Carlos and Smith won their 200-meter semifinals. Carlos had run a hand-timed 19.7 seconds, a world record, at the second of two Olympic trials, in the 7,382-foot altitude of Echo Summit, California, in September. (That mark was later disallowed because he had worn Puma spikes that were deemed too advantageous.) Carlos entered as the favorite, a status solidified when Smith tweaked a groin muscle decelerating past the finish in his semi. (In videos he can be seen limping off the track.)

After the heat Smith retreated to a training room with Bud Winter, his college coach. "Bud loved ice," says Smith. "He put ice all over my leg." As Smith lay on a trainer's table, Evans approached. They had met as adolescents working the fields near Smith's home in Lemoore and Evans's in Madera. "Smith!" Tommie recalls Evans shouting at him. "We picked cotton, we cut grapes. You gonna let this stop you? You better get out there and win that race."

Smith started from lane 3, with Carlos in lane 4. These were the first Olympic track races on an artificial surface rather than on cinders or on dirt. Smith ran a cautious turn, protecting his groin injury; Carlos, the more powerful sprinter, scorched the bend, swallowed up the stagger on the third U.S. starter, Larry Questad, and reached the straightaway with a one-meter lead over Smith. "I was in trouble," says Smith. "I was way behind the fastest man in the world." But with 80 meters to run, Smith burst forward and delivered 60 meters that are among the fastest by any human. Carlos turned to look as Smith shot past (more on this). Smith was a breathtaking runner—knees lifting, shoulders slightly hunched, the rest of his body placid. Where Bolt was a fury of movement and power, Smith was serene.

Ten meters from the line, Smith raised his arms high and wide, then took his last seven strides that way. The automatic timer first froze at 19.78, and then was adjusted to 19.83. With Carlos's previous mark disallowed, Smith's time became the world record, and it stood for 11 years, and there's little doubt he left time on the track by prematurely celebrating. Carlos, staggering at the line, lost the silver to Norman but comfortably took the bronze. Soon afterward came the medal ceremony. The gloves. The socks. The moment.

In the years that followed, Smith and Carlos would be seen as twins in a reductive narrative: tall black men with goatees, fast runners, militants. They were painted with the broadest of brushes and turned into caricatures of the angry black man, reviled and feared by many. The reality was different: aside from being two of the fastest runners on earth, they had little else in common.

Smith was born in Clarksville, Texas, the seventh of 12 children; his family came to California on a labor bus when he was seven. They settled in Lemoore, worked in the fields, and went to church on Sundays. Tommie was serious, thoughtful, pious. Lynda Huey arrived at San Jose State two years after Smith, a blond sprinter raised in San Jose. They dated for a while and later became close friends before drifting apart in the 1990s. "When I met Tommie," says Huey, "he was very aware of his place in society. He didn't think we should be seen together, a black man and a white girl. He would leave the apartment first, and tell me to wait 15 minutes."

Smith's track career was a runaway success. At one time he concurrently held world records for 200 meters, 220 yards, and 400 meters. And if he was quiet, he was not unaware. In 1966, on the day that he set records in the 200 and the 220, he participated in a civil rights march in East Palo Alto. "I was a college student," says Smith. "I was no dummy. And I knew racism."

Carlos was born one day short of a year after Smith and hardened by realities that only New York City can confer. In his 2011 autobiography, *The John Carlos Story: The Sports Moment That Changed the World,* written with Dave Zirin, he describes his childhood as a frenetic hustle, whether stealing food off freight trains (and giving it to poor families), playing the numbers for money, or singing with his friends outside the Savoy Ballroom. His life and Smith's were different versions of black men growing up in 1950s and '60s America.

Carlos earned a track scholarship to East Texas State, spent two years there, and then moved home before transferring out West in 1968. Carlos wrote in his book that it was Edwards who had encouraged the move at a meeting in New York City in January '68, where Carlos says he also met Dr. King. Says Edwards, "I didn't know, or know of, John Carlos prior to him showing up at San Jose State in May 1968. He quickly became one of the most ardent and vociferous advocates of the OPHR. Carlos came on board in May 1968—four months before the Olympic trials at Lake Tahoe—and I'm glad he did."

The arrival of Carlos changed the atmosphere at San Jose State, which was already known as Speed City. "It had been Tommie's kingdom," says Huey. "Then John came, and the energy was different. John's personality could be scary. And Tommie didn't want to be a part of that. I don't think they were ever friends."

Carlos was the archetype of the trash-talking, big-stoned sprinter. In a 1991 retrospective, *SI*'s Kenny Moore, who was a marathoner on the 1968 and '72 Olympic teams, called Carlos "a fountain of jive."

Dick Fosbury, the gold medalist in the high jump at the '68 Games, became friends with Carlos and Smith at Team USA training camps that summer. "John Carlos was a street-smart, very confident, fun guy to be around," says Fosbury. "He had a walk, this strut, the way he carried himself. I was from small-town Oregon. I had never known anybody like 'Los. He struck me as a smart guy who could handle himself and any situation that came up. Tommie was thoughtful and a gentleman. They were different guys whose paths crossed."

Their appearance on the stand remains riveting to this day, every element significant. Single shoes and bare feet covered only in black socks, signifying poverty at home. Carlos's beads, recalling the lynchings of black men. Smith's black scarf, highlighting a deep identity with his race. The gloves, the fists shoved upward for the world to see, suggesting defiance and unity.

Edwards watched from an apartment in Montreal. He started the movement, but he takes no credit for the moment. "That was them," he says. "I didn't know what they were going to do. They had a monumental thing in front of them. First, somebody had to win. Then they had to wrestle with the whole issue of what to do. There was no clear path, no silver staircase. The scope of the demonstration: the beads, the shoes, the gloves. The courage and the commitment that they showed. They deserve every accolade that they get. They deserve to be the faces of a movement that defined an era."

Smith and Carlos knew they would protest somehow; they just weren't sure what form it would take. They have never publicly agreed on who devised the specifics, but they agree that it came together only after the race, in the well of the stadium. "In the dungeon," says Smith. Smith's wife, Denise, had bought a pair of black gloves (Smith wore the right, Carlos the left). Carlos's wife, Kim, had brought beads with her from the United States. Over the years each man has taken credit for orchestrating the moment. And again, the outcome overwhelms the details. In the end, they were together.

At the first notes of the anthem, both men turned 90 degrees to the right and struck their poses. Carlos has said that his arm was bent to shield his face from sniper fire, Smith that his posture was ramrod straight as a remnant of his ROTC training. Smith told me, "I was afraid the whole time. I prayed. I said the Lord's Prayer all the way through. Then I listened to the national anthem, because that's a powerful thing, hearing that anthem knowing how many people died so that belief could remain a part of America."

All three men wore OPHR pins; Norman's had been given to him by a U.S. rower who supported the organization. The ceremony was over in less than 90 seconds. Smith and Carlos raised their fists as they left the stadium floor. Both men remember hearing boos and whistles.

Reaction at home was swift and mostly negative. The most frequently cited response came from Brent Musburger, then a 29-year-old sportswriter with the long-shuttered *Chicago American,* who wrote, "Smith and Carlos looked like a couple of black-skinned storm troopers, holding aloft their black-gloved hands during the playing of the national anthem." Most media accounts found a way to use the term *black power,* which was fair—Edwards calls it a "proto-hashtag"—but simplistic.

The BBC interviewed Smith and Carlos the next day.

BBC: "Do you think the Olympic Games are the right place to do this kind of thing? To use the world stage?"

Smith: "We used it so the whole world could see the poverty of the black man in America."

BBC: "You might say you've got it all. You've got publicity, you've got medals, you've got martyrdom as well."

Carlos: "I can't eat that. And the kids around my block, that grew up with me, they can't eat that. And the kids that grew up after them, they can't eat it. They can't eat gold medals. Like Tommie Smith said, 'All we're asking for is an equal chance.'"

Later that day Smith sat down with ABC's Howard Cosell for a brief live interview. It is Cosell's last question, and Smith's answer, that lives on.

Cosell: "Are you proud to be an American?"

Smith: "I'm proud to be a black American."

Fifty years later Smith sits in his basement and remembers the exchange. "That question stopped me," he says. "I didn't want to say, 'Yes, Howard,' because I was not proud at that particular time. I was confused about how to respond. So I said I'm proud to be a black American. I felt a light go through my body when I said that."

On Friday, Smith and Carlos were suspended by the USOC (though they were done competing) after the IOC threatened to suspend the entire U.S. team if Smith and Carlos were not expelled. The two were ordered to leave the Olympic Village. The front-page headline in the *New York Times:* "2 Black Power Advocates Ousted from Olympics." That night Evans led a U.S. sweep of the 400; all three men wore black berets on the victory stand, but removed them for the anthem. Long jumper Ralph Boston, who won a silver medal behind teammate Bob Beamon's ethereal world record, received his medal in bare feet. The *Times* wrote that their behavior had been "tempered" by the expulsion of Smith and Carlos. No one else was sent home.

There is one other issue relating to the 200-meter race in Mexico City: Carlos says he allowed Smith to win. He first hinted at this in the press conference afterward. Asked why he looked to his left, Carlos said, "The upper part of my calves were pulling pretty hard. I wanted to see where Tommie was and if he could win it. If I thought he couldn't have won it, I would have tried harder to take it."

By 2011, when Carlos wrote his book, that had evolved into, "Whatever drove Tommie, I could tell that for him, the only acceptable ending was to make his political statement from the gold medal perch and the gold medal perch alone. As for me, I didn't care a lick if I won the gold, silver or bronze. I wasn't there for the race. I was there for the after race." In his interview for an NBC documentary, *1968*, which will air this month, Carlos went further and called Smith's injury "Fake. Artificial. He didn't fool me in the least little bit."

There is a long tradition of head games among sprinters. Perhaps Carlos truly settled for any medal that would get him onto the podium. But his insistence on this narrative has deepened the rift between the two. "John says he let me win," says Smith. "Threw the race. You cannot say that. When you don't win, you congratulate the winner for trying his best. I don't believe Carlos means it. I really don't."

In the fall of 2017, Smith met with Kaepernick at a hotel restaurant in New York City. The meeting had been arranged by Glenn Kaino, an artist and documentary filmmaker who is working with Smith. "I told him he will have to find new avenues for his life," says Smith. "He'll need a second plan. I had a plan for my life before Mexico City. But that stopped it. I got home and I was hungry. I lost my food. I lost my house. The price was devastating."

There is a distinction here: Kaepernick's protest has cost him millions, but he has also made millions. And his new contract with Nike figures to generate significant income. His future is sure to be very different from the one Smith and Carlos have lived. Says

Edwards, "Not only is Kaep likely to make millions from his Nike deal, he is also likely to receive every dollar that he would have made on the field by way of a settlement with the league without taking another hit." (The resolution of his collusion claim against the league is pending.) Edwards adds, "On top of it all, he will continue to grow as a sports icon, who will be remembered and revered by tens of millions after all but the most diehard football heads will have long forgotten the likes of Brady, Favre, and Manning." The scope of Kaepernick's legacy is debatable, as Smith and Carlos will attest, but there are differences between a sprinter and a quarterback.

The question of whether their protest was worth it will always hang over Smith and Carlos. It did not instantly alter the course of race relations in America. Edwards argues that the path set upon by Smith and Carlos was never going to be a straight line to equality. "Struggles that are not victories do generate change," says Edwards. "Whether or not they generate progress is another issue. Progress is like profit; at some point it comes down to who's keeping the books." Edwards divides athlete activism into waves: Jack Johnson and Jesse Owens (among others) fighting for legitimacy in the first; Jackie Robinson and Larry Doby (among others) fighting for access in the second; Muhammad Ali, Jim Brown, Kareem Abdul-Jabbar, Bill Russell, and Smith and Carlos (and others) fighting for dignity in the third. And Kaepernick (and others including Malcolm Jenkins and Eric Reid) are the evolving fourth wave.

What did Smith and Carlos contribute most? "Imaging," says Edwards. "Those two men on a victory podium in Mexico City is the most iconic sports image of the 20th century, and that will still be true 200 years from now."

But to paraphrase Carlos, you can't eat imaging. Both men suffered for their protest, drifting in and out of poverty; Smith for several years and Carlos for large slices of three decades. Not long after Smith returned home from Mexico City, his mother's home was vandalized, with feces left in the mailbox and dead animals on the lawn. Both men played pro football, but neither appeared in a regular-season game.

Smith caught a break in 1972, when activist Jack Scott was named athletic director at Oberlin (Ohio) College and hired three black head coaches, including Smith. Smith worked at Oberlin for six years, until he was hired as a coach and phys-ed teacher at Santa Monica, a community college. Smith stayed there for 27 years, speaking out mostly when spoken to. Huey recalls walking down the hall with Smith in the late '80s, hearing a young student heave a little trash talk at him and Smith saying, softly, "They have no idea." Mexico City was always a part of his life. "I don't remember ever not knowing about it," says Kevin Smith, 50, who was born to Tommie and Denise a few months before the '68 Olympics.

But Smith found traction at Santa Monica. "He was quiet, humble, analytical," says Jeff Shimizu, who worked at the college from 1985 to 2016, mostly as executive vice president. "I felt he was happy here, but he had been through difficult times. He was a strong advocate for diversity, and he loved working with students. I loved going into his office and talking. I miss him."

Reentry was more challenging for Carlos. After a few races in the aspirational and short-lived International Track Association (a fledgling pro track league in the era of "amateurism"), he moved to Los Angeles with Kim and their three children in the early 1970s. There, as he describes in his book, he found work as a security guard and a groundskeeper at a park. He told *SI* in '91 that he once worked as a bar bouncer for $65 a week. He wrote of burning furniture in the fireplace for heat. Says Kimme, "There were struggles, but what I remember most is seeing my father get up and go to work every day, no matter what the job was. We had a roof over our heads. We had food. I saw a man of integrity."

Kim died by suicide in 1977, four years after the couple had split. Carlos has long blamed himself and the backlash from Mexico City for her death. But Kimme, a mental health counselor in Trenton, New Jersey, has pushed back against that narrative. "Suicide is much more complicated than that," she says. "My mother was a woman of color in the '60s and '70s. You did not discuss mental illness. You did not discuss whatever pain you were dealing with. The demonstration [in Mexico City] didn't make our lives easier. But any decision my mother made had nothing to do with my father."

In 1984, Carlos was hired by the L.A. Olympic Organizing Committee and spent the year working in youth programs. After that he backslid again, including an arrest in '86 for cocaine possession. (He was found guilty, but after he attended an interventional program, the conviction was expunged from his record.) In 1990, at 45, he was hired by Palm Springs (California) High as a counselor and track coach. He spent 24 years at the school and became revered for his ability to connect with some of the most at-risk students in the community. "John doesn't tolerate any b—," says Ricky Wright, a former college athlete who was the principal for most of Carlos's time there. "He did not pull punches. He loved those kids, and he changed lives."

Paul Grafton, the vice principal of student affairs at Palm Springs High who hired Carlos, says, "There's a point where a kid makes excuses before he tells the truth, if he ever tells the truth. John was able to get kids very quickly from excuses to truth."

Retirement for Smith and Carlos does not snuff out the fundamental question: Would they do it again? They set a course for their lives on that night in Mexico City. They were inarguably heroic (if you think they were something else as well, that is fine, but do not deny them their heroism), but that came at a cost. Still, neither man will look back and question himself because the act endures as inspiration, powerful beyond words.

Says Carlos, "Would I do it again? Absolutely! Yes! When the time came, when I had my one chance in life, I stood up and said, 'This s— is wrong. It's got to be corrected.'"

But now? "The present is not frustrating to me, man. My time was fifty years ago. That's over. Young people today, they need to turn up the volume. They need to come together."

Smith cannot imagine his life without the protest. "It was not a matter of whether I wanted to do it," he says. "I had to do it. My father had a saying: 'When you could, you wouldn't. Now you want to, but you can't.' I was standing on the highest platform in the world. How could I not?"

In his basement, surrounded by history, I ask Smith if there is anyone he would like to talk to about all this, a kindred soul who might understand the struggle and the wounds, the stubbornness of progress and the evil of hate. Smith nods slowly, turns to face me, and offers the slightest hint of a shrug. His answer: "John."

KIM CROSS

The Redemption of Artis Monroe

FROM BICYCLING

BEHIND THE PRISON, outside the wire, hundreds of cast-off bicycles lean in a rainbow of disrepair. There's a huffy cruiser with a rusty cassette and a Schwinn with downtube shifters. A 10-speed from the eight-track era. A Mongoose hardtail with tires so flat they puddle in the dirt. Each week more orphaned bikes arrive in every vintage and appellation. Peugeot. Bianchi. Renyu. Schwinn. Centurion. Bridgestone. Raleigh. They've been outgrown, replaced, discarded, abandoned, or forgotten in the darkest, mustiest, cobwebbiest corner of some garage. Some are in a sorrier state than others. This one needs a drivetrain overhaul. That one just needs lube.

As the sun rises over the tangle of bikes on this day in November 2015, their steward comes out of a dormitory. On one leg of his blue pants, yellow letters spell PRISONER. He's a redwood—six-foot-five, north of 250—with a gentle voice. He has brown, steady eyes and an easy smile with a gap between his front teeth. Despite the streak of gray sprouting from each temple, he looks younger than 63. In the California prison system, this is inmate AA0462. His mother named him Artis. His father nicknamed him "Renny," short for his middle name. The guys here just call him Monroe.

Artis Renard Monroe is one of the roughly 2,500 men incarcerated at California Medical Facility, a state prison 20 miles east of Napa Valley. A little more than half the size of its next-door neighbor, California State Prison, Solano, CMF houses general population inmates, as well as the elderly and sick. Its facilities range in security from Level 1 to Level 4. Charles Manson, briefly, was an inmate here. Most live in cell blocks or open dormitories inside the wire—a high-voltage electric perimeter—in a world of concrete, metal, fluorescent lights, and too many voices bouncing off hard walls.

"Inside, you have to wait for a CO [corrections officer] to open the door to let you go out to the yard," Monroe says. "Out here, I can walk out the door any time I want. Unless it's count time."

"Out here" is what everyone calls the Ranch—the minimum-security quarters where 50 or so Level 1 inmates spend their last few months before parole. They're still counted several times a day and watched from towers by armed corrections officers. But they have relative autonomy and considerable perks: sunshine and basketball courts and a million-dollar view—velvet hills studded with oaks and roaming cattle. They also have jobs—moving furniture, picking up cans beside the highway, landscaping the prison grounds—that pay 15 to 32 cents an hour.

Monroe's job is fixing bikes. "There's no better job on the Ranch than this," he says. It's "freedom within prison."

On his daily walk to work, he signs out a box of bike tools from a corrections officer in the tool room, where such things are locked up every night. He loads the box onto a little red Roadmaster wagon and pulls it through the dirt to his office: a corrugated metal shed with a desk and a workshop. Above the door hangs a sign:

THE BIKE PROJECT
REHABILITATION THROUGH RESTORATION

This barrel-roofed shed is the headquarters of a prison recyclery where inmates restore donated bikes and give them back to the community. The program is designed to give them job skills and a chance to contribute something to the community they will soon reenter. This has been happening, quietly, for more than three decades.

Monroe is in charge of the recyclery, overseeing the flow of bikes in and out of the prison, and the handful of inmates who fix them. The program has waxed and waned through the years. Under Monroe, it's seeing a renaissance. Other Bike Project workers come and go, but he has been a near-constant for the four years he's been at CMF.

Monday through Friday, he arrives at the shed at 6:45 a.m.—a good hour before anyone else. He can view the sunrise, listen to birds, watch deer wander by in the slanting light. He scatters bread for wild turkeys that waddle across the Ranch. It's a moment of something like solitude, a rare chance to be alone in prison.

"I look forward to coming to work," he says. "If you like what you're doing, you forget you're in prison for the hours that you're here."

He hangs a plastic baggie filled with water in the doorway (keeps the flies out) and reorganizes his tools. The officers in the tool room count them every night and leave them in disarray. He counts them too as he puts the box back in order. This is a privilege, being trusted with a whole box of tools. Most inmates are allowed only one at a time. He walks over to a Napa Auto Parts calendar hanging on a metal cabinet and draws an X through another day.

He flips through a blue paper folder to review his handwritten inventory. As of today, there are 96 bikes restored and ready to go to new homes. They wait in a shed behind the workshop, out of the sun and salty Pacific air that wafts past Alcatraz, crests the East Bay hills, and stirs the towering palms lining the road into the prison. On pretty days, he imagines the eucalyptus trees rustling in Stern Grove or the waves crashing on Ocean Beach. So close. And so unreachable.

Monroe's supervisor, Landon Bravo, is the prison's community resource manager, and oversees several programs. He wears stylish suits and shiny shoes and doesn't hover over the shed. As long as Monroe has enough inventory, Bravo leaves him mostly alone. They like each other, and they like the arrangement. Bravo drops by now and then to deliver bike requests. A teenage boy wants a mountain bike. The Moose Lodge needs a raffle prize for a fundraiser. A recovering alcoholic lost his license and needs a ride to AA meetings.

Monroe walks among the fixed-up bikes and chooses just the right one for each new owner. He pulls them aside, tags them, and delivers them to the prison gate, where drop-offs and pickups take place. It's kind of like playing Santa, or Cupid, for strangers he will never meet.

Sometimes he imagines the face behind the handlebar. He envisions some little kid's smile as he gets his very first bike. (He remembers being that kid.) He especially likes the image of one of his bikes carrying a drug addict down the road to recovery. Someone who was a victim of the reasons he's here. It's his second time to prison, he says. (Prison records say it's his third.) What got him locked up the first time, in the 1980s?

"Possession for sale of narcotics," he says. "Distribution."

Back in his twenties, he did time in San Quentin, California's oldest prison, which has its own zip code. "I didn't learn anything," he says. "I was young." He got out. Grew up. Cleaned up his act. After his mother died in 2000, he got angry. "Lost perspective." Fell back into trouble.

"I go back to doing stupid stuff around people who have no morals," he says, "and end up back in prison for conspiracy to run a drug organization."

Out here, in the shed, he says he has time to think about that. He speaks about his renewed faith in God, and the peace he finds in helping someone quietly and anonymously. "This is an opportunity for redemption," he says.

One of the first bikes he fixed was for a recovering addict who needed transportation to appointments to graduate from drug court. Monroe picked out a black three-speed Schwinn cruiser. It came in with flat tires and a broken chain. He pulled fresher tires from another bike and shined the chrome until it winked in the sun. When he was done, the bike looked so badass that one of the prison staffers coveted it. Monroe called it "the Deebo bike," from the 1995 Ice Cube movie *Friday*.

After he left the bike at the prison gate, he didn't give it another thought. He didn't know the guy who got the Deebo bike was a father in his mid-forties, a drug addict and alcoholic who had relapsed over and over since his first recovery at age 16. His license revoked, he was ashamed to ask his parents to drive him to all the places he needed to be in order to graduate from drug court. AA meetings. Drug tests. Appointments with his case manager. At least four meetings a week. Monroe didn't know his Schwinn had gotten the man to every one of them, that he had never been late. Or that after getting sober (and staying sober) the man gave that bike—which he really wanted to keep—to another addict entering drug court.

In a way, these details don't matter that much to Monroe. "It's fulfilling something," he says. It's enough to feel the sun on his neck and his hands on a bike, helping some stranger in this one small way.

Once in a while, Monroe comes across a special bike. It might be a European relic from the days when Tour de France riders smoked cigarettes in the saddle. Or an early Schwinn with original parts. Sometimes brakeless fixies come in, or carbon road bikes worth four digits. Two unicycles of different heights lean against the shed.

Today he pulls out a little red bike that has seen a lot of miles. It's heavy and dated and so old-fashioned it's actually back in style. Butterfly handlebar. Twenty-inch wheels. A chain guard and a coaster brake. The banana seat has long been removed and re-placed with a BMX saddle, shoved low and tilted back.

The name on the frame is obscure: Vista Torino 400. Monroe has never heard of that brand, but it looks familiar. He recognizes a perfect knockoff of a Schwinn Stingray. That was the bike ev-ery kid in the universe wanted when Monroe was 10 years old. It needs work. The chain is black, coated with the grit of a thousand backyard odysseys. Its frame bears the scars of every crash, and its head badge is missing. The tires are worn thin by a million turns through vacant lots and magnificent mud puddles. The faded paint is a testament to an endless parade of summers. If bike years are like dog years, it's well beyond ancient. In people years, it's around 50. But even through a half-century of grime, Monroe can see the bike it was—and could be.

A bike is a vehicle for so many things. A ride to school. A paper route. An escape from the world of parents. Through the years, it becomes whatever its owner needs it to be. Then one day, its kid stops needing it, or wants things it cannot be. That's the day the wheels roll to a final stop, or maybe spin for someone else.

"These little bikes," Monroe says. "They bring back real memo-ries." This one carries him to the shadow of Candlestick Park, and his first great love: the Giants. He was 10 years old in the sum-mer of '63, when Juan Marichal, known for his high-kick windup, tossed a near-perfect game against the almost-perfect game of the Milwaukee Braves' Warren Spahn. Monroe's hero, Willie Mays, hit a home run in the 16th inning, before roughly 16,000 Candlestick fans, to win the game 1–0.

While he works, Monroe often listens to baseball games on a radio that was state-of-the-art during the Reagan era. The crack of a bat sends his heart soaring, and the hours disappear in the roar of the crowd. In his mind, he is threading a baseball glove over the handlebar of a borrowed bike and racing his buddies to Candlestick Point.

When he wasn't playing sandlot ball, he was hurtling down hills on his best friend's bike. Those were the days of skinned knees and no helmets. Curly had a Schwinn Stingray. Curly let him ride it—they had to take turns—but young Artis longed for a bike of his own.

One day, when he was in middle school, his father surprised him. This is one of his favorite stories, though each time he tells it the details change. In one version, his dad tells him to get in the car, they're going fishing. In another, they're going to a barbecue. Yet another has them going to the Candlestick parking lot for a driving lesson. Once they get to the parking lot—it's always Candlestick—his dad tells him to wait right there.

"Go over there, Renny," his dad says. "I'll be right back."

His dad disappears. Then someone comes and leads Artis Monroe to where his dad is standing for the big reveal. Two bikes—a big one and a small one. They pedal to a hill on the other side of Candlestick and ride down it together, flying.

That's one of the lovely stories. In another, the bike (just one this time) is hidden in a wood-paneled Country Squire wagon. Sometimes the father and son race across the shimmering tar of the parking lot. Or he rides off with Curly, who also gets a new bike. In another telling, the bike is leaning up against a tree at the Gilman Playground, near Candlestick, where everyone's having a barbecue.

"There's a little bike there, Renny," his father says, nodding at the tree.

"Jump on it. It's yours!"

He can still see it, a blue Schwinn Stingray with three speeds and a banana seat. (In some versions it's not a real Schwinn, but a knockoff from Sears, Roebuck and Company.) Whatever it was, that bike carried him to the edge of the world and back. He recalls rattling through fields, riding with no hands to impress the girls, and jumping mud puddles (or aiming for the middle). He remembers the feeling of racing down San Francisco hills as steep as ski slopes.

Some of the details may be warped by time, age, or nostalgia. The one thing that doesn't change is the feeling. That feeling is as true today as it was a half-century ago. Freedom.

Monroe knows just what to do with the Vista Torino 400. He scavenges for newer grips, a banana seat, and whitewall tires. It takes parts from three bikes to make this one whole. He wipes away cobwebs, douses the frame with Simple Green, and scrubs off five decades of dirt. Underneath, she is still a beauty. Timeless. She has plenty of miles left to go.

On a tense day in October 2016, the prison is on lockdown. Last night there was an escape. The fugitive did not dig a tunnel or cut a hole in a fence. He simply walked off the Ranch.

Monroe won't go to work today. Neither will anyone else. During lockdown, all inmates stay put in whatever place they go when it's count time. Monroe is the only inmate allowed outside, a generous exception made by the warden for this writer, who traveled 2,000 miles to talk with him again. Their one-arm, nice-to-see-you-again hug is aborted by a corrections officer in a spectacularly awkward moment.

A lot has changed in the last year or so. Other guys paroled. Landon Bravo, the supervisor with the shiny shoes, got a promotion. Which means Monroe got a new supervisor. He wasn't too happy about that. The thought of starting over, building trust, was almost enough to make him quit. But the new guy looks him in the eye, treats him with respect, and asked him to stay. So here he is.

A lonely baseball sits on his desk in the shed, beside the radio, calendar, Giants' schedule, and pictures of pretty places. It has been a year since Candlestick Park was torn down to make way for an $8 billion development. The guys who once played softball on the Ranch have long since gotten out. New men sleep in their beds. These new guys don't care about baseball. They just want to play football and basketball.

"Times change," Monroe says. "We change." He still goes through his daily motions on the Ranch. He walks to the prison entrance to pick up the bikes that donors have left. On an average day he'll find three or four. There are 200 bikes ready to go in one shed. Forty-seven more in another. There's a queue of 127 bikes waiting to be fixed, and around 99 organ donors.

Mornings are still his sanctuary. Bent over a bike, he thinks a lot. He imagines buying an ice cream cone in Golden Gate Park, attending a free concert in Stern Grove, and watching the sun sink into the endless waves crashing on Ocean Beach. He plans his first meal on the outside—it changes from catfish to oysters to lamb. He thinks about driving up to Lake Tahoe with friends.

"Just being able to do what I want to do," he says, is what he thinks of the most. "Appreciate the freedom we have so willfully given up by doing stupid things." It turns out that those "stupid things" are other shifting details. "Conspiracy to distribute narcotics" is not what the prison records say. They say robbery. Burglary. Theft.

Gently asked about that, Monroe begins to sweat. Mopping his face with a blue shop towel, he mumbles something about being "caught doing the theft of taking back something that was mine," and getting the charges reduced for a shorter sentence.

Months later, after considerable digging, an old newspaper story will turn up another set of facts. It will name Monroe as a suspect known as the "Live-to-go-home bank robber." Accused of robbing five San Francisco banks in five months, the suspect allegedly brandished no weapon—only a note. The note promised tellers they would "live to go home" if they gave him the money he asked for. In court, Artis Renard Monroe plead not guilty to 13 felonies, including robbery and burglary. The DA's office confirmed his case had nothing to do with drugs.

What happens when the facts don't line up? Where does that leave the truth?

We know this much is true: A prisoner fixed bikes. The bikes helped people. This may or may not add up to redemption. But it matters.

Monroe has a bike set aside for himself. He parks it near his desk, where it leans on a rusty kickstand. It's a red-and-black Genesis RoadTech with a triple chainring and a gel-padded saddle. Walmart sells it new for $129. It may not be much of a bike, but it has been his constant companion in a world where everything else seems to flow in one direction: out.

He has been told he can keep it when he leaves. Maybe he will.

He hasn't decided. Maybe that gives him something to think about for four months and seven days before he walks out of the prison gates. Every day after work Monroe rides 15 laps around the shed. He may be going in circles, but it feels like moving forward.

A few blocks from the prison, in a park with playgrounds and bike trails, a little girl smiles shyly at the Vista Torino 400. Her name is Amaya. She is seven years old. She has big brown eyes and red earrings. She knows how to ride a bicycle, but this one seems foreign. Not what she expected.

"You can touch it," says her mother, Tresa Andrews. "It's yours! Touch it, baby!"

Her old bike was purple, with princess stickers. But both tires are flat, and besides, it's too small. This one looks and feels a little weird. The handlebar is a funny shape. Her new helmet, donated by a stranger, won't fit over her braids. The seat looks like nothing she has ever seen.

"This is a banana seat," her mother says. "See how it's long and skinny? That's exactly what Mommy used to have when I was growing up!"

The bike reminds Amaya's mom of the yellow-and-white Schwinn she'd shared with her little brother. Tresa rode it barefoot, in a bathing suit, all summer. For a minute, she's that girl again: missing teeth, freckled cheeks, sun-kissed hair flying behind her. It took Tresa's mom months to save up for that bike. Her brother got a pink hand-me-down. A few nights before Christmas, Tresa helped her mom spray-paint it blue. He didn't know it was a girl's bike, but the other boys informed him. He didn't care. It was his.

That freckled girl is now a single working mom. Photos of her kids—two girls, two boys—are taped to her waitress's notebook. Her oldest child is about to make her a grandmother. Her youngest is smiling with shy confusion at the bike she couldn't afford, a gift from the local prison.

The Vista Torino 400 is a little too big for Amaya. She has to balance on the tips of her toes and sit on the nose of the seat. She scooters around, afraid to lift both feet. Then she pedals, timid and wobbly. The front wheel wags back and forth. Her mother runs next to her, holding on. Amaya keeps looking at the ground.

Suddenly Amaya's gaze moves from the ground to the horizon. She pedals fiercely, steady now. Her shy smile transforms into something else. Her mother lets go.

Postscript: By the time he was released on February 24, 2017, Monroe had restored more than 800 bikes. He did not take the one he'd set aside for himself.

JOHN M. GLIONNA

Who's Lookin' for a Fight?

FROM CALIFORNIA SUNDAY MAGAZINE

MICROPHONE IN HAND, Michael John Karaitiana stands atop a narrow wooden plank seven feet off the ground. Behind him is a circus tent with mustard-yellow banners that read ALL WEIGHTS. NOBODY BARRED! and WE CHALLENGE ALL COMERS. CASH PRIZES. With his graying hair tied in a neat ponytail, wearing an embroidered Western shirt and a beaver-skinned cowboy hat, he resembles a range hand dressed up for a night on the town. His body is muscular, his stomach taut, even at age 54. Broken knuckles jut like bony spikes from his oversize fists.

Flanking Michael are six boxers dressed in satin robes. Two have been with him for decades. Part Aboriginal, they are distant relatives from the cotton-growing town of Moree, their lives marked by anger and prison time. Brendan Prince, who is 49, fights as the "Moree Mauler," his large face flattened by too many punches. He bangs a bass drum with a *boom-ba-boom* beat. To his left is Michael John Jenkins, known to everyone as "Fugzi," who is 53 and missing his front teeth. He rings an old cowbell in a ragged rhythm.

"Shake 'em up, boys. Give 'em a good rally!" Michael tells the pair over a tinny sound system. "Let's show 'em that Roy Bell's Touring Stadium is back in town!"

It's 3 p.m. on a cloudy July day in Alice Springs, an isolated dot of humanity located at the center of Australia. Michael and his boxing tent are part of the annual agricultural fair, the biggest event of the year for this frontier town. He's driven 1,400 miles from his home in New South Wales to get here. Boxing tents have enlivened rural Australia since the early 1900s, when tent fighters faced off against challengers from small communities across the Outback. Michael's grandfather Roy Bell first came to Alice Springs in 1924, his father joined the troupe in 1957, and Michael has been running the tent for the past 36 years.

The drum-and-bell racket draws a crowd that's a cross-section of the unpeopled Northern Territory, where 244,000 residents inhabit an area twice the size of Texas. The audience is predominantly Aboriginal: elders in bush hats and flannel shirts, teens in hoodies clutching rugby balls, and women with baby strollers. There's a scattering of whites, mostly men, some toting sons on their shoulders, others with trucker caps and sagging bellies.

"Holda! Holda! Holda!" Michael says to halt the beat, waving a wooden cane and flashing two gold front teeth, mementos from a crashing tent pole. "Now, ladies and gentlemen, if ya cast your eyes along, you'll see all those girlie rides and bouncy things. But you're not gonna find an old-time boxing tent like this. My men are here to challenge all comers, so if ya have any fighters in the crowd, have 'em ready."

Michael is a "spruiker," a carnival barker, whose twangy auctioneer's patter has a loose relationship with the truth. His task is to lure fairgoers inside the tent to take on his fighters. Winners can earn as much as $200 and a year's worth of bragging rights. Losers can at least claim they had the gumption to strap on the gloves. "Take a look at this big joker here, folks," he says, pointing to Mauler. "He once did a nude shot for *Playboy* and used to fight in the pubs and clubs. He fought with the tent for 35 years before he left to have heart surgery. Now he runs on batteries."

The boxing tent reached its heyday in the two decades after World War II, when half a dozen troupes crisscrossed the country. Nowadays, Michael says, the working-class men who once clamored to the mat have given way to "soft kids who fiddle with smartphones." By the time the spectacle faded in the 1970s, many Australians associated tent boxing with a shadowy and violent past they would rather forget. Michael's tent is one of only two that's still going, and neither tours full-time.

"Okay now, fellas, put your hands up," he tells the crowd. "Who's lookin' for a fight?"

Michael summons a handful of volunteers to the plank, known as the lineup board, and assigns each one a nickname. He dubs a slender man "The Fishing Rod." Another he christens "Hendrix" for his Afro. A third he calls "The Alien." "You sober, son?" he asks him. "Do you know what you're doin'?" When asked what he does for work, The Alien raises his hand to his mouth as though taking a drink, making the crowd cackle.

Two hundred spectators file into the boxing tent, paying $20 apiece to witness a six-bout card. They pass fading canvas posters of long-dead fighters crouched in their pugilist poses. Rather than a roped-off ring, large mats are laid at the center of the tent, allowing spectators to press in so close that when boxers are hit hard, they're sent reeling into the crowd. Between rounds, the fighters rest on milk crates.

During each match, Michael offers a running commentary that celebrates challengers whose punches land anywhere near their target. These are decidedly amateur fights with three two-minute-long rounds and bulky 16-ounce gloves—twice the weight that professional boxers use—to slow the speed of blows and to provide additional cushion. The challengers see the bouts as a serious test, but for the tent fighters, they are part theater. Michael tells his boxers that bashing a local would discourage volunteers, so Mauler and Fugzi give each a chance to prove himself in the first two rounds, then go for a knockout in the third after their opponent is exhausted.

Fugzi takes on an undersized challenger named Justin, whose head barely reaches the tent fighter's shoulders. Both men tap gloves. "Box on!" Michael says. The bout is a mismatch, even with Fugzi fighting barefoot. With a straight-backed posture that harks back to boxers of another era, he glides and jabs, orbiting his foe, using his superior reach to swat away any attack. Justin's punches are undisciplined, his defense nonexistent. Seconds into the fight, Fugzi lands a blow to the jaw, dropping Justin to his knees. A woman screams in delight.

"Let him throw a few punches, Fugz," Michael rasps over the microphone. "Good boy. That's the way." But Fugzi's benevolence doesn't last. He soon lands two quick strikes to Justin's midsection, and the challenger is helped to his milk crate. "Stay away from him, Fugzi," Michael scolds at the beginning of the final round. "We don't want to see the little fella get hurt." As a quick left jab sends a spray of sweat from Justin's head, Michael ends the fight.

Hours later, Michael paces his tour bus. The Alice Springs fair lasts only two days, a small window to earn money for petrol, food, and salaries. He needs an evening fight card to make ends meet, but only if the crowd is large enough for a decent profit. One last look, though, confirms the fairgrounds have emptied. He gives Mauler and Fugzi the news: there will be no fights tonight.

A tattoo on Michael's back depicts a white boxer facing off against a grass-skirted Māori warrior wielding a spear. On his left temple, Māori tribal marks morph into a snake, for him a symbol of Australia, its long tail curling around his ear. It's no coincidence the country's fraught history of race relations plays out on Michael's body: the narrative of Australia's mistreatment of its indigenous people, the story of the boxing tent, and Michael's travails with his own extended family are intertwined.

Tent fighting got its start just a decade after Australia became a nation. At the time, almost all indigenous people were confined to remote "missions," or reservations, could not travel without government permission, and were not considered citizens. It wouldn't be until 1965 that indigenous people throughout Australia were allowed to vote and another six years before an indigenous person was elected to Parliament. For most of the past 50 years, the prevailing view in Australia has been that the boxing tent didn't just reflect the country's systemic racism but perpetuated it. Aboriginal boxers were paid less than whites and sometimes not at all, and they were often presented on the lineup board with the invitation of "Who wants to fight the darkie?"

Recently, though, historians have taken a more nuanced view. The boxing tent, they point out, was also a rare public place where races mixed. The boxers who traveled with Roy Bell and others were both white and Aboriginal, as were the audiences. Richard Broome, who teaches Aboriginal history in Melbourne, believes that the boxing tent offered indigenous Australians a sense of empowerment in a nation that denied them basic rights. "They became heroes to their own people," he writes. Michael agrees. The tent, he says, was the one arena where a black man dared raise a fist against a white man and knock him to the mat.

Michael's father, Lester, was a Māori who emigrated from New Zealand in 1956 and joined Roy Bell's caravan soon after. It was the golden age of the boxing tent. Bell's fighters traveled year-round, making 100 stops in towns and work camps that were among the most desolate places on the continent. Fighting under the name the "Māori Chief," Lester performed the haka war dance before each bout, often facing the toughest challengers, known as "takes." Within the country's strict racial hierarchy, he existed in an in-between space—a cut above indigenous Australians but well below whites, a man of color who was still subject to the country's pervasive racism. Reliable, hardworking, and a nondrinker, he eventually became Bell's camp boss, responsible for keeping the fighters in line.

Trouble came when he and Bell's teenage daughter, Nita, started a secret romance and she became pregnant. Bell banished them. The way he saw it, Lester had risen above his station: the black men who fought under him were employees, not sons-in-law. He vowed never to speak to his daughter again. After seven years, they reconciled, and the family rejoined the tent, but the old man's relationship with Lester remained strained, even though he was the star of the show. Bell insisted on calling him not by his name but as "Māori."

Michael, Lester and Nita's second-born son, talks about growing up among the "showies," carnival men and women, with almost dreamy reverence. He helped handle snakes in the reptile act and at night wandered Sideshow Alley to watch Sampson the Strong Man, Vanessa the Undresser, Pygmy performers, and Indian rope-trick artists. He also learned to box—his first tent bout, at the age of six, made the local newspaper—and for years scrambled for the coins spectators tossed onto the mat to award boys who had the spunk to fight.

In 1971, Bell retired the troupe in the wake of new laws that restricted boxing tents in all but two federal territories. When he died the following year, he left nothing to Lester. In the end, Michael says, his father was treated no better than the hired help. "Lester was a good man, but he worked for us," says Elwin Bell, Roy's youngest son. "Michael might take offense to that, but that's how it was."

A decade after his grandfather's death, Michael decided to revive the boxing tent. "It was in my blood," he says. "I had thought about it at school. I had always thought about it." He studied videos of the old man spruiking to memorize his words, inflection, and movements. He went to a shed and retrieved the musty tent equipment—gloves, mats, and canvas portraits—and took Roy Bell's Touring Stadium back on the road. In the early years, the show was a family affair: Lester fought; Nita managed the money. Michael soon married a girl who had also grown up on the show circuit, and their children romped the fairgrounds.

Michael quickly learned just how much the tent-boxing circuit had shrunk since Roy Bell's death. By then, television had come to the Outback, and entertainment like the boxing tent suddenly seemed antiquated. To make money, he traveled to Aboriginal missions in the equatorial jungles of northern Queensland, far beyond where most showies had ventured.

Fighting as "The Afghan" ("His mother was a full-blooded Aboriginal, his father, an Afghan camel driver"), Michael took on the takes, as Lester once did. He fought two men at once, even on his knees, anything to draw customers.

When the tent was down for the season, Michael trained as a professional boxer. His career was short-lived, but he continued to fight in the tent into his late forties until a skull-rattling blow stopped him cold. For months, he couldn't focus or make decisions, and he still worries that boxing has made him punch-drunk. An earlier hit left him with so much pain that a doctor had recommended he have a steel plate inserted into his jaw. To bring in steady income, Michael has worked as a truck driver and a mechanic and, in recent years, has hunted wild goats—a task he calls "a mongrel of a job." Supporting his wife and five children has kept him from taking the tent out every season, and the past decade has been especially hard, with several years passing between tours.

Roy Bell's sons, who remain fixtures on the carnival circuit operating thrill rides, are baffled by Michael's insistence to prolong an entertainment they believe has had its day. "The boxing tent died with my father," says Arnold Bell, Roy's oldest son. "It should have been left in the shed where it belongs."

Michael, though, relishes being an outlier. He has always considered himself more Lester's son than Roy's grandson, proud of being on the dark-skinned side of the Bell clan. He keeps the tent alive, he says, in honor of his father. At Lester's funeral in 2003, dozens of Māori performed the haka dance. A spruiker challenged mourners to raise a hand if they wanted to step up and fight the big man. The casket was lowered to rest on a section of boxing mat covered by a swath of Roy Bell's canvas tent. Lester's second-born son had seen to that.

*

Behind the wheel of his bus, Michael leads his convoy north along the Stuart Highway. Known as "The Track," it is the interior's principal north-south route, stretching more than 1,750 miles along the path forged by Scottish explorer John McDouall Stuart, who in 1861 led the first successful expedition across the nation's then-uncharted center. The two-lane road runs ramrod straight past fields of termite mounds towering like desert cathedrals and settlements whose names seem pulled from a children's storybook: Cutta Cutta Caves, Banka Banka Station, Jingaloo, Mungkarta, Amoonguna, and Humpty Doo.

Michael's secondhand bus—its destination sign reads SPECIAL —pulls an old trailer he refitted himself, while his son-in-law drives a battered truck with another ancient trailer in tow. With his own pickup, Fugzi peels off to stock up on chilled cans of bourbon-and-soda for the road, reappearing to speed ahead of the caravan, honking and pointing and laughing.

Michael bought the Special for $2,000, and it has no heat, air conditioning, or shower. He is proud that his road show is "patched together with tape and glue" in contrast to the upper-class Bells with their shiny thrill rides. He forgoes modern conveniences not just because he's on a tight budget, but because it's a way to re-create a bygone era when Roy Bell and his boxers traveled dirt tracks, forded rivers, hunted game, and camped in the bush for weeks on end.

The bus lacks a "roo" bar to protect against the kangaroo's suicidal hops into the path of passing vehicles. When he spots one, Michael flicks off his high beams and slows to a crawl. The Special passes thousands of kangaroo carcasses. It's not just roos he must avoid; there are wallabies, goats, donkeys, porcupines, emus, Brahman cattle, boars the size of boulders, and flocks of bush parrots that dive-bomb his windshield. One morning, the crew awakened at a roadside camp to find a dead 30-foot python hanging from a nearby tree.

Averaging 50 miles an hour, the Special is an obstacle for the diesel-powered semis known as road trains. Hauling as many as four trailers, the freighters can be as long as a 14-story building. Drivers resist applying their brakes to prevent jackknifes as they bear down on lumbering vehicles like the Special.

After a long day on the road, the piercing headaches from his jaw can leave Michael testy. One moment he's calm, and the next he's clenching his fists, ready to scrap. The time he considers most sacrosanct is when he retreats to the bus to prepare for a show, making his transition from truck driver to carnival showman. Everyone knows to leave him alone. The pressures Michael faces are substantial. Unlike the days of Roy Bell, he has only two boxers accompanying him, Mauler and Fugzi, and at every stop must recruit fighters to represent the tent. He also negotiates with show officials, keeps the books, and does his share of the cooking. His biggest stress, though, is that his audience is diminishing; with each tour, fewer whites are coming out to the bouts. He views this as a personal insult—a rejection of the thing he loves the most. Without white audiences, he's convinced, the tent is in peril. "In the small towns, there's just not enough money going around," he says. "It's bad for the other showies as well."

All of this can make him desperate. One morning in Alice Springs, a wiry white teen with a shaved head asked to fight for the tent. Michael had him throw a few hooks and jabs and liked what he saw. He nicknamed the kid "Jailbait." Michael boasts he can instantly size up anyone's ability to fight, a necessary expertise when volunteers try to downplay their skills to gain advantage inside the tent. He looks at their nose and knuckles. Have they been broken? Do the men have balance, a fighter's stance? He knows matching boxers of equal strength will ensure a good match and bring customers back.

That afternoon, Michael matched Jailbait up against an Aboriginal challenger nearly twice his size. Once on the mat, Jailbait never threw a punch. He ducked and danced to avoid his opponent, who was slow and powerful and relentlessly moving forward. By the end of the first round, the crowd was jeering. In the second round, the challenger caught up with Jailbait and connected with a straight-on blow to the nose. "Why does he have to punch so hard?" Jailbait yelled. "Now I've got a headache!" The crowd erupted in laughter. Michael had seen enough. "Take the gloves off him!" he shouted to Mauler. "Throw him out!"

Later, Michael admitted he selected Jailbait because he was white. He sat in his tour bus, flicking ashes from a cigarette into his palm. "Nobody wants to come watch the black fellas," he says. "My kids, they won't want to run this—it's too much work. This is the hardest show there is. It's as rough as guts."

*

Before each tour, Michael puts the word out that he's going back on the road. For years Mauler and Fugzi have answered the call. When they join the caravan, there are long man-hugs and back-slapping. But once en route, Michael becomes a cloying perfectionist.

Setting up the tent, with its rusty spikes and iron bars, is arduous work. The tear-down is no easier; heavy ropes, banners, and wooden planks are stored in cramped, hard-to-access compartments on the trailer's sides and undercarriage. "Here, let me do it," Michael invariably tells his men. "That way it'll be done right the first time." He brags that he could put up the tent by himself, a claim that might have been true years ago but not anymore. And nobody touches the wooden box that holds the electric wiring, a relic once used by Roy Bell himself. Along with the canvas fighter portraits, it's Michael's most treasured possession. While he observes no color line, he follows a generations-old rule that places showies above their workers. "I'm the boss," he reminds them.

By nature, Michael is a loner, but the boxing tent requires him to manage Mauler and Fugzi, men who size up every stranger through one prism: Can they knock him out? Fugzi is Michael's best worker, but he's also an agitator and complainer who picks fights in camp. Mauler, though, presents the bigger challenge. He's a self-destructive slacker but impossible to dislike. Michael has a strict set of rules. No alcohol on the bus or in camp. Everyone showers before hitting the road. No urinating near the tent. No women allowed. Before the tour is over, Mauler breaks every one.

He showed up in Alice Springs fat and out of shape. Arriving by bus from Katherine, 735 miles away, his small duffel bag containing all he owned, he immediately bummed a cigarette, helping himself to four from the offered pack. Mauler has spent much of his life "long-grassing," sleeping in fields or public parks, scrounging cigarette butts and money for liquor and pot. He met Fugzi growing up in Moree, a rough New South Wales town split along racial lines. He never met his father, he says, and his mother rejected him at birth. Raised by his grandmother, who ran a gambling house, he was expelled from school at 15. "Teachers hated me. I hated them," he says. "My grandmother was angry. She wanted me to get the best education. I let her down."

He committed petty crimes—breaking into cars, getting drunk in public—and has spent several years in prison. His body is covered with scars, the vestiges of street fights, pub brawls, and the time a girlfriend hit him with a brick that left an angry pink welt below one ear. He was long-grassing when he joined Michael's tent in 1993. "He was a big black fella with a few scars on his head," Michael recalls. "I thought, *This bloke will be all right in the tent.* He's got a bit of character. He can mix with any crowd. Back then he wasn't drinking like he does now." For several years, Mauler has collected government disability after doctors diagnosed fight-related brain damage. "But really," he says, "I've been this crazy all my life."

The first morning in Alice Springs, Mauler vanished as the men labored to set up the tent. On past tours, he's pulled "a midnight," abandoning the tour. Michael rarely allows anyone back who's left him, but he always accepts his feckless fighter. "He's like family," he says. Mauler is also fiercely loyal to Michael. "It seems like the day of the tent is over, but it's not," he says. "Success will come. And I want to be by his side when that day happens."

In Tennant Creek, the tour's second stop, the crew sets up camp beneath a copse of eucalyptus trees on ground crowded with anthills. The bush flies immediately descend, invading the men's eyes and mouths, drawn to the sweat and stink. Mauler makes do with a World War II–era iron bed with stained, hand-me-down cushions, blankets, and pillows. While others do chores, he lounges in his tent reading a newspaper, discoursing on discrimination against indigenous Australians, and smoking hand-rolled cigarettes, a money-saving habit in a country where singles sell for $1.50 each and packs go for up to $40.

When Michael last came to Tennant Creek, in 2013, an official told him that his tent attracted only "drunken Aboriginals." "I'm a man of color," he says. "I was offended." Tempers flared, and police were called, with officers ordering him to leave town just before his first show. He stalled for time, saying he needed to pack up, but when the police left, he told the crowd he would defy the lawmen even if it meant going to jail. "I'll have my bacon and eggs behind bars!" he proclaimed and went on to stage several matches. Officials first told him they didn't want him back this year but eventually relented.

Mauler had refused to box in Alice Springs, claiming he'd lost his mojo. But after Fugzi's fight with Justin appeared on YouTube, his competitive spirit was aroused. Sitting around the campfire the first night in Tennant Creek, Michael offers a bit of advice. To outdo Fugzi, he says, Mauler should take on two contenders at once and post his own video. Mauler likes the idea and the next morning trudges over to the public bathroom to shave his head as part of his prefight routine.

Mauler loves the mat, but he also suffers from terrible stage fright. "I'm just a brawler," he says. "I don't know any moves or repertoire, but I do have a big right punch." He's convinced he can't fight unless he's drunk or stoned. "It gives me the wind," he says.

On the morning of fight day, he starts swigging from a fifth of rum. He wears sunglasses, a black knit cap, a faux-gold chain, and a STRAIGHT OUTTA MOREE T-shirt.

"Mauler," Michael snaps, "you can't wear that beanie or glasses on the lineup board. When you're in the tent, you dress like a boxer. Go put on a gown."

"I'm on it," Mauler replies, finishing off the bottle. "I'm confident now."

He fights two men—a white cowboy whom Michael nicknames "Rampaging Ricky" and an athletic young black man named Darryl. Dripping from a rum sweat, Mauler plays to the crowd, jokingly running about the mat. The two men buzz around him, careful to avoid his powerful swipes. "Look out for the little fella behind ya, Mauler," Michael warns. "Don't run around too much, you'll run out of air!"

Mauler dashes between the pair, extending his arms to throw a simultaneous punch at each. By the second round, he is gasping. He knocks down the cowboy with a left hook, but Darryl sends him to the mat with a flurry of short punches. In the last round, woozy from the alcohol, Mauler goes down twice without even being hit. Michael awards the bout to the challengers, but Mauler insists his mojo is back. "At least I didn't cough up any phlegm," he says. "That's gotta count for something."

At Katherine, the next stop, both Fugzi and Mauler pull a midnight. Michael isn't entirely surprised they took off, he says, but "it's a kick in the guts. You carry them along, and then they're not there for you on show day. You need them just for that one hour so you can earn enough money for the week."

The day before the matches, several of Michael's old boxing

pals arrive to help out. Lucas "Cool Hand Luke" Warren, a 65-year-old concrete worker and former pro boxer with gray dreadlocks, volunteers to take on challengers half his age. Ken "Rocky" Couzens, a former tent boxer who coached Michael in a few pro fights, agrees to referee. "How can you put up a tent like this and announce you'll take on anyone in town when you don't have any fighters?" Rocky asks, letting out a huge laugh. "Now that's balls." The men sit around the camp on lawn chairs trading stories as Michael plays his guitar and sings a song he wrote about his father.

That night on the lineup board, before Michael starts to spruik, a fighter rings a cowbell in honor of a professional boxer who had recently died—10 times, one for each round of a fight. "That's the 10th bell," Michael tells the crowd, "and he's not getting up." Then, as he promotes the evening's first match, Mauler appears in the crowd. He's been partying for days. Somebody asks him if he's ready to fight. "I can't," he says. "I've got a headache." He disappears before Michael can spot him.

The fights are a success, attracting a large, mixed crowd, many of them ranch hands who participated in the rodeo next door. After the last bout, an indigenous Australian named Norman George approaches Michael. Decades earlier, George had fought for Roy Bell under the nickname "Crow" before he left to earn a college degree and a good government job. On this night, he's nostalgic. "I loved the tent," he says. "I loved being around the other boxers. For all of us Aboriginal kids, the fights gave us a way out." As Michael squats on the lineup board, Crow reaches up to shake his hand. "I miss the drumbeat," he says softly. "*Boom-ba-boom-ba-boom!*"

On the final morning, as Michael breaks camp, Mauler shows up to collect the money he says is due him. Sitting in the bus stairwell, smoking a cigarette, Michael doesn't look at the boxer, a gesture meant to wound. "So, ya come for your money after we're all packed up," he says, exhaling smoke. "You let us down, Mauler. We needed you, and you weren't there."

"Aw," Mauler says. "It was just the grog and the cones"—bong hits.

Michael hands him a tight wad of bills, and Mauler takes it without looking. He suggests he might show up in Darwin, the tour's final stop. "We'll see how I go," Mauler says. "Well, we won't need ya," Michael lies. It's a rerun of the same sad scene. Mauler walks away in a Bob Marley T-shirt, his head already sprouting gray hairs.

Darwin brings more bad news. Fair officials won't allow Michael to set up his tent. His application arrived late, they claim, but he is convinced he's being blacklisted after the 2013 Tennant Creek incident. He parks his caravan outside the front gate in the hope that officials will change their mind. "If I drive away," he says, "I've given up." Fellow showies stop by to offer encouragement and a few dollars, which he refuses.

In the end, the Darwin officials don't budge. Michael was counting on the proceeds from Darwin to pay for the 2,200-mile drive back to New South Wales. To cut down on expenses, he decides to leave the pickup and trailer behind, but that isn't enough. He will eventually have to ask his mother for a loan to make the trip home.

By any definition, the tour has been a failure. Michael's lost his boxers and was nearly banned from half of the four stops. Most of white Australia has turned its back on the tent. The indigenous people are the only ones who haven't abandoned him, but he knows he can't continue with them alone. Despite the tour's abrupt end, Michael is smiling. Behind the wheel of the Special, he begins singing out loud and talking about the future—his plans to open a boxing museum and sparring ring in his hometown, how he's going to keep the tour alive at least until 2024, the 100th anniversary of when Roy Bell started the boxing show. "This trip has shown that I've still got it," he says. "I can still spruik. I can still get 'em in the door, just like I used to." Before he is out of town, he's on his phone, calling Mauler.

MAGGIE SHIPSTEAD

Another Voyage for Madmen (And, This Time, One Woman)

FROM OUTSIDE

ON JULY 1, 17 skippers in 17 boats left the French port town of Les Sables d'Olonne and sailed west into the Bay of Biscay. Their destination? Les Sables d'Olonne, but from the other direction, a journey of about nine months and 30,000 miles. The boats are unremarkable. The sailors are a mixed bag: hotshot pro racers, ambitious yachties, ultracompetent old salts, young upstarts, dedicated adventurers, a hopeless dreamer or two—16 men and one woman representing 12 countries, all with a common intention. They're racing around the world without stopping, without benefit of modern technology, and alone.

This is the second-ever Golden Globe Race. The original, which has been immortalized in several books, including Peter Nichols's classic account, *A Voyage for Madmen,* as well as the documentary *Deep Water* and the recent Colin Firth film *The Mercy,* began in the summer of 1968 and, by its end, turned into an epic blend of historic triumph, human tragedy, and utter shitshow. Nine sailors started and one finished. One killed himself. This race marks the 50th anniversary of that event, and besides some allowances for safety, the rules limit the racers to technology available in 1968. Sextants, not GPS. Radio, not sat phones. Film cameras and Super 8s, not DSLRs and GoPros. No digital anything. No high-tech materials like Kevlar or carbon composite. No electric autopilot, desalinization, or refrigeration. No blog posts, no video chats, no selfies at sea.

Such restrictions might seem suspiciously like pedantic hipster nostalgia for all things analog, but the throwback nature of the race is an earnest attempt to reclaim radical simplicity in a world addicted to interconnectedness. Just think—no email, no texts, no news alerts for the better part of a year. But no family or friends either. No human touch. Just one person, one boat, one planet. This is a race about intangibles. The skippers will sail a very long way to see pretty much only a disc of water and a dome of sky, their progress marked by changing angles in the sextant mirrors, lines drawn on charts. Whoever wins won't even win money—more on that later—but will be symbolically awarded a perpetual trophy.

Not all will finish. If half the fleet succeeds, everyone will be pleasantly surprised. Following the fastest route, as the skippers are obliged to do, means sailing down the Atlantic, turning east around the bottom of Africa, passing below Australia and New Zealand, rounding Cape Horn, and crossing back up the Atlantic. This, in turn, means spending something like four or five months in isolated latitudes known as the Roaring Forties and Furious Fifties, in the ring of water around Antarctica that sailors speak of, with caution and respect, as the Southern Ocean. Strong and reliable westerly winds, unimpeded by land, make for fast sailing but also build into severe gales and massive seas that will break anything on a boat that can be broken and wear on the physical and mental fortitude of any sailor. Boats will fail. Injuries will happen. People will decide they've had enough. It's a war of attrition.

The obvious question is why. Why choose to sail alone in a small boat through the world's most furious seas, far from comfort or help, guided by the stars? Why attempt such a journey knowing full well that at times you will be horribly lonely, at others frustrated beyond measure, sometimes bored, sometimes afraid, that death by drowning out in the middle of big blue will be a constant possibility?

If you have to ask, you'll never really understand the answer. In a way, there is no answer.

Les Sables d'Olonne has a broad, curving beach edged by a well-strolled, almost supernaturally shadeless embankment and presided over by a long row of blocky apartment buildings interspersed with elegant Belle Époque villas. It's a sailing town with a steady breeze, best known as the start and finish of the Vendée

Globe, an extravagantly high-tech singlehanded circumnavigation race that happens every four years. Faded posters from the 2016 iteration still hang in windows.

For the second half of June, the Golden Globe boats were tied up at a floating dock, *les pontons*, in Les Sables d'Olonne's densely occupied marina for final preparations and inspections. Flags flapped in their rigging. A steady stream of well-wishers, gawkers, and autograph seekers walked up and down the row of boats, chatting in French to the skippers, even those who spoke no French. The French are big sailing fans, and many clustered around the boat of Jean-Luc van den Heede, the oldest racer, a 73-year-old French sailing hero with five solo circumnavigations already under his belt, including two Vendée Globes. Nearby was Susie Goodall's red-hulled sloop of the same design, a Rustler 36 called *Starlight*. Goodall, at 28, is the youngest skipper and the only woman. Kevin Farebrother, a firefighter from Perth, Australia, christened his boat *Sagarmantha,* the Nepalese name for Mount Everest, which he has summited three times.

Mark Slats, a strapping Dutchman, had two gigantic oars on the deck of his boat, which he planned on using to row through calms. (Dread of calms and a strong preference for storms was universal among the sailors. Calms are boring and leave you too much time to think.) Slats thought he could row for about 10 hours a day, getting maybe 2.5 knots. This past December, he rowed solo across the Atlantic in 30 days, 7 hours, and 49 minutes, smashing the world record.

Aside from the sponsor logos on hulls and sails, the boats were decidedly basic—cruisers you'd see in any marina. Race rules required them to be single-hulled, mass-produced, designed before 1988, and between 32 and 36 feet in overall length. Farther down the dock, their masts towering over the rest, were a handful of IMOCA 60s, the boats used in the Vendée Globe. Recent designs resemble 60-foot-long squared-off *Star Trek* insignias and are capable of levitating above the water on retractable foils, reaching speeds over 30 knots. If they are the monohull equivalent of Formula One race cars, then the Golden Globe boats are modestly tricked-out camper vans. Get six knots out of one and you feel pretty good. The Vendée Globe record is 74 days. Golden Globe sailors are planning for 300, even if the speediest hope to shave more than a month off that. But modesty is part of the point.

"All the other races are incredibly expensive," said Golden Globe race director Don McIntyre. "They're great to watch, but it's now got exclusive, very exclusive, and it's going more so that way." A competitive Vendée Globe campaign costs millions of dollars, but the Golden Globe requires only a fraction of that. According to McIntyre, $100,000 would be enough to get in the race, and at the end you'd still own your boat, which, he pointed out, you could live in. Some might have to. While a minority of the sailors were comfortably covered by sponsors or personal wealth, five sold or mortgaged their houses to fund their circumnavigations. Others, lacking houses to sell, have had to hustle hard.

"I had no money and no boat," said 31-year-old Irishman Gregor McGuckin. "I did an overseas in the Caribbean to help get a bit of capital to buy a boat, or at least help trick banks into thinking I had a steady income so they'd give me a loan to buy a boat." Just a month out from the start, McGuckin was still relying mostly on blind faith and dogged determination when, after much pavement pounding, he secured a sponsorship. But costs still loom for when he is away—payments on the boat loan, for example, even if the repo man wouldn't have an easy time tracking him down. Taking advantage of a technological recourse unavailable to the 1968 skippers, he has set up a GoFundMe.

As of the start, the race itself was also short on funds. The original plan was for a purse of 75,000 euros (around $87,000), to be split among the four fastest circumnavigators, but without a major sponsor, pride and a sense of accomplishment would have to suffice. (Banners on each of the boats, beneath the sailors' names, had a blue place-holding rectangle that read simply "Sponsor?") According to McIntyre, only 35,000 euros in sponsorship funds had come through, and while the local government of Les Sables d'Olonne had contributed the cost of the race village and each entrant had put in a start fee of just over $10,000, he said he'd personally invested nearly three-quarters of a million dollars.

McIntyre, an Australian, has made a colorful career for himself seeking out and facilitating adventure. In the 1980s, he started marine equipment importing and yacht-building businesses to fund his own participation in the BOC Challenge, a solo circumnavigation race with stops. McIntyre was second in his class in 1990. After that, he started running and guiding tourist trips to Antarctica; currently, he and his partner have a long-term lease on an island in Tonga, where they run whale swimming trips. McIntyre's initial concept for the Golden Globe reboot, which first occurred to him in 1995, had been simpler: he would sail around himself for the 30th anniversary. At the time, he was spending a year in an 8' × 12'–foot hut on Antarctica with his then-wife. "I was sitting there in the box in the middle of winter thinking, what's next, what's next?" McIntyre said. He made plans and designed a boat, but life got in the way. He missed the 40th anniversary as well when he chose instead to re-create Captain Bligh's 3,600-mile Pacific journey in a 24-foot open boat. These things happen.

"Finally," McIntyre said, "we were in Tonga, treasure hunting —this is in 2014, long story—and I thought, jeepers, four years to the anniversary." The timing had come right. Then he thought, *Why not make it a race?*

In 1968, no one had ever sailed around the world alone and without stopping. This may not seem like a problem, but to rivalrous sailors from France and the UK, it was. People had sailed around the world singlehanded, but they'd always come ashore at some point for repairs or supplies or to have a good meal and a chat. The first solo circumnavigator was Joshua Slocum, a former clipper captain from Nova Scotia who, rendered professionally obsolete by the rise of the steam engine, set off eastward from Boston in 1895 in a 37-foot oyster sloop and returned three years later. He made many stops, navigating with spooky accuracy despite relying on a rudimentary combination of lunar sights, dead reckoning, and an old tin clock instead of a proper chronometer.

Eighteen others had followed suit by 1967, when an Englishman named Francis Chichester became first to sail around with only one stop. What was left to do but cut out the stop?

The *Sunday Times,* a weekly newspaper in the UK, hit on the idea of offering a trophy, the Golden Globe, to the first sailor to complete the feat and a cash prize of £5,000 for the fastest circumnavigation. No official entry was required, nor was any kind of qualifying experience. Skippers could sail whatever kind of boat they wanted, no matter how unsuitable. The only nod to safety was the paper's stipulation that, to be eligible, sailors had to leave between June 1 and October 31, 1968. Departing earlier or later would mean near-suicidal conditions in the Southern Ocean. In the end, the field was made up of six Brits, two Frenchmen, and one Italian.

In early February, four were left. Carozzo, the Italian, had made it only as far as Portugal before stomach ulcers forced him to retire. Others dropped out due to boat damage or the realization that life would be much more pleasant elsewhere. Who was left? In the lead, 29-year-old Robin Knox-Johnston, a straitlaced merchant marine officer who considered hegemony over the sea a British birthright, was on the homestretch, crossing back up the Atlantic in his 32-foot teak ketch, *Suhaili*. He had left earlier than anyone else remaining, in mid-June, and was likely to be the first back but very unlikely to be the fastest. The only sailor with a chance at overtaking him was the famous French sailor and nautical memoirist Bernard Moitessier, who was sailing very fast in a 39-foot steel ketch named *Joshua* (for Slocum). Moitessier had just rounded Cape Horn. British naval lieutenant Nigel Tetley was in third, having just passed New Zealand in his increasingly beat-up 40-foot trimaran named *Victress*. Tetley would not catch Knox-Johnston, but if he continued as he had been, he would be faster.

Then there was Donald Crowhurst, the dark horse, whose exact whereabouts were unknown.

In Les Sables this June, skippers and support teams came and went to their boats like bees to a favorite flower. They hauled out and put away sail bags and boxes of hardware and giant plastic bins of canned and dehydrated food, hung off sterns to tinker with the self-steering gear, politely signed autographs when visitors couldn't be dodged, went up masts, drilled and cranked and coiled and generally enacted sustained, miscellaneous marine busyness.

The busiest boat was Italian Francesco Cappelletti's, because it was nowhere near ready to sail. While the other skippers had all raced to Les Sables by sea from Falmouth in the UK, Cappelletti, running far behind schedule, had been forced to ship his yellow ketch overland from the south of France. At Les Sables, he'd put it in the water and stepped the masts, but with days to go, countless tasks remained undone, including major ones like wiring and installing pumps and radio. Before he could leave, he'd need to pass an involved safety inspection and spend three days at sea doing 300 additional qualifying miles, and things were *not* looking good for Cappelletti. His one bittersweet ray of hope was that racers who didn't make the July 1 start were permitted to start as late as July 7. In fact, in the 1968 race, the only Italian competitor, Alex Carozzo, faced with a similar situation, had repaired to a mooring after the start deadline passed for another week of preparation before setting out.

Russian Igor Zaretskiy's ketch, *Esmerelda*, was another hive of activity, due not to desperation but an abundance of helpers: a large and unsmiling crew of men in Yacht Russia T-shirts and shin-length denim shorts who, when Igor went out for a test sail, followed unsmilingly behind in a rigid-inflatable boat, flying the Russian flag. Among Zaretskiy's supplies were 600 packs of cigarettes —a disincentive against quitting the race, because if he put into port abroad, he'd have to pay duty on them.

Other boats were oases of tranquility. Sailors knew to casually swing by *Lazy Otter* around lunchtime, when Turkish-born British skipper Ertan Beskardes and his wife, Arzu, purveyors of military regalia in their onshore lives, would inevitably insist they stay for lunch. Abhilash Tomy, a pilot in the Indian navy who'd completed a previous solo nonstop circumnavigation in 2013, sometimes slept the morning away, rolling in midafternoon to do some languid boat tinkering. "It's just a circumnavigation," Tomy said. "I don't know why everyone's making such a big deal out of it."

As far as anyone back in Britain knew, in February 1969, Donald Crowhurst was more than a thousand miles east of Cape Town, in the southern Indian Ocean, sailing at incredible speed. They thought this because he had been radioing home false daily mileages and deliberately vague positions, and his overzealous, highly credulous publicist had been spreading and embellishing his story. In actuality, Crowhurst was dawdling off the coast of South America. An inexperienced sailor and struggling electronics entrepreneur with an unfortunate knack for convincing others to believe in his self-delusions, Crowhurst had finagled the sponsorship to build a 41-foot trimaran, *Teignmouth Electron*, in exchange for a contractual promise that if he didn't finish the race, he would repay the cost. In effect, Crowhurst would be ruined, and he had a wife and four children to support.

At the time of the first Golden Globe race, multihulls were in their infancy. They were known to be fast, but many doubted their capacity to endure heavy seas. One major problem was that when a multihull capsizes, its submerged mast and sails become a keel, and it does not right itself. *Teignmouth Electron,* even setting aside its questionable basic design, especially had no business going anywhere near the Southern Ocean. It was leaky and rattletrap. Its decks were sealed only with paint, not fiberglass, and the great invention Crowhurst had talked up to sell his voyage—an automatically triggered self-righting buoyancy bag at the top of the mast —existed only as bunches of wire running through the trimaran's cabin, attached to nothing.

Within a few weeks of leaving port, his boat already falling apart with alarming speed, Crowhurst understood that proceeding with his planned journey would mean almost certain death. In December, ensnared by pride and shame, he had begun keeping a second logbook, documenting a false journey. He calculated navigational sights for positions thousands of miles from where he actually was (not an easy bit of math) and cobbled together guesses at distant weather from radio reports. In January, feigning radio trouble, he had cut himself off from the outside world. Crowhurst planned to loiter in the South Atlantic until the other homebound racers passed him, at which point he could fall in line behind them and finish respectably. Hopefully no one would look too closely at the logbook of the third- or fourth-place sailor.

In mid-April, Crowhurst reestablished radio contact, claimed to be approaching Cape Horn, and asked for news of the other racers. Knox-Johnston was nearly home, he learned, and Tetley was in the Atlantic, about two weeks ahead of Crowhurst. Bernard Moitessier, always something of a mystic and concerned about the corrupting effects of competition and fame, had decided to abandon the race and continue on toward Tahiti in pure communion with the sea. In a message he slingshotted onto the deck of a passing tanker near Cape Town, Moitessier informed the *Sunday Times,* "I am continuing non-stop towards the Pacific Islands because I am happy at sea, and perhaps also to save my soul."

On April 22, Knox-Johnston arrived back in Falmouth, an immediate hero and celebrity. On May 20, only a thousand miles from home, Nigel Tetley's trimaran, badly weakened by months at sea, finally fell apart and sank. When he was informed by cable of the sinking (and Tetley's subsequent rescue), Crowhurst understood, inescapably, that if he continued on, he would be laying claim to the fastest time around and subjecting his account of the journey to impossible scrutiny. There was no way his deception would not be exposed.

His progress slowed. His track became aimless. Early in June, his radio failed, and Crowhurst spent two weeks working obsessively to repair it while the *Teignmouth Electron* drifted through the doldrums. Once the radio was repaired, Crowhurst tapped out a flurry of messages to his wife and publicist. After that, becalmed in the Sargasso Sea, he opened his logbook and spent eight days writing down incoherent, exclamation point–studded ramblings about Einstein and mathematics and intelligence and morality, working himself up to the less-than-realistic conclusion that "[m]athematicians and engineers used to the techniques of system analysis will skim through my complete work in less than an hour. At the end of that time problems that have beset humanity for thousands of years will have been solved for them."

On July 1, reaching the end of the logbook, he stopped mid-sentence and wrote no more. Nine days later, *Teignmouth Electron* was found adrift in the middle of the Atlantic. Crowhurst was gone, and so was the ship's chronometer. Presumably he'd jumped overboard, leaving behind a confession in the form of the two logbooks.

A few nights before the start of the 2018 Golden Globe, in the tented bar in the Les Sables race village, Jean-Luc van den Heede's band was playing. Couples waltzed around whatever floor space they could find while the septuagenarian sailor happily crooned away, pausing occasionally to banter in French. Late in his first set, van den Heede invited up a special guest. Robin Knox-Johnston climbed onstage, bearing two beers. He is now 79, Sir Robin, elder statesman of singlehanded sailing with three more circumnavigations under his belt, including another solo voyage in 2007. In 2016, he finished restoring *Suhaili* to its original low-key, slightly tubby glory, and he'd sailed it across from Falmouth with the Golden Globe fleet. Knox-Johnson downed his beer and gave the other to van den Heede. The two men launched into a baritone duet of "Molly Malone." "Cockles and mussels," they sang. "Alive, alive, oh." The crowd went wild.

Bernard Moitessier died in 1994, but *Joshua,* also restored, was in Les Sables, docked beside *Suhaili.* (*Victress,* of course, was at the bottom of the Atlantic, and in a sad and puzzling epilogue, Nigel Tetley had been found hanging from a tree in 1972.) Francis Chichester's yacht *Gypsy Moth IV* was also at *les pontons*. Alex Carozzo, the Italian who'd been undone by ulcers, put in an appearance. Jesse Martin and Jessica Watson were around, both Australians who'd completed solo nonstops as teenagers (Watson with significant assistance from Don McIntyre), and there was a prevailing atmosphere of fellowship among the circumnavigators, both veteran and hopeful, a sense of being at a rare gathering of usually solitary creatures.

"The thing about singlehanded sailors," said Mark Sinclair, a 59-year-old Australian skipper known to all as Captain Coconut, after his orange Lello 34, *Coconut*, "is by nature they don't conform. They don't obey rules. They do their own thing. So having an event for singlehanded sailors is like an oxymoron. It's impossible."

Or certainly not easy. The competitors complained about all the rules. (The notice of race—the official regulations—was more than 60 pages long and involved the purchase of many expensive bits of safety equipment, including satellite phones they weren't allowed to use to call anyone except race officials for required check-ins.) The race organizers complained about the competitors complaining. There was some whispering about whether anyone might smuggle aboard a GPS. Not everyone was comfortable with the sextant yet. The rules—those rules again!—mandated that the racers pass a specific mark in the Canary Islands, but not everyone was confident about finding it.

"The reality is," said Don McIntyre, "the only way you will finish this is if you have a burning passion to finish it. It's all in the brain. You can have the best boat and the best gear, but if you're not there for the right reasons, you'll find a reason to retire."

But these reasons, the right reasons, resist definition. All the sailors seemed to have decided more or less instantaneously to enter the race as soon as they heard about it, as though the idea had broken a pane of glass inside them, releasing an implacable spirit. They described obsession, sleeplessness, a rush to lock down a spot in the lineup without knowing how they were possibly going to get the money together. But as far as why, they couldn't do much better than offer platitudes about the challenge or say, well, this is just the kind of thing I do, this is who I am. Fundamentally, the desire to be in the race was just that, a desire, as instinctive and unpredictable and inarticulable as lust.

Minnesotan Nabil Amra, who is competing under the Palestinian flag and is one of the more novice sailors, was something of an exception. When he first heard of the event, he wasn't initially seized by a personal mania. First he suggested to Mahfouz Kabariti, an activist and president of the Palestine Surfing and Sailing Federation, that a Palestinian enter. Kabariti told him Palestinians are prohibited from competing internationally. "Maybe it was my Midwestern sense of fair play, but that burned me up," Amra said. "So I thought I would do it. I had an interest in cruising, not necessarily in sailing around the world without seeing anything. But sometimes we make a sacrifice for a greater good."

He added, "Sometimes anger can be a powerful motivator if you harness it."

Will a lofty sense of the greater good be enough when you've been cold and wet for four months in the Southern Ocean? No one can predict what will happen out there. There's a randomness to how environment and boat and human will chafe and collide, an unpredictability to internal and external breaking points. At any moment, anyone might hit a submerged shipping container and sink. And there is the uncertain capacity of the self to cope with existence as the solitary center of a disc of empty water. You can't know how you'll manage until you try. Some find they can't get enough.

Abhilash Tomy couldn't wait to leave Les Sables. He was sailing a newly built replica of *Suhaili* that had been constructed, like the original, in India. "I know what the mind is going to be like," he said. "I know what the body's going to feel. And you just go through it." What does the mind feel like? "Empty. Blank. Happy. In control. Without emotions." And the body? "Shit."

On his previous circumnavigation, Tomy said, "I became very clairvoyant. I could see far into the future, far into the past." What did he see? "Many, many things. I saw everything."

Tomy said he would come back completely wiped clean, without memory or guilt or morality or cravings. "Completely deconstructed," he said. For him, that was what was critical. A self so distilled it became a kind of nothingness. That was what he was looking for.

*

On July 5, four days after the start, Francesco Cappelletti officially withdrew from the race, acknowledging that he would not be able to meet the safety requirements in time for the July 7 deadline. He still planned to sail around the world, but, no longer bound by the race rules, he would be using GPS, not the stars.

Later the same day, Ertan Beskardes headed for port in northern Spain. In a Facebook post announcing his withdrawal from the race, Beskardes wrote, "After few days, not talking to my family regularly to share the daily experiences has sadly taken the joy and happiness from this experience. The feeling gradually felt worse until nothing else mattered except to talk to them."

He had not been afraid of loneliness, but it got him anyway.

Before that, though, before the race was quite a reality, the morning of the start was hot and sunny with only a breath of breeze. One by one, the skippers steered out of the marina and through a channel to the open sea, where they raised their sails. A hundred or so boats had gathered to send them off. There were dozens of recreational yachts, a tall ship, a couple IMOCA 60s. There were race officials and support teams in rigid inflatable boats. A helicopter darted and hovered among the masts. "We love you!" Beskardes's family shouted to him as they motored past. He blew a kiss.

At noon, the boats gathered behind an imaginary line in the sea between *Suhaili* and *Joshua*, both under sail. A cannon fired, and they passed between the two old yachts, racing toward the horizon at a sedate pace. Eventually, all the other boats turned back, and they were alone.

JEFF JACKSON

Paradox of Paradise

FROM ASCENT/ROCK AND ICE

AT ABOUT EIGHT o'clock on Saturday morning, January 13, I
was standing in my kitchen in Makawao, Hawaii, eating a pancake
and working on a haiku. I was teaching haibun—linked prose and
verse—and wanted to try to write a haibun about a climb. The 17th-
century Japanese master poet Matsuo Basho had written his classic
travel sketches as haibun, and what is a climb if not a journey?

For inspiration, I'd been reading Basho's *Narrow Road to the Deep
North*, a haibun travelogue about his years-long road trip into wild
and dangerous Edo-period Japan, where travelers risked brutal
cold, illness, and meeting roving brigands who'd chop your arm
off with samurai blades to take the gold out of your fist. Basho sold
his house in 1689 and took off for two and a half years, traveling
over a thousand miles and living on handouts as a Zen-influenced
pilgrim. In 1694, five years after starting his northern journey,
Basho died back in his home province at the age of 50.

That morning in January, I was standing, eating, looking at a
haiku I'd written, holding a book, and hollering at my two boys to
be quiet so I could get in the right mood to tell the story behind a
route that Guillermo Marun, Coco Dave Elberg, and I had put up
a couple years before.

The route is *Sky Turtle* (5.10+). A long, steep hike past ancient
petroglyphs and shelter caves leads you to a room-sized hole in
the mountain, the remnants of a giant gas bubble. You make five
rappels out of the hole past orange, black, and purple streaks that
trail down the gently overhanging trachyte (a close geological relative to the syenite of Hueco Tanks).

Foggy, green, rainbow-laced valleys rise northward toward the crest of the West Maui mountains jutting like pyramids from the Pacific Ocean, which shines like a 2,500-mile-long grow light behind you. From the halekoa tree at the base you climb back up the only crack, 100 feet of 5.9+ protected by cams up to six inches. A pitch that will keep away the riffraff. Continue up ladders of tacky finger buckets and wormlike lava flows for six more pitches, all bolted. Wandering, bulging, cutting across the big wall, they take you places where you can really feel the mana (spiritual power) all around.

Sky Turtle is a metaphor for the mystery that hovers above us all the time. Climbs can be portals into that mystery; you just have to step outside the familiar confines of habit. Or something like that. Honestly, I was having a little trouble with the metaphor.

After some stern hectoring from me, the boys quieted down, and I tried again to conjure a poetic frame of mind.

Looking for insight, I opened my book and read the introduction: "In other words, the *Narrow Road to the Deep North* was life itself for Basho, and he traveled through it as anyone would travel through the short span of his life here—seeking a vision of eternity in the things that are, by their own very nature, destined to perish."

That's the contradiction of life, I thought. Everything we love dies.

At precisely that moment my phone buzzed, and I saw on the screen a little exclamation point in a triangle.

I'd seen that before. It was a flood alert, but instead of the familiar flood warning, in a glowing light-gray box, under the heading *EMERGENCY ALERT,* were the all-cap words: *BALLISTIC MISSILE THREAT INBOUND TO HAWAII. SEEK IMMEDIATE SHELTER. THIS IS NOT A DRILL.*

Perhaps you're wondering: Did he really read that heart-rending line from Nobuyuki Yuasa's intro at precisely the moment the missile alert went out? The answer to your question is: Yes.

My mind went blank. Then my guts melted. I called my boys over and hugged them tight for a long time.

My mother-in-law goes by the name Unci, which is Lakota for grandmother. She came in from the ohana (grandmother's cottage) and pointed to her phone. "Did you get this? Ballistic missile inbound to Hawaii?"

My 10-year-old, Kai, perked up. "Missile?" he asked. I could tell he thought it was cool.

Blond and long-limbed, into baseball, Norse myths, and playing the violin, Kai trusts in the universe. I don't think he had any sense of danger. He's also into that fearless boy-stage of broken collarbones and chipped teeth, and to him maybe missiles were just another name for a rocket ship.

Isaac, seven, is more perceptive. He picked up on the vibe, hugged me harder, and said, "I don't want missiles to come here."

"I don't either," I said.

What do you say to your still-pudgy, blue-eyed, soft-cheeked first grader about the inbound-missile alert? I couldn't think of a single honest way to assure him of its impossibility.

I wanted to believe it was a hoax or some hacker or a mistake—that it couldn't be true because nuclear war is MAD (mutually assured destruction) and crazy and unthinkable, and just the dumbest fucking thing human beings could do to each other.

And yet Trump had been tweeting, engaging in a nuclear pissing contest with Kim Jong Un of North Korea. Just a month earlier, Hawaii had started testing nuclear sirens for the first time since the end of the Cold War.

I thought about what might happen in the next few moments. Would we be wiped out in a flash of white light? Vaporized or turned to glass?

The missile, I thought, would probably be targeted on Honolulu, Hawaii's largest city, with a metro population of nearly a million people. Honolulu is on the island of Oahu, about 116 miles away. But I didn't know how far the blast—or whatever you call it—would travel or whether we'd have radioactive ash raining down like red-hot cinders for a decade. The alert had said to seek shelter but there are no shelters. We live on Maui. Our house is single-wall construction, built in 1957. I looked around at the open windows and felt again the knee-weakening sink, and in an ironic moment lamented never finishing my haibun.

I thought about all the things I'd left unfinished. The climbs and stories—raising my sons. I've had a great life and was surprisingly okay with dying in a flash. In some ways a quick death would be easy, maybe even a relief from the existential ennui that troubles everybody from time to time, some of us more than others. But not these little boys, who had all of life unlived—their fate couldn't be so senseless.

I held them in the kitchen for a little longer, gaming it out— wondering how to survive the blast and the fallout and the horror-show of what was going to happen to North and South Korea and Japan and China and the Pacific Ocean and the Mainland. War, martial law, power outages, contamination, burns, shortages, starvation, disease, and death. At any moment there could be a roaring concussion and mile-high drifting radioactive cloud only 100-some miles away. What was I gonna do?

I learned to climb in southwestern Oklahoma in the late 1970s and early 1980s at a time where difficulty was measured not by the grade of the climb but by its survivability. None of the routes at Quartz Mountain were super-hard, mostly 5.10s and 5.11s, but almost all of them had sections where if you fell you'd die or be horribly broken. Many of the routes were between 100 or 200 feet long. Many only had a couple of bolts or pieces of gear to protect the entire span. But it was also the only place to learn to climb within five hours of my home in North Texas.

One day I worked up the nerve to try a climb called *The Big Bite,* a 5.10 put up by Duane Raleigh, or maybe it was the *S Wall*? It's been so long I can't recall. Let's just, for obvious reasons, say it was *The Big Bite,* an infamous line responsible for at least one 100-foot fall when Mark Herndon slipped and tried to slow his plunge by dragging his hands across the hot granite. He survived, but he scrubbed his palms down to the bone.

I smeared up the low-angled first 50 feet and clipped the lone bolt and charged on higher and higher till I stalled, over 100 feet off the deck, the distant bolt a tiny glint no bigger than the point of a star. I tried to move off the crystal, but my foot slipped, and I clasped the bald slab tighter, pushed my butt out, and lifted my heels. I started to slide again but leaned back and brought my weight over my feet. The rubber gripped. My slide stopped, and I scrambled onto the desert-island-like foot crystal and tried to get my breathing back under control.

Five minutes passed. Ten minutes. It was hot, and sweat dripped off my nose and splattered onto the rock, dampening potential footholds. I slapped chalk on the wet marks and resolved to go. Just move. But I couldn't. Because what if?

Fifteen minutes later my feet hurt too bad to hang out any longer. I had to go or melt off. When I finally went, the climbing was wobbly but easy.

That was the lesson. Just move. Even when you think you can't, move.

I called Uncle Lance Endo, my ex-military, Maui-born, kama'aina who'd taken part in missile-tracking exercises when he worked at the military telescope on Haleakala. He always knows what to do in big rains and hurricanes, and he's related to everybody in Hawaiian government.

Lance said, "I made calls. It looks real."

"What do we do?" I asked.

"I'm closing my windows. You shouldn't come outside for 15 days. We'll know in 40 minutes."

"Okay, Uncle Lance," I said.

"Aloha, Uncle Jefe," he said unsteadily.

I hung up, even more shaken.

"Can we go outside and play with the chickens?" Kai asked.

"No, buddy. Help me close the windows. Help Unci fill up the jugs."

As I filled the bathtub I called my mom and she asked me to "just stay on the line with me, let's just stay on the line," but I wanted to keep the line clear for any glowing gray screens I hoped might pop up and read:

OOPS. WE MEANT NO BALLISTIC MISSILE THREAT INBOUND TO HAWAII TODAY.

I called my wife, Hannah, who was in Colorado at the time, but she didn't pick up so I sent her a text, which felt awfully banal. As I took inventory of the canned food and calculated days, I called my brother and choked up a little bit about the boys.

Over 40 years of climbing I've had plenty of scares but nothing like this ugly lack of agency. When you're climbing you can always do something: downclimb, rig a rappel, or press on—just move. This was different, but I kept moving anyway, breathing, getting ready, keeping my boys close, and calling everyone I loved.

*

For a little while that morning of January 13 I believed a nuclear
warhead could momentarily impact near my home and annihilate
my family and possibly kick off a conflict that would poison the
entire world. That I'd ever be in a position to believe in such a
scenario strikes me as terribly sad.

The experience also prompted a few questions. To wit: Is it always better to be well informed and available for the ballistic missile alerts? Or would it be better to simply disappear up the Narrow Road to the Deep North? How am I going to travel through
the short span of this life? Listening to depressing news, governed
by liars on both sides, and checking my phone every few seconds?
Or by loving things that are destined to die? The responsible citizen wants to keep voting and texting. The wild one wants to take a
hammer and beat his phone into a scrapyard.

Uncle Lance said it takes 40 minutes for a missile to travel to
Hawaii from North Korea. Thirty-eight minutes after the first alert,
my screen lit up again (with some lower-case letters this time):

> EMERGENCY ALERT: *There is no missile threat or danger to the state of Ha-
> waii. Repeat: False Alarm.*

One month since the missile alert, and I'm looking for some resolution—or is it consolation? I reach for the Buddhist sop of inter-
connection versus dualism. Black and white, me and him, us and
them—illusions that lie at the root of all suffering. They damn
sure lie at the heart of missile alerts.

I want to feel connected to all things, but I can't. Perhaps I'm
still too sad and unenlightened? Or maybe, as a friend once said,
that's the point of being human—to love despite death, to live
like everything is connected despite bumping against edges every
moment?

Today is a Wednesday, and the boys are at school. A rooster
crows in Makawao but otherwise it's peaceful and quiet, so I open
my haibun and begin writing:

If you're a climber and you've surfed Thousand Peaks on the
west side of Maui, you've looked in at the 700-foot plug of trachyte
Hawaiians call Honu (Turtle) and wondered if it's climbable. It is.

When it rains, my shoulder hurts. Silver strands lace my hair.
Forty years of climbing cliffs and mountains have tracked my face

and hardened my toenails. Older than Basho when he died: Who is this travel-worn stranger in the mirror?

My older son stands taller than my shoulder and writes his age in two numbers. Soon he'll be gone, and then the little one will go away too, each son taking all my heart. What will remain of me?

All loves are doomed. Nothing withstands time. The days spiral like elm seeds in a windstorm, and I wonder: Am I missing everything?

The cure for these heart pangs is a project into which you can pour life force. A chalice. And so the rust-colored rock calls me.

Old as igneous
sweat drips feet slip
on cinder cone—we begin.

Contributors' Notes

Notable Sports Writing of 2018

Contributors' Notes

JOHN BRANCH has been a sports reporter for the *New York Times* since 2005. In 2013, he was awarded the Pulitzer Prize in feature writing for his tale of a deadly avalanche, titled "Snow Fall," and was a finalist the previous year for his story about the late NHL enforcer Derek Boogaard, who died of a painkiller overdose and was found to have CTE, the degenerative brain disease. He is the author of two books, including 2018's *The Last Cowboys,* about a family of saddle-bronc rodeo champions. He lives near San Francisco.

VIRGINIA OTTLEY CRAIGHILL resides in Sewanee, Tennessee, and has been teaching English at the University of the South since 2001. A native of Atlanta, Georgia, Craighill grew up with, and now lives with, people who love to watch football but considers herself more of a sports anthropologist than a fan. Recent publications include commentary on the letters of Tennessee Williams in the *Sewanee Review* and a chapter in *Teaching the Works of Eudora Welty.*

KIM CROSS is the *New York Times* best-selling author of *What Stands in a Storm,* a literary nonfiction account of the biggest tornado outbreak in history. A national champion water skier, she has competed in 10 sports, most of them laughably obscure. She lives in Boise, where she teaches creative nonfiction and mountain biking.

BETH DAVIES-STOFKA is chair of liberal studies for Colorado Community Colleges Online and serves on the Faculty Advisory Council of the School of Graduate Studies at Excelsior College. A career academic, she has written for *Africa Today, Political Theology, Sacred Matters,* and *Patheos,* among others. She is also a career humanitarian, most recently writing and fundraising for Hôpital Albert Schweitzer Haiti and safe houses in the United States for children and teens rescued from commercial sex trafficking. She earned her doctorate in ethics from the University of Toronto and lives with her husband in Denver, where she occasionally performs original fiction and poetry for live audiences and writes for *Baseball Prospectus.* More of her work can be found at eirwenes.blog.

HEATHER DINICH joined ESPN in 2007 as a college football reporter for ESPN.com and now covers the College Football Playoff as a senior writer and studio analyst. Throughout the season, she is a regular contributor on ESPN Radio's *College GameDay* and the *Campus Conversation* podcast and also on *SportsCenter.* Dinich previously worked for the *Baltimore Sun* as a sports reporter, mainly covering University of Maryland athletics. She graduated from Indiana University with a bachelor's degree in journalism and is the mother of three boys.

NATHAN FENNO is a sports enterprise and general assignment reporter for the *Los Angeles Times.* A Seattle native, he previously wrote for the *Washington Times,* the *Ann Arbor News* in Michigan, and the *King County Journal* in Bellevue, Washington.

BONNIE D. FORD is an ESPN.com senior writer whose coverage of international sports often focuses on stories of remarkable women, along with issues common to all athletes such as mental health and working conditions. She spent her formative years in Paris, France, and graduated from Oberlin College. Her newspaper career included stints at the *Ann Arbor News,* the *Detroit News,* the *Plain Dealer,* and the *Chicago Tribune.* She could not do what she does without the unwavering support of her husband, *Philadelphia Inquirer* sports columnist Bob Ford.

JOHN M. GLIONNA is a nonfiction writer whose work has appeared in numerous national publications, including *California Sunday Magazine, The Guardian,* and the *New York Times.* He specializes in writing personality profiles and delving into subcultures. After 26 years as a staff writer at the *Los Angeles Times,* he is now a Las Vegas–based freelance writer.

NICK HEIL is the author of *Dark Summit: The True Story of Everest's Most Controversial Season,* which received the Mountain Literature Award from the Banff Book Festival. He is a contributing editor at *Outside,* where he writes often about human performance, adventure sports, and people in the outdoors. Heil holds an MFA from the creative writing program at the University of Montana. His fiction has been published in *Cutbank,* and his nonfiction work has appeared in *Outside, Men's Health, Reader's Digest, Skiing, Backpacker, Men's Journal,* the *Daily Beast, Vice,* and elsewhere. Heil has reported from three continents and more than 20 countries, including Tanzania and Afghanistan. He lives in Santa Fe, New Mexico.

BOB HOHLER is a sports investigative reporter for the *Boston Globe*. A Boston native, he joined the Globe in 1987 after reporting for the *Monadnock Ledger* and *Concord Monitor* in New Hampshire. He served in the *Globe*'s Washington bureau from 1993 to 2000, covering government and politics, including President Clinton's impeachment case. He was the *Globe*'s beat writer for the Boston Red Sox from 2000 through the 2004 championship season. His writing honors include the Dick Schaap Excellence in Sports Journalism Award from Northeastern University's Center for the Study of Sport in Society, the Award for Excellence in Coverage of Youth Sports from Penn State's John Curley Center for Sports Journalism, and the Salute to Excellence Award from the National Association of Black Journalists. Hohler has been cited 10 times since 2005 by the Associated Press Sports Editors for writing one of the nation's top 10 investigative or explanatory stories. He is the author of *I Touch the Future . . . The Story of Christa McAuliffe*.

KERRY HOWLEY is the author of the critically acclaimed book *Thrown*, which follows the comedic adventures of two very different MMA fighters. She is a contributing writer at *New York* magazine, where she has profiled Serena Williams and Manny Pacquiao, and where her work has been nominated for a National Magazine Award. Since 2015, she has been an assistant professor at the University of Iowa's MFA program in nonfiction writing. As a kid, her favorite sports team was the Miami Dolphins, because she liked dolphins. She still doesn't know how football works.

JEFF JACKSON is the at-large editor for *Rock and Ice* magazine. His work has appeared in *American Short Fiction, At Large, Lonely Planet, Climbing,* and many other books and magazines. He has three screenplays in development with Chockstone Pictures, teaches writing at the University of Hawaii at Maui, and likes to surf and climb.

TIM LAYDEN has been a senior writer at *Sports Illustrated* since 1994. He worked previously at *Newsday,* the *Albany Times Union,* and the *Schenectady Gazette.* At *Sports Illustrated* Layden is a feature writer and previously covered college football, college basketball, and the NFL. He has also covered the last 14 Olympic Games. This is his third appearance in *The Best American Sports Writing.*

JEFF MACGREGOR is a writer-at-large for *Smithsonian* magazine. He is the author of the critically acclaimed *Sunday Money* and has written for the *New York Times* and *Sports Illustrated*. His work first appeared in *The Best American Sports Writing* in the 2000 edition.

JACKIE MACMULLAN is a senior writer and television analyst for ESPN. She worked at the *Boston Globe* for 19 years as a reporter and associate editor and as the first full-time female sports columnist in the paper's history. She was a senior writer at *Sports Illustrated* from 1995 to 2000 and has authored five books, including the *New York Times* best-seller *When the Game Was Ours.* In 2010, MacMullan was the first female recipient of the Naismith Basketball Hall of Fame's Curt Gowdy Award, recognized for "outstanding contributions to basketball," and in February 2019 she became the first female to be awarded the PEN American Lifetime Achievement Award in Literary Sports Writing.

KATHRYN MILES is the author of four books, including, most recently, *Quakeland: On the Road to America's Next Devastating Earthquake.* A regular contributor to *Outside,* she has also appeared in publications including *The Best American Essays,* the *Boston Globe,* the *New York Times, Popular Mechanics, Politico,* and *Time.* Miles serves as a scholar-in-residence for the Maine Humanities Council and as a faculty member for several low-residency MFA programs. She resides in Portland, Maine.

SAM MILLER writes about baseball for ESPN. He is the co-host of the *Effectively Wild* podcast and the co-author of *The Only Rule Is It Has to Work: Our Wild Experiment Building a New Kind of Baseball Team.*

ADAM RITTENBERG is an award-winning national college football reporter for ESPN. His work primarily appears on ESPN.com and *E+,* and he also makes regular appearances on ESPN television and ESPN Radio. He is a regular host on ESPN's college football podcast *Campus Conversation,* as well as with the Sirius XM college networks. Rittenberg serves as an adjunct lecturer in DePaul University's College of Communication and has taught journalism at Northwestern University, his alma mater. Before joining ESPN in 2008, he spent five years covering college and professional sports at the *Daily Herald* in Arlington Heights, Illinois. Rittenberg is a San Francisco Bay Area native who lives in Chicago with his wife and three children.

MAGGIE SHIPSTEAD is the *New York Times* best-selling author of the novels *Astonish Me* and *Seating Arrangements,* which won the International Dylan Thomas Prize and the *Los Angeles Times* Book Prize for First Fiction. Her work has appeared in *The Best American Short Stories,* and she has twice been a National Magazine Award finalist for fiction. She is a dedicated armchair sailor and non-armchair travel writer, with a particular passion for the polar regions.

CLAY SKIPPER is a staff writer for *GQ,* focusing on sports and wellness. His major sports features have included Draymond Green, Kirk Cousins, Jalen Ramsey, and Josh Gordon. Skipper also stars in the new *GQ* sports docuseries, *Above Average Joe,* and he hosts *Level Up,* a *GQ* podcast about living smarter. A graduate of Vanderbilt University, he is based in New York City.

CHRISTOPHER SOLOMON is making his seventh appearance in a volume of *The Best American* series. He is a contributing editor at *Outside* and lives against the shoulder of the North Cascade Mountains in north-central Washington State. More of his work can be found at www.chrissolomon. net.

ABE STREEP is a contributing editor at *Outside* and a contributing writer at the *California Sunday Magazine.* His work has appeared in the *New York Times Magazine, Harper's, Wired, The Atavist,* and elsewhere. In 2019 he was awarded the American Mosaic Journalism Prize for excellence in long-form reporting on underrepresented groups in America.

LOUISA THOMAS is a contributing writer to *The New Yorker* and a former writer and editor at *Grantland.* She is also the author of *Louisa: The Extraordinary Mrs. Adams* and *Conscience: Two Pacifists, Two Soldiers, One Family—A Test of Will and Faith in World War I,* and the co-author, with John Urschel, of *Mind and Matter: A Life in Math and Football.*

WRIGHT THOMPSON is a senior writer for *ESPN The Magazine.*

TOM VANHAAREN covers college football and recruiting for ESPN. A graduate of Central Michigan University, he has been with ESPN since 2011 and resides in southeastern Michigan with his wife and three children.

CAITY WEAVER is a writer for the *New York Times.* Previously, she was a writer and editor for *GQ.*

PATRICIA WEN is the editor of the Spotlight Team, the *Boston Globe*'s investigative unit that includes six reporters. She took over in 2017 after having worked as a reporter on the team more than two decades ago. Over the years Wen has specialized in covering social service, legal, and medical issues. She has been a finalist for the Pulitzer Prize three times—in 2004 for feature writing, in 2013 as part of a team for national reporting, and in 2018 as Spotlight editor overseeing a seven-part series on race issues in Boston. Wen has twice won the Casey Medal for coverage of children and family issues, each time in the category of major projects in large publications. Before joining the *Globe,* she worked at the *Star-Ledger* in Newark, New Jersey, and *The Advocate* in Stamford, Connecticut. A native of East Lansing, Michigan, and a Harvard graduate, she is married with three children.

Notable Sports Writing of 2018

Selected by Glenn Stout

MICAH WIMMER
In the Shadow of a King. *Fansided,* May 31

DENNIS YOUNG
Freestyle. *Victory Journal,* Fall

THE BEST AMERICAN SERIES®

FIRST, BEST, AND BEST-SELLING

The Best American Comics

The Best American Essays

The Best American Food Writing

The Best American Mystery Stories

The Best American Nonrequired Reading

The Best American Science and Nature Writing

The Best American Science Fiction and Fantasy

The Best American Short Stories

The Best American Sports Writing

The Best American Travel Writing

Available in print and e-book wherever books are sold.

Visit our website: hmhbooks.com/series/best-american